MY LIFE

AS A REBEL

O

ANGELICA BALABANOFF

MY LIFE
AS
A REBEL

GREENWOOD PRESS, PUBLISHERS
NEW YORK   1968

And if, in the course of this great battle for the emancipation of the human race, we should fall, those now in the rear will step forward; and we shall fall with the consciousness of having done our duty as human beings, and with the conviction that the goal will be reached, however the powers hostile to humanity may struggle or strain in resistance. *Ours is the world, despite all.* . . .

—August Bebel.

Introduction

THE first impulse to write this book was given me by an American—John Reed. When I first met Reed I was secretary of the Zimmerwald movement, which at that time had its headquarters in Stockholm and was the chief link between the new Russian government and the revolutionary labour movement of other countries. Here I worked in direct contact with the leaders and institutions of the Soviet Republic and thus John Reed was sent to me from Moscow. I do not remember now whether his visit was preceded by a letter from Lenin, Chicherin, or Sverdlow; but after our first few moments of conversation I understood that Reed was a true revolutionary, burning to serve the new Russia and the labour movement in general.

There in Stockholm, after we had come to know each other better, Reed once said to me: "Angelica, you must not go to your grave with your experiences untold, with your knowledge of contemporary history and the men who are making it, unwritten. Why don't you write your memoirs?"

I told him that I had no intention of doing anything of the sort. At that time I did not think that my activities had any objective historical value. Later, in that decade of tragedy which followed the high hopes of 1918, I began to realize that the experience of the individual in relation to historic events does not belong to oneself alone. It should be put at the disposal of those who can make use of it.

Today, after twenty years in which the international labour movement has been defeated and dismembered, humanity is again on the verge of self-destruction. The failure to learn the lessons of experience between 1914 and 1922 has led the world to a new cycle of tragedy which today threatens to engulf all of Europe and perhaps America.

I have been an intimate witness of many of these events from their beginnings. I was an active member of the great international movement that collapsed in 1914 and I was one of those who tried to rebuild it and to rally the workers of all countries to an international banner during the World War. I was a leader of Italian Socialism both in its isolated adherence to internationalism and when it became the victim of an infamous betrayal—that of Benito Mussolini. I watched, day by day, the triumph of the new Russia, its energies enriched by the spirit of revolution; I saw its achievements threatened by blockade, starvation, and intervention at the hands of its enemies, and later by the unpardonable mistakes of its friends within and without its borders. Finally, I have known closely and collaborated with the masses of men and women who have been the instruments— and often the victims—of these events, and with the men who most influenced their development—Lenin, Trotsky, Mussolini.

The World War created a rift between the generations which cannot be ignored. The millions who were slaughtered took with them into their graves not only their hopes and sufferings, but the traditions and the knowledge they had inherited and acquired. The physical and moral horrors of our epoch are possible only because of this. The war cancelled a whole period of human progress and the wisdom of its artisans. It made possible a generation that knows nothing of what has gone before—nothing except what its rulers tell it. History has been falsified without shame by the Fascists and, unfortunately, also by the Bolsheviks. The truth was never more necessary than it is today.

This is not a conventional autobiography. I write of myself only as a witness and protagonist of the events described. Something of my background must be told in order that the reader become acquainted with the author. Though the movement of which I was a part has been destroyed in half of Europe, not even in this tragic hour do I believe that the work of the generation of revolutionaries to which I belong has been altogether in vain. If there is hope for our civilization beyond the black night of war and totalitarianism, I am convinced that it lies only in the movement to which we—the living and the dead—have given our lives.

The author wishes to express her appreciation for the assistance given by Lillian Symes and Travers Clement in the preparation of the manuscript of this book.

MY LIFE

AS A REBEL

1

THE TELEGRAM WHICH SUMMONED ME TO AN emergency meeting of the International Executive in July, 1914, reached me in a remote section of Tuscany. On my way to Pisa, I consulted my timetable again and again. Unless I could make connexions with the express at Milan, I would not be able to reach Brussels in time for the meeting. I knew only too well the nature of the emergency, the historic significance of this occasion. In the solidarity of the millions of workers who would be represented at this conference might lie the last chance of saving Europe.

I boarded the night train at Pisa, and as it pulled out of the station I congratulated myself on the fact that now there would be no difficulty in making the necessary connexions. When the conductor came for my ticket I asked him if he would knock on my door just before we reached Milan, as I wished to take a nap.

"Milan!" he exclaimed, in astonishment. "But, madame, this train goes to Rome."

My heart sank. For more than a decade I had been travelling about Italy, even in the most remote sections, and never before had I taken the wrong train or missed a meeting or appointment. And now—the most important meeting of my life! The train was an express and would not stop before it reached Rome. I could not possibly get to Brussels from Rome before the first session would be over. I explained my dilemma to the conductor.

"I have seen you so often at the station," he said, "and I know who you are. Is it important for the Party that you get to Milan tonight?"

I knew that I could speak freely. "Listen, comrade, the war has begun. We must stop it if we can or keep it from spreading over all Europe. The International Congress in August will be too late. The Executive Committee must act now. We meet in Brussels tomorrow."

"Don't worry, comrade. You will be in Brussels in time."

Half an hour later, as we approached a station, the train slowed down. The conductor entered my compartment and opened a window. Lifting me in his arms, he thrust me through the opening and lowered me into the outstretched arms of a startled station employee who came running along the platform in response to the conductor's shouts. The train gathered momentum and disappeared in the darkness.

"What are you doing here at this time of night, Comrade Balabanoff?" the station master asked. I explained my situation.

"There is no passenger train to Milan tonight, but I will see that you get there."

I arrived at Milan in a baggage-train just in time to catch the express for Brussels.

I had made this trip on several previous occasions, but never before had it recalled my first flight to Brussels from Russia, sixteen years earlier. That too had coincided with a major crisis in my life, though not in the movement of which I had become a part. It marked the final break with my family, my home, with all the luxurious and conventional life I had hated for so long and against which I had struggled so fiercely. Before me lay the realization of all my adolescent dreams—the university, knowledge, freedom, the opportunity to give some meaning to my life, though I had not known yet just what this last might mean. Among the dozens of men and women who travelled with me in that succession of third-class coaches during the long, six-day journey, I was sure that none was as happy as I. I wanted to tell them what was happening to me, that my life was beginning, that I was going to the university; I wanted them to share my joy. I had never travelled alone before, but I felt more secure and at home in that crowded train than I had ever felt with my own family. One thing only frightened me as we neared Brussels. I had never been in a hotel alone, and when the train stopped at four in the morning my heart stopped too. The town seemed dark and forbidding, the many military statues which loomed out of the darkness were both menacing and ridiculous. During the trip to the hotel I revived my courage by reminding myself of all the other girls who had to face life without the protection of friends and family. But after the door of my hotel room closed upon the porter who had brought my luggage, I looked under the bed and opened the clothes-press after much trembling. I had just read in the papers about a man who had hid in a wardrobe and during the night had attacked a sleeping girl.

In the sixteen years that had elapsed since that first morning of my new life I had realized in action all of those vague but compelling ambitions with which I had first come to Brussels. The generalities in which my inexperience had clothed them—freedom, equality, the right to live my own life, dedication to humanity, the struggle against injustice—had found concrete expression. I knew that I was a very fortunate person. The suffering and struggle of these intervening years—unlike those of my childhood and youth—had meaning and dignity because they were linked to those of humanity. Life lived in behalf of a great cause is robbed of its personal futility.

I was returning to Brussels now as the representative of Italian Socialism on the Executive Committee of the Second International. The end of this journey was to mark the end of a period both in my personal life and in that of the movement to which

[3]

I had dedicated these intervening sixteen years. I did not know then, as I neared Brussels, the sense of hopelessness and defeat, of inevitable calamity, which was to mark the next two days and which would overshadow even Jaurès' magnificent speech at our closing session. I did not know that a few days later this speech was to be answered by an assassin's bullet in Paris; that as Jaurès' murder was to mark the beginning of international slaughter, that of two others of our Executive Committee, Rosa Luxemburg and Hugo Haase, was to mark the beginning of the brutal peace which followed. This was July 28, 1914.

Whenever I am asked how I came to turn my back upon my family, upon the comfort and luxury of my home in southern Russia and to become a revolutionist, I am at a loss for an answer. No definite date or fact suggests itself to me. All the years of my childhood, as far back as I can remember, seem to have been years of rebellion—against my mother, my governesses, the conventions and restrictions of my life, and against the destiny for which I was being trained.

Serfdom had been abolished in Russia before I was born and I had been told of the "magnanimity" of Alexander II who "freed the peasants and made them happy, whereas before they had belonged to the landlords, just as animals or merchandise." But mother's treatment of the "free" servants in our household always aroused my indignation. (I visited few households and had no standard of comparison.) Once when I saw some peasants on our estate kiss the border of my father's coat when he returned from a long journey, I cringed with shame.

My first realization of inequality and injustice grew out of these experiences in my early childhood. I saw that there were those who commanded and those who obeyed, and probably because of my own rebellion against my mother, who ruled my life and who for me personified all despotism, I instinctively sided with the latter. Why, I asked myself, should mother be able to rise when she pleased, while the servants had to rise at an early hour to carry out her orders? After she had raged at them for some mistake, I would implore them not to endure such treatment, not realizing that necessity held them as tightly

[4]

to our home as it had held the peasants to the feudal landlords.

I received my first glimpse of actual poverty and misery when I became old enough to accompany mother on her visits to the poorhouse. Here were crowded together not only the poor but also the sick and insane. I was allowed to distribute the gifts we had brought—aprons, dresses, linen, etc.—in the manner of a small Lady Bountiful. The inmates seemed overjoyed with these presents and some of them kissed my hand in gratitude. Once mother gave me a silk scarf to give to a beggar woman who called at our door. Taking her into a secluded part of our grounds where I was sure we could not be seen, I asked her to promise to do as I asked. After she had promised, I gave her the scarf, and after she had accepted it I knelt down and kissed her hand. In this way I felt that I had established a balance between those who were able to give and those who were compelled to receive.

Father died when I was quite young and I remember very little about him. He was a landowner and business man, very much absorbed in his affairs. He did not interfere with the training of his children except when mother—much more energetic than he—appealed to his supreme authority. The only conflicts I ever had with him were those mother provoked.

Mother had borne sixteen children, seven of whom had died. I was the youngest and my older sisters were already married when I was born. This accounts in part for the manner in which I was raised—for the fact that I had no playmates, was not permitted to go to school or to play with my brothers who associated with other children. In the Russian idiom, and in mother's eyes, I was to be "the crown of the family." My training was such as would fit me for my destiny—marriage to a wealthy man, a life of ease for which the conventional accomplishments and social graces were a necessary preparation. Good manners, languages, music, dancing, and embroidery—these were the requisites of a Russian lady. In school I might learn bad manners from "ordinary" children. The solution was a succession of governesses and isolation from playmates.

My resentment against mother was intensified by the manner in which her plans for me and her conventional habits of mind were expressed in the simplest incidents. "Who will marry you

[5]

if you do not drink milk or if you do not take your cod-liver oil?" she would ask. "Where has one seen a girl of good family who does not play the piano?" And this exasperated me most of all: "What will people think of you?"

In spite of her tyrannical temperament and harshness, mother had been devoted to all her children and sacrificed herself continuously in their behalf. If she devoted herself particularly to me, it was probably due to some subtle intuition on her part that, for all her efforts, I would not follow the beaten path of her other children, that she would lose me as soon as I was old enough to make my own life, and that, therefore, she needed to provide me with greater physical strength and resistance than the others. She never admitted these motives, of course, even if she knew them. She would proclaim frequently that I was the worst of all her children, that she would be happy to be rid of me; in my absence, however, she would say the contrary. She was especially severe with me in the presence of others and although this deepened my resentment, I soon came to understand her temperament, with the result that she ceased to have any influence upon me.

We lived at this time just outside the town of Chernigov, which is near Kiev. The house had twenty-two rooms and was surrounded by a beautiful garden and orchard. Though I now feel at home in any country, I cannot think of those early surroundings without intense nostalgia. The house, the garden, the trees, the quiet town, and the beautiful river which flows through it—I saw them last forty years ago, but even now I can remember every part of that garden, the trees to which I confided the doubts and despairs of my childhood, the bushes that pricked my fingers, the blackberries I picked and with which I spotted my dresses to the disgust of mother and my governesses. About sixteen years ago, when I was a member of the Ukrainian government, I was about to go back to my native town to see all this once more. I had actually boarded the boat which was to take me there from Kiev and which had been rechristened *Third International* in my honour. Then I discovered that I could not face these scenes of my youth and bid good-bye to them a second time. Too much had happened to me since I had left home and the gulf that divided me from that childhood was now too deep. I left the boat and the trip was abandoned.

It may have been a recognition of Russia's social backwardness, even while they defended the conditions which contributed to it, which turned the interest of the aristocratic and rich bourgeois classes towards western "cultures" before they had explored their own. This and a desire to be as unlike the "ordinary" Russian as possible.

In our family we spoke mostly foreign languages. I had to learn my own language secretly from books hidden from my mother and governesses. These governesses were all foreigners and now I can scarcely remember their names or the number of them. None of them had any solid training or any real intellectual interests. They were hired to teach me languages and the superficial accomplishments. None of them could answer the questions which were constantly puzzling me or arouse in me more than a perfunctory interest in my studies. They took their cue from mother, at whose pleasure they held their positions, and if any of them ever guessed how much I wanted and needed understanding and love, they never showed it. Though I was never on good terms with my mother, I preferred her company to theirs, because she had a certain sharp intelligence that attracted me and I felt that her severity was more apparent than real. I preferred even that severity to the cold, impersonal attitude of my governesses.

Years later, after the Russian Revolution, I was to meet one of these governesses again in Germany. Fascism was rising in Italy and I had been invited to speak at a public meeting on this subject in Leipsic. Leipsic was the "reddest" spot in Republican Germany at this time and the headquarters of the intransigent Marxists. It was here that I had received my own training in Marxian thought and here Rosa Luxemburg had published her most brilliant articles before her murder in 1919. I was received in an immense hotel belonging to the workers. I had retired for a moment to my room to concentrate upon my speech when a woman entered with an armful of red carnations. She was bareheaded and poorly dressed. When I did not recog-

[7]

nize her, she introduced herself. She had been my last governess.

The meeting was held in the largest hall in the city and was crowded with more than ten thousand people. Several times during my speech I met the eyes of my ex-governess. They expressed sympathy and enthusiasm. After the meeting she came forward and caught my hand. "I am so proud of you, Angelica," she said. She added that she was a member of the Party, that she had always sympathized with the movement.

"Then why did you not help me when I was a child?" I asked.

She replied that she had not dared to encourage my rebelliousness because of my parents and her own dependence upon them for her livelihood. But I could not help but doubt her sincerity. She had joined the Party after the collapse of the monarchy, when it was not only safe, but also fashionable to do so, and when the Social Democracy was the dominant political influence. She was a teacher and most of her pupils were Socialists.

I was eleven when mother became aware that it would be impossible to cope with my determination to go to school. I don't know which was the strongest motivation behind this determination—the desire to learn, to be with other children, or to escape what I considered a prison, my home. We had travelled a great deal, particularly in Germany and Switzerland, but these trips, during which we visited the conventional places and lived in fashionable hotels, seemed merely an extension of life at Chernigov. I felt now that I would be overjoyed if I could be taken into the lowest class of some public school. Instead of sending me to the gymnasium, as I had wished, mother finally struck a compromise and agreed to send me to a fashionable school for girls in Kharkov. One of my older sisters and her husband lived there and they could keep an eye on me. Though I was delighted even by this concession, mother soon found a pretext for postponing my departure. I did not know enough Russian to pass my entrance examination in this subject, she insisted. She did not know that I had been studying it secretly, so I assured her that a brief, intensive period of study with a tutor would be sufficient. At Kharkov I was admitted to a higher class than I had anticipated, and before the end of the first year was promoted for "striking linguistic ability."

As the life of the boarding-school was somewhat less conventional than that of my home, I was very happy and could not understand why the other girls complained because our food and material surroundings were not so good or comfortable as they might have been. As the tuition fee was high, the student body was not large and the teachers were chosen from among the best qualified. If it had not been for their obligation to train us for a parasitic life, our academic standard would have been much higher. The uniforms which we wore indicated the social character of the school and I have often thought of them when I have seen the schoolgirls of western Europe in their simple costumes. We wore sky-blue dresses, short sleeves trimmed with white lace, and white aprons.

When the Tsar planned to visit Kharkov, the pupils of our school and one other, attended by girls of the nobility, were the only ones who were to be permitted to greet him at the station. I remember my excitement awaiting his arrival with an enormous bouquet of flowers, and then my disappointment when we were told that an "accident"—in reality it was an attempt upon his life—had prevented his arrival. The following day I wrote about this experience in school and in my composition I thanked God for having spared the life of His Imperial Majesty.

I was seventeen when I finally left Kharkov. Soon after my return home, mother and an elder sister insisted that I accompany them to Switzerland. I escaped the boredom of hotel life at Montreux by enrolling in a language school for young ladies. Though mother had considered my education complete when I left Kharkov and had hoped that this sojourn in Switzerland would mark the beginning of that "social" life which would lead inevitably to matrimony, it was difficult for her to object to this plan.

One day at the school a teacher was ill and the director asked me to take charge of a class. At the end of the day she told me that I would make an excellent teacher. It was the first time any one had suggested to me a career other than idleness, and by the time we returned to Russia the word "teacher" had become synonymous for me with the word "escape."

As I look back over the two years that followed, I realize that they represent the real *sturm und drang* of my whole career. After Kharkov and Switzerland, it was far more difficult than it had been in my childhood to adjust myself to life at home. I was no longer a child and I knew more definitely what I wanted. I knew also that I had reached an age at which I was supposed to fulfil the destiny of my sex. In the sense in which my family understood that phrase, such fulfilment had but one meaning— a suitable marriage arranged by my mother and brothers. As my resistance to her plans for me became more determined and mother's tyranny became more repressive, the struggle between us developed into daily warfare—a warfare that exhausted me emotionally and physically and that finally resulted in serious illness.

In Chernigov, as in other Russian towns, there were girls— daughters of the petty bourgeoisie, professional men, minor government officials—who were preparing to enter foreign universities. Entrance requirements abroad demanded a knowledge of certain languages which they had not been taught in the "public" schools. I realized that I could give them this preparation.

Mother was willing that I should teach "the children of the poor." This would be charity and therefore a suitable avocation. But to associate with, and possibly become friendly with, these girls of the lower middle class who had attended the public schools, who were training themselves for useful careers, for the free—and therefore dangerous—life of the university—this was another matter.

To spare myself the storm of her wrath and my pupils from the possible embarrassment of her insults, I planned to teach some of these girls secretly. I went to their homes when mother went on her shopping tours into the city, or met them in some far corner of our garden. Most of the Russian students of this time went to the University of Zürich, but one of the girls to whom I taught German and who had lived abroad for several years told me about a university which immediately excited my imagination—the Université Nouvelle in Brussels. I had read nothing of any radical philosophies at this time, and though I knew vaguely about the illegal revolutionary movement in Russia and instinctively sympathized with its aims, I had never met an avowed Socialist or Anarchist. Here was a place where such people lived and talked freely, where they were honoured and admired, and where students came from all over Europe to sit at their feet. As this girl described the life of the students, the atmosphere of free inquiry, the men who taught there, I knew immediately it was to Brussels, rather than to Zürich, that I must go.

I can scarcely bear, even now, to think back over the scenes which followed the announcement of my decision. Even my brothers were shocked, though they knew little about the Université Nouvelle. Like mother, they believed that a university was no place for a girl, especially for a girl who did not have to make her living.

Emotionally and intellectually, I had already broken completely with my family and with every tradition they represented. I knew that now the time had come when I must make the physical break which I had been looking forward to for years. The storms and hysterics of this period merely confirmed me in my determination to make it as quickly and cleanly as possible. I felt that the money I was to inherit from my father's estate was a chain which bound me to the past, to my family and to Russia. It too must be broken. I told my older brother that I wanted none of it, that I would leave empty-handed and make my own way. He reminded me that I could not travel without money, that even at the university I would need food and shelter, clothing, books. Finally his common sense overcame my scruples and I agreed to accept a very small allowance—just enough to keep me "like a working girl," to permit me to travel third class. We made an agreement by which he was to send me this sum each month and I renounced my share in my father's estate in his behalf.

When I left home, mother was not present to bid me good-bye or give me her blessing. My last memory connected with her was to be her curse upon me. But I was happier than I had ever been in all my life.

[11]

2

AFTER A FEW DAYS AT THE HOTEL WHICH I HAD entered with such fear in the early morning hours upon my arrival in Brussels, I succeeded in finding a room. It was a miserable little room without heat and furnished with only a bed, a table and two rickety chairs. My landlady ran a third-rate stationery shop. As it was in one of the most poverty-stricken districts of Brussels, her customers were very poor. She catered primarily to school children, the majority of whom appeared sickly and undernourished. My room was above the shop and I took my meals with my landlady, whose living-quarters at the rear of the store were as bare as my own. But even on the coldest days and at a time during the winter when I was sick and half dead from a combination of cold and undernourishment, I would not have surrendered one dark corner of my room for all the big, well-heated house at Chernigov.

The university was only a short distance away, and as soon as it opened my days were divided between its lecture-halls and the public library; my evenings spent at various meetings or informal gatherings of students. The meetings I attended were usually held at the People's House, then an extremely modest institution occupying an old building near by and not the fine, coöperatively-owned structure it was to occupy later—a building costing over a million francs and containing an auditorium, theatre, offices and committee-rooms for the Belgian Socialist Party and the trade unions, the café, stores and shops of the Coöperatives.

The Université Nouvelle, housed in two old residential buildings, was far from impressive from the physical point of view. It could not boast of million-dollar endowments. Its intellectual equipment, however, was a different matter. It had been created by Belgian intellectual radicals in 1894 primarily as a field of activity for Elisée Reclus, whose work had begun a new era in the annals of scientific geography. Reclus was a revolutionist as well as one of the most brilliant scientists of his day; he had participated in the Paris Commune and had been expelled from France because of his Anarchism. He was typical of the intellectual Anarchists of that time. His own life was a daily exemplification of his views. Any victim of inequality, whether good or bad, innocent or guilty, appealed to his altruism and courage. His wife would allow him only a few cents a day for pocket money because she knew that he would give away whatever he had, often to those who abused his confidence and kindness.

From a friend who worked closely with Reclus I heard that he preferred me to his other students. I still do not know why. I was an extremely poor student in his subject. He had no way of discovering my deficiencies, however. He was impatient with all academic formalities and never interrogated his students. When I came up for my finals in my major subjects, literature and philosophy, he startled my other professors, who knew his distaste for such proceedings, by appearing suddenly in the examination-room. I was extremely flattered. He often invited me to come and visit him; but, with one exception when I took dinner with him and his wife at their home, I was too shy to do so.

[13]

Much as I was impressed by the personality of Reclus, his lectures did not altogether satisfy me. They were interesting and instructive, but his social philosophy lacked the element that I passionately sought—causality. I came to the conclusion very quickly that I was not and never could be an Anarchist, despite my intense admiration of individual Anarchists, of the spirit of sacrifice and high idealism they bring to the movement.

Elisée Reclus was only one of many brilliant international radicals who lectured at the university and before great audiences at the People's House in those days and who influenced my development. I listened eagerly to sociologists such as Maxim Kowalevsky, to criminologists like Enrico Ferri and Edmond Picard; economists such as Hector Denis, Émile Vandervelde, Emile deGreef; and studied with Elie Reclus, brother of Elisée, who lectured on mythology and the history of religion.

Many of the students at the university were foreigners—mostly Russians, Bulgarians, and Rumanians. Through the People's House, I also came in touch with a few Italian *émigrés*, some of whom had come to Brussels to escape the persecutions which followed the riots of 1898. I felt drawn to them at once. This was the first intimation of the existence of what has seemed to some of my friends an almost mystical bond of sympathy between me and the Italian radicals—a bond so strong that it was more or less to shape the entire course of my later life. Of course to me there is nothing mystical about it. I was a moody, shy young girl and the child-like simplicity, generosity, and warmth of the Latin temperament fascinated me. In the presence of Italians I seemed to emerge from a dark, cold place into the brilliance of Mediterranean sunshine.

At this time Russia was not the only country where girls encountered difficulties when they looked forward to university careers, to graduation and ultimately, perhaps, to entering professional life. Yet despite the barriers that existed for women even in the comparatively free atmosphere of Brussels, there were quite a few girls and young women studying at the Université Nouvelle. I had no intimate friends among them, however. I made my adjustments quickly and was almost completely absorbed by my studies.

My compatriots, the Russian students, were for the most part well advanced in radical theory. Many of them had been active in the underground movement in Russia and they had little in common with the young unaffiliated students of other nationalities or with persons like myself, who, though speaking the same language, had come from sheltered, completely bourgeois backgrounds. I looked up to these Russians who could discuss by the hour the theories of Marx and Bakunin, who had participated in demonstrations and other revolutionary activity. In comparison with those of us who had not yet done anything for the Cause, who had not faced persecution, police terrorism, exile, they were heroes. I did not want to seem to them indiscreet nor to reveal to them my naïveté, so I worshipped them from afar.

Thus it was also with my professors. To me they were Olympians not to be approached by ordinary mortals. I came, however, to make one exception. This was in the case of Célestin Demblon, our professor of modern French literature and an enthusiastic disciple of Victor Hugo. In order to understand my attitude towards Demblon, however, it is necessary first to write of another man who was one of the founders of the university and whose lectures at the People's House I attended—Émile Vandervelde.

Vandervelde later became president of the Socialist and Labor International on whose Executive Committee I was to sit with him years later. In 1914, he became Belgian Minister of State and in 1925, Minister of Foreign Affairs. At this time he was considered one of the most ardent and gifted of European Socialists, an authority on economic and juridical questions. He was a very rich man, charming, physically attractive, an excellent speaker. In fact, he seemed endowed with every possible attribute to enhance his prestige among such romantic idealists as comprised the majority of our student body. The girls, particularly, adored him.

Demblon, in contrast, was poor and ugly. He dressed like a workingman, though with what I now realize were dramatic touches which added a romantic effect of which he was not entirely unconscious. To me he was the embodiment of the

[15]

downtrodden and oppressed, while Vandervelde, so charming and so much admired, represented Success. The more the young women students gushed over Vandervelde, the more I resented him and the higher Demblon rose in my estimation. With no reasons other than my own private emotional ones, I came to dislike the one and to worship the other.

Demblon was a good speaker, and when he read poetry, which he often did, I could actually see and hear the men he was quoting—Lamartine, Chateaubriand, Victor Hugo. His revolutionary temperament manifested itself in violent outbursts of indignation against social inequality. These unrestrained outbursts, burning with the fire of his complete sincerity, were never tempered for the occasion. Demblon expressed what he thought and felt in no uncertain terms whether he was speaking in the classroom, a public meeting, or in the Belgian Parliament, of which he was a popular member.

During my first year in Brussels, the newspapers reported one violent scene, an altercation leading to blows between a reactionary deputy and Demblon, the Socialist. The admiration this stirred in me led to my first literary effort, an allegory with Demblon symbolizing Truth and Justice. While I was reading my composition to a group of students before class next day, Demblon entered the room without my noticing him. I glanced up suddenly from my manuscript and he was standing before me, smiling quizzically. I felt the blood rush to my face. He asked me to go on reading, to begin at the beginning. I was trembling all over, but I managed to read back over what I had written. When I had finished, he assumed a very objective tone and, though praising my literary ability, tactfully avoided giving any indication that he realized the personal application of my allegory.

Shortly after this he approached me as I was arranging my notes at the end of one of his lectures. He began talking, and almost before I knew it we were walking along the street towards the stationery shop. In my room I served him tea while he talked on and on. After that he came to visit me often. Those were hours of intense joy for me—to share the thoughts of a great Socialist, of a man who had dedicated his life to the oppressed, a man with such experience, such courage! Like most people with similar temperaments, he repeated himself often, but I listened always with the utmost concentration, scarcely daring to offer him a second cup of tea for fear of interrupting him. About three o'clock in the afternoon he had to be in Parliament and I often accompanied him, parting with him only at the last possible moment to take my seat in the visitors' gallery while he proceeded to his place on the floor of the Chamber. Parliament seemed to me then a sacred place where Science, Truth, and Justice, given voice by the Demblons, were to conquer the forces of Tyranny and Oppression for the working class.

On my way home—my head still in the clouds and with glorious phrases ringing in my ears—I would usually stop at the public library. Here, too, I hoped to find the way to Truth and to prepare myself to defend the have-nots against the haves.

Many years later I was addressing a vast audience at the World Congress of Freethinkers in Rome. Suddenly, in the middle of a sentence, my eyes focussed on the upturned face of a man standing near the platform. The question flashed into my mind, "Where have I seen that man before?" In the next instant it was answered: "Université Nouvelle—Demblon!" My voice faltered. I thought I would be unable to conclude my speech. I was the shy young girl again who had just glanced up from her manuscript in that lecture-hall in Brussels.

Back in Brussels again, long after the Russian Revolution and after I had severed my relations with the Bolsheviks, Demblon's daughter came to see me. She told me that her father, then dead, had often spoken of me in his later years, that he had followed every step of my career. She indicated that it would make her happy if she could give me something in his memory. I went to her apartment and chose the pen with which Demblon used to write. I still have it.

While I was not drawn into the main stream of the labour movement at this time, I attended countless lectures on labour history and tactics. I had come to Brussels an instinctive rebel rather than a conscious revolutionary, and as I attended these meetings at the People's House and listened to the discussions among the workers who came there after a long day's labour, I began to realize how much I had to learn. My own personal aspirations had been clothed in such abstractions as Knowledge, Truth, Justice, and Liberty, but now I began to understand how much more than mere passion for social justice was required of a revolutionary. The eloquent libertarianism of Reclus had stirred my enthusiasm while it had failed to satisfy my intellectual curiosity. How could these abstractions be clothed in reality?

In Belgium, as in other western countries, political democracy was accompanied by the most abject poverty. The revolutions of the past, fought in the name of these beautiful abstractions, had left the working class enslaved. Only a new social revolution, a new economic system could emancipate them. And how was this to be achieved?

From the lectures of Vandervelde, deGreef, Demblon, and other Socialists at the university, I began to get my first insight into economic theory, the mechanics of capitalism, and the history and meaning of the revolutionary labour movement. But the most decisive factor in my intellectual life at this time—as in the lives of a whole generation of Russian revolutionaries—was the work of George Plekhanoff.

Plekhanoff was at this time the outstanding philosopher and theoretician of the Marxist movement in Russia, although he had been in exile in western Europe for a number of years. He might be said to have created that movement, and his books and pamphlets, circulated throughout underground circles, were the textbooks of the men who were to make the Revolution of October, 1917. When some of the Russian students at the university recommended to me his work on the monistic approach to history, I found it exactly what I needed at the time, a philosophy of method that gave continuity and logic to the processes of history and which endowed my own ethical aspirations, as well as the revolutionary movement itself, with the force and dignity of an historical imperative. In Marx's materialist conception of history I found a light which illuminated every corner of my intellectual life.

Plekhanoff, like so many of the Russian revolutionary leaders, combined the qualities of a man of action, a professional revolutionist, with the reflective intellectual capacities of a philosopher. Though trained as an engineer, he had abandoned that career at the age of nineteen, when he had addressed the first great public labour demonstration in St. Petersburg. Thereafter he participated in the intense and dangerous life of the underground movement. Before his time, the efforts of the utopian revolutionary intelligentsia had been directed largely towards the peasants. As a Marxist, Plekhanoff recognized that the industrial workers in the cities, even in such an undeveloped country as Russia, would constitute the vanguard of any revolutionary upheaval and with Axelrod, Vera Zasulich, and Deutsch he founded the historic Group for Emancipation of Labour. It was as the leader in exile of the Russian Social Democratic Party, and its representative on the Executive Committee of the Second International, that he came to Brussels soon after I had read his books.

When I heard that he was to speak at the People's House in behalf of the victims of Russian despotism, I could scarcely wait for the night of the meeting. I went to the hall in a mood of combined anticipation and anxiety. His writings had affected me so profoundly that I could not bear to think that his personality might disappoint me in any way. The moment he walked onto the platform that anxiety was allayed. His physical appearance was as striking as the brilliance of his speech. He looked more like a Russian aristocrat than a revolutionary and as he spoke one realized immediately that here was not merely a master of logic, a brilliant polemicist, but a man of wide cultivation and the aesthetic sense of an artist. As he spoke in fluent French of the new wave of persecutions in Russia, he moved about the platform seeming to search the conscience of each man and woman in the audience with his piercing dark eyes. This was shortly after Zola had shaken public opinion in western Europe with the challenge of his *J'Accuse*. As I looked at and listened to Plekhanoff in bashful veneration, he seemed to me a Russian personification of that challenge.

If any one had told me that a few years later I was to know the speaker of that evening as a friend and comrade, that I was to serve as his aid and alternate on the Executive Committee of the International, that one of the most bitter experiences of my life was to be my break with him at the beginning of the World War, I would have laughed at such fantasy. Nor could I foresee that nearly twenty years later, Plekhanoff, as a Menshevik, would share the fate of all non-Bolshevist Marxists and would be denounced as a counter-revolutionary by the men whose minds he had helped to mould.

I spent some months in London, working on my thesis at the British Museum. I often went to Hyde Park, where, among other speakers, I remember listening to Hyndman and Tom Mann. In order to supplement my allowance, which was not sufficient in England, I took care of a small child in a stuffy bourgeois home in the suburbs. Returning to Brussels, I graduated from the Université Nouvelle with the degree of doctor of philosophy and literature, but I knew that my education was far from finished. I had found at Brussels the intellectual affirmation of all that I had felt and believed, but I was too self-critical not to realize how one-sided my training had been. At the Université Nouvelle, the work of the orthodox economists and philosophers had been presented under the searchlight of a revolutionary critique. But what if the process were reversed? What would have happened had I first entered some German university where these subjects were taught by the most noted defenders of the *status quo*? How did I know that my new-found Marxism would stand the test? It was in an effort to answer these questions and to establish my own intellectual security that I decided to spend the next two years in Germany; a few months later I enrolled at the University of Leipsic.

After Brussels, university life in Leipsic was like a step from the future back into the past. As I look back upon that period now—both my year at Leipsic and the next in Berlin—my life at that time seems to have been enveloped in a damp fog, those two years a chilly interlude between Brussels and Rome. The atmosphere at the German universities was that of a well-disciplined army post over which ruled the faculty as the general staff. The chasm between teachers and pupils was symbolized in

[20]

the curt and arrogant nods with which the former acknowledged the military salutes and heel-clicking of the latter. The incredible formality and authoritarianism of academic life appalled me, but even more incredible was the complacency with which the students accepted the régime. One looked in vain for some hint of rebellion, of irreverence, of good-natured mockery. If there were any radicals among the Leipsic students, I did not discover them—and this in one of the most revolutionary Socialist centres of all Germany.

There were few women students at Leipsic and these were subjected to special restrictions. Perhaps because of a threefold combination of circumstances, I aroused particular scrutiny. I was a girl, a Russian, and I wanted to study, not arts and letters, but political economy. I found that I had to receive personal authorization from each professor to follow his course and the more conservative the professor the more reluctant was his consent.

The absurd insistence on form and hierarchy that prevailed at this time, and which would have amused me if I had been more objective about my surroundings, was illustrated by an incident which occurred during my second semester. I was halted in the midst of a desperate plea that a doctor be sent to a student who was dangerously ill because I had omitted one of the three titles of the physician.

"You mean *Geheimrat* Professor Doctor X, do you not?" interrupted the professor.

The tedium of academic life was made bearable by the meetings I attended several nights a week. It was here that I first heard and met August Bebel, leader of the German Social Democracy, Rosa Luxemburg and Clara Zetkin, who were later to become my friends.

I remember in particular my first meeting with Rosa Luxemburg. I had been reading one of her books on the development of capitalism, which she had written during her frequent sojourns in gaol in Poland and Germany, and when I heard that she was to speak in Leipsic I determined to meet her if possible. On the evening she was to speak I went early to the Leipsic

People's House. As she was to address Socialist women and I was not yet a member of the Party, I was not sure that I would be admitted. As she was entering the building, I recognized her from descriptions of her that I had read, and summoning all my courage I approached her.

"Comrade," I inquired, "would you allow me to attend your meeting? I am a Russian student, a believer in Socialism, though not yet a member of the Party."

She was very gracious towards me. Her eyes lighted up. "Of course," she said. "I shall be happy to have you at my meeting." She kept me at her side until it was time for her to take the platform.

While she was speaking I realized why she was considered one of the greatest speakers and teachers of the movement. Her simplicity, her enthusiasm, and deep sincerity, together with her wit, combined to produce a profound effect upon her audience. She was extraordinarily endowed intellectually. While still a very young girl, a university student, she had impressed authorities on political economy with her precocious writings on this subject. She had an exceptionally keen critical mind, and at an age when most girls are interested in little except clothes, romantic novels, and dancing, she was already a regular and highly-respected contributor to the scientific Marxian journals.

Rosa Luxemburg belonged to that generation of famous women who had to struggle against almost insurmountable obstacles to gain opportunities which the men of her day accepted as a matter of course. For a woman to acquire intellectual recognition at that time demanded an authentic thirst for knowledge, much tenacity and an iron will. Rosa Luxemburg had all of these qualities to an exceptional degree.

But there was also a softer side to her nature. When, after her tragic death, some of her letters to her intimate friends were published, they were a revelation to the public—particularly perhaps to that section of it which read the conservative press, which usually referred to her as "the Red Fury." Those letters were poetic in the truest sense of the word. The intense political activity and scientific work of Rosa Luxemburg expressed but one aspect of her mind and personality.

[22]

After a year in Leipsic, my Marxian faith was affirmed rather than shaken, but I was determined to put it to still another test. I went to Berlin to study under Adolph Wagner, the most noted of the academic political economists at this time.

In Berlin, too, though the atmosphere was somewhat more sophisticated, my academic surroundings seemed to belong to the past rather than to the present or future. There were few radical students there and the same worship of authority prevailed. Though Herr Doctor Wagner had a reputation as a "liberal," I soon discovered that he was a true Prussian militarist. In this he was typical of the German academicians of that time; and it was this combination of abstract liberalism, innate servility, and blind nationalism with which so many of the German intellectuals were to astonish the world in 1914. When I first interviewed him early one morning at his home in order to secure permission to attend his classes, he was inclined to refuse —on the ground that as a graduate there was no reason for me to pursue my studies further. A graduate, a woman, why should I spend more time at a university? And why, of all things, did I want to study political economy? I sensed his suspicion. My confusion saved the day for me. I merely stammered, "But I know so little, Herr Professor, and your lectures are so famous." The inadvertent flattery of this reply pleased him. I received his permission to enrol.

One morning as I entered the classroom, I noticed an extraordinary excitement among the students. As Professor Wagner arose to speak, he was greeted by that boisterous stamping of feet by which the German students expressed their patriotic excitement. It was only after he sat down at the close of his remarks that I understood the meaning of this demonstration and the extraordinarily chauvinistic tone of his address. Beside him on the platform an elderly gentleman in military uniform and many decorations sat in an arm-chair which had been covered by a Gobelin tapestry trimmed with gold. At the end of the session I learnt that the visitor was a member of the Hohenzollern family.

Long before the end of the year I had made up my mind that I had had enough of German university life.

3

EVER SINCE I HAD BEGUN THE STUDY OF MARX-
ism, one name had become increasingly familiar to me.
This was the name of Antonio Labriola—not to be confused
with Arturo Labriola, the spirited leader of the Italian syndicalists. Antonio Labriola was a professor at the University
of Sapienza in Rome. Whenever a group of Socialist students
at any of the universities I had attended gathered for discussion,
one was almost certain to hear him quoted. Any student who
took the revolutionary movement seriously in those days would
have been tempted to give his right arm for the opportunity to
study with him. What interested me most in Marxism was its
philosophical approach, and Antonio Labriola, like Plekhanoff,
had this approach. At this time I had never been in Italy
and the thought of living there and coming to know the Italian people first hand, coupled with the opportunity of working
under a man with such a brilliant international reputation,

constituted an irresistible attraction. At the end of the semester, after I had packed up my books and had boarded the Berlin-to-Rome express, the train seemed to me—in my impatience—to be scarcely moving.

I had no intimate friends in Rome, but I remembered vaguely that a Socialist refugee whom I had met in Brussels in 1898 lived there. I wrote him a note in care of *Avanti* and he came to my hotel and helped me look for a room. We found a suitable one in a boarding-house. The only woman member of the Party in Rome, Elena Pensuti, lived there, too. She became my intimate friend and remained such until the war. Though we lived in the "modern" part of the city, we were near one of its oldest churches, the famous Santa Maria Maggiore. While I began at once to study at the university and to frequent the public library, I spent much of my time admiring the treasures of Italian art in the churches and galleries. From these excursions into the past I learned much more than I did from books. But for me at this time the past with all its glories was only a prelude to the new civilization which I hoped to help inaugurate.

The university atmosphere in Rome was as different from that of Germany as was the climate. That absurd formality and insistence on academic form was entirely absent. The professors passing among the students greeted them and were greeted in turn with informal courtesy. The highest ranking members of the faculty could be stopped and questioned at length about any point that was interesting or perplexing to the student. There was no difference in the treatment of men and women students; no special requirements or restrictions set up for the latter. Many lectures were open to the general public as well as to the students and were free.

Many of the young women who attended classes came from wealthy and conservative Roman families. They dressed with a certain elegance and were usually accompanied by nuns acting as their duennas. Many of them would leave their nun chaperons in the library or elsewhere and steal away to some rendezvous. They took much greater liberties than the few radical women who believed, as a matter of principle, in "sex freedom."

I was not disappointed in Labriola. Possessed of a deep, keen, and critical intellect, he was undoubtedly one of the most outstanding teachers of his generation. In fact, I still consider him one of the most remarkable men of modern times. Earlier in his academic career he had been a professor of philosophy at the University of Naples, where his scientific investigations had brought him into contact with the works of Marx.

Labriola's method was both scientific and creative. Though a Socialist, he never attempted to impose his Socialist convictions upon his pupils. He would lead us through history, philosophy, through the past and the present; he would uncover the facts and let us draw the conclusions ourselves. He taught us to doubt so that we would learn to investigate and to develop our own critical approach to social theory, to art and science. He wrote in one of the few books he left to posterity: "A professor using the university to make *propaganda* for socialism ought to be put into a madhouse."

We were all the more deeply moved then when, at the close of the last lecture of the semester, he paused a moment, looked at us with tired, friendly eyes and said: "In the forty lectures I have given you this year I have shown you that society is divided into exploited and exploiters. Those of you who choose to fight with the former against the latter are fulfilling a generous, noble task. As your Professor of Morals and Philosophy, I tell you this. I have finished."

I have never applauded any one so vigorously, so gratefully, as I applauded him.

Soon after I had enrolled in Labriola's class, it was evident that I had aroused his curiosity. Though I sat in a far corner of the room, he would often look at me inquiringly when dealing with certain questions, especially when he alluded to Russia. Finally he spoke of a book I had translated from Russian into French and introduced me to the class. That was the beginning of my personal relationship with him and thereafter I became one of a small circle of students who would accompany him to a café after his lectures. At these discussions, which became a sort of academic forum, he would deal frequently with contemporary events and politicians, and here we came to know not only the tremendous scope, but also the caustic and ironic quality, of his intellect.

I remember how angry he would get when some one would ask him whether Arturo Labriola (also a professor, a Socialist of the extreme syndicalist type and a native of southern Italy) was related to him. Poor Antonio Labriola! If he had known how many people outside of Italy not merely think of these two so different men as related, but even consider them the same person! A witty French Marxist once made the statement: "Yes, Italy has two Labriolas—Antonio, a very great one; Arturo, a very insignificant one."

Labriola had a serious throat ailment and as his voice grew weaker and weaker, those most interested in his course were allowed to sit close to his lecture table. His doctor had forbidden him to smoke or snuff tobacco, but inevitably, a few minutes before he was to begin his lecture, he would look over his audience, which contained several monks and priests. Singling out one of them, he would approach him and say, alluding to his own atheism: "Your Christian God has punished the organ I have sinned with most." (Here he would point to his throat.) "Be a good Christian and give me a little tobacco." There would be an exchange of smiles between the great iconoclast and the humble servant of the Church as the latter produced his tobacco-pouch from beneath his cassock.

Near the end of the year, Labriola called me to his table before class and showed me a new book on Marxism in which he thought I would be interested. "Look here, Signorina," he said, sadly, as I was about to return to my seat, "I am the only Marxist in Italy. When I die, you will be the only one. You must be the executor of my Marxist will."

I was so deeply moved not only by what he had said, but by his manner, that I could not concentrate on the ensuing lecture.

At the close of the year I had an experience which was a revelation to me. Labriola had two children, a son and a daugh-

[27]

ter, neither of whom shared any of his intellectual or political interests. The son developed into a most colourless employé of the government. The daughter was a pretentious, pseudo-intellectual. From her father she had inherited a certain caustic quality; but whereas Labriola used his sharp tongue as a weapon for creative criticism and analysis, she used hers as an outlet for her rancour and disappointment in life. She, too, became a professor at the university, but it was common knowledge that her father not only used his influence to secure her appointment, but also helped her to write her doctor's thesis and exerted pressure upon his own students to compel them to attend her lectures.

At the end of the term I wanted to show in some small way my appreciation of what Labriola had done for me intellectually, and I had a small medallion of Karl Marx made by a Roman artist. When I went to Labriola's home to present my gift, he escorted me into his ample, sunny studio. Bashfully, I tried to explain what had induced me to bring him the medallion and how grateful I would be if he would accept it as a souvenir from a very thankful pupil.

He accepted the gift most graciously, and I was about to leave when he asked me an unexpected question—"Have you seen the bust of my daughter?"

Before I could reply he took me to a place which seemed to be a sanctuary to him—a silent, dark room. Here he drew aside a velvet curtain and revealed a portrait bust of Teresa Labriola mounted on a pedestal.

"How do you like it? I am sorry the artist did not reproduce her coiffure exactly," he said, in such a serious tone that I abstained from any comment.

Before we left the sanctuary he once more looked at the bust, touched the head with one finger so as to be sure that there was no dust, no mark of profanation, upon it. He then closed the curtains and we left the room very quietly, as though afraid of disturbing a sleeping child.

The fact that such a man, so inexorably critical, so impatient of human imperfections, was so blind where his own feelings

[28]

or affections were concerned gave me new insight into human nature.

During my early days in Rome, I had no direct contact with the Party. While Elena was a member, she, like myself, was too shy to approach the Party leaders. But even to see these men, many of whose names were well known throughout Italy, was to us a great joy. As we knew that most of them took their meals at restaurants in the neighbourhood of Parliament in Piazza Firenze, we usually lunched there. It was here I first saw Prampolini, Morgari, Turati, Treves, and many other Socialist deputies. Elena and I would sit in some remote corner, listening eagerly to their animated discussion. During the whole meal there would not be a single moment of silence at the table where they were gathered. But other patrons, too, were very noisy and we were often disappointed in not being able to hear what the Socialists were saying.

Though I am reviving these memories after almost forty years, during which I collaborated and was in close personal touch with most of these men, I am happy to say that they did not disappoint me. As a whole, they remained to me what they were when I worshipped them in my naïve youth—honest men, thoroughly devoted to the working class, and whose errors and defeats, however fatal they may have been for the movement, were not due to personal opportunism or lack of fidelity to the ideals they had espoused.

The first of the Socialist deputies whom I came to know personally was Leonida Bissolati, one of the founders and then chief editor of the official organ of the Italian Socialist Party, *Avanti*. For my work with Antonio Labriola I needed current German Marxist literature which I knew could be obtained at the headquarters of the Party press. Those small, bare editorial-rooms surrounded by historical buildings and old churches, and presided over by the man who seemed to me to speak for millions of oppressed workers, filled me with awe.

Bissolati was one of the most typical of Italian Socialist leaders of his day. Before he had finished his studies at the university he had already decided to give up his career as a lawyer and

[29]

devote all his time and energy to the labour movement. Born in Cremona, which was surrounded by vast estates owned by absentee landlords whose managers were expected to squeeze every possible centesimo out of their holdings, he had early gained first-hand knowledge of the misery, degradation, and suffering of the Italian peasants. He had watched malaria and pellagra wipe out whole districts. His first polemical writings, dealing with the suffering and injustice he saw all round him, caused him to be denounced as a "utopian" and "mutineer."

At the time I first met him, the Italian Socialist Party was already divided into two warring factions—a left wing which emphasized the revolutionary goal of the movement, a right wing which believed in "gradualism" and stressed immediate reforms. The left tendency, which I passionately approved, was represented by Enrico Ferri; and the right, which I just as passionately opposed, was led by Bissolati. Yet, despite my principled agreement with Ferri, I had little respect for him as an individual. His arguments and manner of defending his position impressed me as being superficial and even demagogic. His reputation as Italy's greatest criminologist and his brilliance as a speaker gave him a standing in the movement which, judging him as a Marxist, I did not feel he deserved.

Bissolati was the antithesis of Ferri in many respects, and though I disagreed with him politically, I came to have great personal admiration for him. He was the personification of the anti-demagogue. Just as courageously as he had defied public opinion in his native province when he joined the labour movement, he later faced the disapproval of the masses and the criticism of his own comrades when he was accused of being a reformist. In neither case was he concerned about, nor would he make the slightest concession to, public opinion.

When I first met him, though I was young and inexperienced, he treated me as an equal. Thus it was not difficult for him to induce me to express my opinion, my criticism of his viewpoint. When I came the second time, he was even more kind and encouraging. When I apologized for taking up so much of his time, he said: "Don't say that. I feel so much younger when

I am talking with you. Please come again soon—as soon as you like."

He then picked up the volumes of the German Marxist review, *Neue Zeit,* which I had asked him to lend me, and accompanied me home, continuing our discussion *en route.* Who would have thought that the time would come when the young woman walking beside him and listening so eagerly would be the one to advocate his expulsion from the Party he had founded?

My revolutionary convictions enforced by the lectures of Antonio Labriola, by avid reading of *Avanti* and other periodical and scientific literature, and by my discussions with Italian Socialists, I felt that the time had now come for me to join the Party. It was the next logical step in my development. It was not as if I had experienced a sudden emotional conversion while attending a mass meeting and listening to some eloquent speaker. I had approached the movement gradually and had contemplated this step for a long time. Joining a revolutionary party is not necessarily an exciting and dramatic experience. There is no elaborate ritual. One makes out an application card, appears before a small membership committee, and then takes one's place in the ranks.

As a member of the Party, my life went on for a time as it was before. I continued to devote myself to my studies. Near the end of the year, however, I grew restless. I wanted to begin active work as a propagandist. But where and how? For advice, I turned back to my own people and discussed the problem with certain Russian leaders in addition to consulting those Italian Socialists for whom I had come to have such a deep respect.

My Russian comrades advised me most emphatically to remain in Western Europe. I had had no experience in the underground movement, and Russia, they told me, was quite impossible except for professional conspirators. As an *émigrée* returning home after years spent in European universities, it would be taken for granted that I had been "contaminated" by the liberal tradition and I would be suspect at once. My every move would be watched by the police. For the sake not only of the Russian movement, but also of the international one, I must remain abroad. My Italian friends agreed with this. The decision was hard to accept, for I had always considered my sojourn in Western Europe as preparation for work in the movement in Russia.

I yielded, however, to the arguments of those whose judgment was undoubtedly more objective than mine and based on more experience. But if not in Russia, where? The solution of this problem, now that Russia was eliminated, did not prove difficult. When I had travelled about Europe with my family, it had seemed to me that the most heavy, dangerous and degrading work in Europe was done by the "cheap labour" of Italian emigrants. This was particularly true in Switzerland, where thousands of them came each year to escape unbearable conditions at home. I learnt that the Swiss town of St. Gall, with its great textile mills employing thousands of Italians— particularly young girls and women—and its many Italian masons, was an important *émigré* centre. I went to St. Gall.

The town is located in what is known as German Switzerland and German is its official language. The People's House, which served as the headquarters of the Swiss trade unions, was also the gathering-place of the foreign workers, among whom the Italians were the predominant group. I saw at once what handicaps the foreigners suffered in their relations both with their employers and with their fellow unionists. With my ability to speak many languages, I realized I could be of assistance as a translator and interpreter to the Italian workers. I talked the matter over with the Swiss trade-union officials and they approved of my plan. I had offered to work in the headquarters without compensation and I was furnished with an office and desk. Within a few weeks I had all the work I could handle.

One day the manager of the People's House stopped at my desk and made a request that astonished me. Would I speak on the revolutionary movement in Russia before the German Socialist Club?

[32]

"Speak—why, how can I?" I asked. "I have never spoken before an audience in my life. I wouldn't know how to begin."

He went on insisting, in his calm, Teutonic fashion. Was I not a member of the Party, with duties to perform like other members? They wanted some one to speak on Russia on this occasion, and I was a Russian and a revolutionist. Did I not believe in Party discipline?

It was difficult to answer his arguments, even though I was certain that I would never be able to speak. I decided, however, that I must at least show my good will, regardless of the result. I would not talk about Russia because I did not know enough about the movement at that time, but I agreed to give a Socialist propaganda speech—and if the affair was a fiasco, well, I had warned him in advance.

In preparing my speech, I think now—as I look back upon it—that I understood intuitively what many people have to learn from experience—in what measure an agitational speech must stem from the emotions and how gradually an audience must be prepared for the absorption of abstract ideas. First one must understand one's audience and establish a psychological *rapport* with them. I had taken as my own, Antonio Labriola's slogan: "Put science at the disposal of the masses." How to do it only my Marxist training and my intuition could suggest.

When the evening came for the meeting, I was surprised to find that I felt no concern about the result. This was a duty to be performed and I believed that if I expressed myself honestly and sincerely, it would not matter how badly I failed in other respects. There was work for all in the movement and I should be no less valuable to it after the workers realized that I did not know how to speak from the platform.

I was so sure of the negative result of this experiment—which I was certain would be my first and last public address—that I decided to take a small dog that a comrade had entrusted to my care to the meeting with me. After saying a few words, I would certainly have to stop and the chairman would try to save the situation by apologizing for my lack of experience. Then, after I had shown my good intentions, I could leave the hall and take the dog with me for a long walk. It was only this feeling of complete indifference as to the outcome which enabled me to face the audience. I had written what I had intended to say, but once I rose to speak I never thought of looking at my manuscript. After a few minutes, I found that I was speaking freely and spontaneously. Not even the repeated applause interrupted my flow of words. I must have spoken for over an hour and the poor dog did not get his usual exercise that night.

After this experience, I might have spent all my time in making speeches and within a year I had become one of the most popular propagandists in Switzerland, speaking often four or five times daily in four or five different languages.

I had been in St. Gall nearly two years when new and important work took me elsewhere. One day, while I was away on a trip, I received word that a young Italian teacher, an ardent propagandist for Socialism, was coming to St. Gall. She had only recently fled from Italy to escape imprisonment for an article she had written. I wrote the comrades at St. Gall that Maria was to have the use of my room. When I returned I found I had a rather difficult situation on my hands, for Maria was experiencing her first pregnancy. She eventually became the mother of seven children and the object of considerable gossip. She kept her private affairs very much to herself and there was a great deal of speculation as to who the father, or fathers, of these children might be. I happened to know that only one man was involved and that Maria was as faithful and devoted to him as any bourgeois wife to her husband. Several years later, in Italy, the editor of a clerical journal made slurring remarks about Maria's morals. Meeting him in the marketplace one day, Maria, in a loud voice that all round her could hear, inquired of a vegetable woman if this was the man who had gossiped about her. The startled woman, whom Maria knew to be a devout Catholic, was taken off guard and nodded her head affirmatively. Maria then stepped in the path of the astonished editor and, before the crowd which had already assembled, gave him a resounding slap in the face. There was little more talk of Maria and her children after that. The man who was the father of Maria's children was killed in the war and she afterwards lived with another man who had an equal number of children by a former wife. Their household was a lively one.

At the time Maria lived with me in St. Gall, the Italian Socialists had no special propaganda paper for women. We conceived the notion that one should be started and decided that Lugano, where some Italian comrades had a coöperative printing-shop, would be a good place from which to launch it. Both Maria and I were hostile to any form of "feminism." To us the fight for the emancipation of women was only a single aspect of the struggle for the emancipation of humanity. It was because we wanted women, particularly workingwomen, to understand this, to learn that they had to fight not *against* men but *with* them against the common enemy, capitalist society, that we felt the need of this paper. Moving to Lugano, Maria and I founded *Su, Compagne!* (*Arise, Comrades!*). It was an almost instant success, gaining wide distribution throughout Italy, Switzerland, and wherever Italian workers congregated throughout the world.

One day in Lugano as I was writing an editorial for *Su, Compagne!*, a young worker stepped into my room.

"I come from Stabio," he said. "It is a small town off the railroad. A reactionary place, but a few of us are beginning to wake up. Will you not come and speak for us?"

I asked him a few questions and agreed to go. I was to speak in the only meeting-hall in the town, which was in a hotel, but when I arrived I found the few radicals who had congregated there in a state of great excitement. The town priest, when he heard that I was coming, had denounced me from his pulpit as a "she-devil" and was organizing a group of women to disrupt the meeting. The police, too, were opposed to the meeting.

The owner of the hotel had been intimidated and refused at the last moment the use of the hall. My friends begged me to call off the affair. I answered as I always have in such emergencies, "A revolutionist does not yield to threats."

We finally assembled at a public square near the church. When we were ready to start the meeting about forty or fifty

[35]

people, both friends and enemies, had gathered about a table which was to serve as a platform, while many more assembled at a distance, afraid to approach closer. I had scarcely begun speaking when all the bells of all the churches in the town began ringing. Indignation and fear were registered on the faces of my friends. I realized that if I stopped speaking, there might be a panic or riot. Notwithstanding the clamour of the bells, shouts—both hostile and friendly—from the audience and the screams of frightened children, I continued, though I realized I could not make myself heard.

Suddenly a man's angry voice rose above the tumult. "Why don't they let this woman speak? I am not a Socialist, but I want her to be heard. Are they afraid of her? Let us go to my place."

"Bravo! Bravo!" shouted people from all sides.

The man led the way to a large shed. My audience had been growing and by now the whole town had turned out and the shed was filled to overflowing. The priest's followers milled round outside, shouting imprecations and raining stones on the building. Neverthless I finished my speech.

We were just leaving the shed when two excited men came running in, breathless and hatless.

"Quick!" they said. "You must get out of here. Hundreds more women are coming with forks and sticks. They will kill you."

"The doctor's house is the only safe place," some one said. "We can get there by going round through the fields."

The tall grass had not been cut and was wet from recent rains. We stumbled along as best we could, the men insisting on carrying me whenever I got out of breath or the going became difficult. In the doctor's house at last, we barricaded the door and windows. The mob, now composed of both men and women, howled outside, threw rocks and garbage.

One of the men who had been especially solicitous as to my welfare while we were crossing the fields, but who had not uttered a word, suddenly knelt at my feet and began to remove my wet shoes.

"Please don't," I said, touched and displeased at the same time.

He looked at me a moment without saying a word, then carefully removed my shoes and put them beside the stove to dry. After that he took a crumpled piece of paper out of his pocket, sat down in a corner, and labouriously began to write. When he had handed this paper to me, I read:

Dear Comrade Balabanoff:

I would like to give my life to save yours. I am a stammerer and have always felt inferior to others. My parents died when I was very young and I was supported by public charity. During my childhood other children teased and laughed at me. I can't take part in the discussions of the workers. But when I heard you speak I understood at once that you feel and speak for people such as I—for all the oppressed, the unhappy, the downtrodden.

This tribute, paid to me as the mob screamed outside and stones beat a tattoo on the walls of that house in Stabio, I cherish above any other that I have received in my long life as a propagandist.

When the time came for me to catch my train, a carriage that had been ordered drew up in the street outside. The mob, sensing an opportunity at last, gathered about it. I was determined to leave and would not listen to my comrades' objections. I insisted that only one man accompany me. As I stepped out of the door, a frenzied horde of women surrounded me. They threw dust in my face and spat on my dress. I saw the man beside me fumbling at his pocket. I knew the meaning of that. "Don't touch that revolver!" I shouted. Despite all the noise they made, the women gave way before me. I was in the carriage, the horses reared and plunged for a moment, and then we were off.

As a result of this episode and the publicity it received throughout Switzerland, the whole labour and radical movement rose in protest. A new meeting was arranged and workers from all over the canton poured into Stabio to guard against a repetition of what had happened on my first visit. This meeting was very successful. The Party began to gain strength throughout that entire area and an active branch was established in Stabio itself. Some of the very women who had howled and cursed at me eventually joined it.

During the period I lived in Lugano, I would leave every Friday for propaganda engagements in the German or French cantons, returning Monday morning to work on the paper, which went to press Thursday. The most difficult part of the work was editing articles we received from the women in factories or on the rice plantations. We encouraged all of them to write regardless of their capacities as we wanted to develop their self-confidence. They described the conditions under which they worked, exchanged opinions and impressions; thus a spirit of comradeship was engendered among them.

At that time nuns would go from Switzerland into the Italian provinces where Catholicism was strongest and from which many Italian workers emigrated. Parents who were afraid to let their daughters travel and live alone were willing to let them go in care of the nuns. In Switzerland these nuns ran "boarding-houses" which were practically convents in the neighbourhood of the textile mills in which the girls worked. The wages of these girls were paid by the factory owners directly to the nuns, and after payment for board, penalties for "sins," and various religious "donations" had been deducted, the girls received practically nothing.

Among the letters Maria and I received as editors of *Su, Compagne!*, was one from a mother of one of these girls complaining of the treatment her daughter was receiving. Wishing to make sure that the situation was as she described it, I made a personal investigation. As soon as I had gathered authentic material, I began a campaign on the subject in *Su, Compagne!* and carried the exposé into the German and French labour press. The reaction of public opinion was violent not only among Socialists and trade unionists, but also among freethinkers, Freemasons and the public generally. Finally, after my material had been incorporated into a pamphlet, the government was forced to intervene.

While I was conducting the campaign, an Italian Socialist lawyer asked that I be sent to speak at the World Congress of

Freethinkers which convened in Rome on September 20, 1904 to celebrate the abolition of papal power in Italy. It was to be an impressive gathering of rationalist and scientific forces from all over the world. The railroads had made special arrangements to handle the crowds as ten thousand people were expected to join this pilgrimage to the land of such martyrs of free thought as Giordano Bruno, such fighters for freedom as Garibaldi. The Pope, who was then living a prisoner in the Vatican, had ordered all the Catholic churches closed for the entire week of the Congress as a counter-demonstration.

The Congress itself was to be divided into sections dealing with anti-clerical, scientific, and social problems. I was to report on my investigation and to submit a resolution calling for the abolition of the work system sponsored by the nuns. I could see little use in attending such a gathering made up largely of anti-clericals who believed in the profit system. But I was finally persuaded by the argument that my report would be published in free-thought journals throughout the world and read by many workers.

At the Italian frontier I found that the train service was disrupted by the first great general strike in modern Italy. Most of the travellers protested against the consequent difficulties of the journey and were indignant at the strikers. But I was proud and happy to return to Italy in the midst of this impressive demonstration of proletarian solidarity.

I had not been in Rome since I had left the university and the city seemed more beautiful and the sun more glorious than ever. The Congress was to be held at the university. Antonio Labriola was dead but I felt that I had inherited from him an inexhaustible treasury of knowledge.

When I arrived at the university the Congress was already in session and Ernest Haeckel, the outstanding biologist of his time, was speaking. I was shocked by the conduct of the audience, which made so much noise that he could not be heard. (He was speaking in German.) He was an old man with a weak constitution and his voice could not compete for an instant against the shuffling and confusion in the hall.

The younger people attending the Congress were especially

impatient. A parade had been planned for this morning, it was time for it to start, and still Haeckel went on talking. The sun, the music, the many banners, the huge crowd already gathered outside invited them into the streets.

When the parade finally moved it was not the disciplined demonstration which had been planned. Thousands of men and women who had just stepped out of their houses to see what was going on were carried away by the colour, the singing and laughing, and joined in. The occasion took on a spontaneous character which increased its effectiveness as a demonstration a thousandfold. All the latent rebel instincts of the people seemed to awaken. Nobody had ordered them to demonstrate. On the contrary, there was the veto of the Church. But there they were, the masses of Rome, singing revolutionary songs, waving aloft impromptu banners, and mocking all the forces of ecclesiastical and secular power which in their everyday life held them in subjection.

If the foreigners who speak and write today of the enthusiastic unanimity of the Italian people for Fascism could have seen the spontaneous demonstrations of pre-Fascist Italy, they might not be in such a hurry to rush into print with their meaningless and stupid generalities.

The sessions of the Congress continued almost as turbulent as the inauguration. While the delegates were engaged in their discussions, people would enter the hall and leave it as soon as they realized that they were not interested in the subject or did not understand the language of the speaker. I was sure that when my turn came to speak I would be prevented from making myself heard by the disorder.

When I began talking I fully intended to give only the barest outline of the speech I had originally had in mind. I soon noticed, however, that all noise had ceased. Not only were those present listening intently and in complete silence, but more people were coming in. By the time I had warmed to my subject every seat and all available standing room was taken. When I finished, I could not submit my resolution because of the applause which broke out again and again. Eventually when the resolution, which not only condemned the work system of the nuns, but also called for the abolition of private ownership of the means of production, came before the delegates, I was amazed that it passed unanimously. Though I was inexperienced, I understood that this vote was much more the result of enthusiasm than of conviction.

Among those who seemed most impressed by this demonstration were people—among them professors at the university—who had taken no notice of me whatever when I had lived in Rome. When I went to the Café Aragno, where I had gone so often with Antonio Labriola and other Socialists in my student days, I found that I had suddenly become the centre of attention.

After I had returned to Lugano, friends sent me hundreds of newspaper clippings reporting my speech and its effect on the Congress. Invitations to address other meetings poured in. I had become "famous."

4

A MEETING TO CELEBRATE THE THIRTY-THIRD
anniversary of the Paris Commune had been organized
by the Italian Socialist branch in Lausanne and I was asked to
be the principal speaker. I had spoken frequently enough by
this time to have lost all self-consciousness on the platform but
on this occasion I found my attention distracted throughout
the meeting by one individual in that large and attentive audience. He was a young man I had never seen before and his
agitated manner and unkempt clothes set him apart from the
other workers in the hall. The *émigré* audiences were always
poorly dressed, but this man was also extremely dirty. I had
never seen a more wretched-looking human being. In spite of
his large jaw, the bitterness and restlessness in his black eyes,
he gave the impression of extreme timidity. Even as he listened,
his nervous hands clutching at his big black hat, he seemed more
concerned with his own inner turmoil than with what I was
saying.

At the close of the meeting, during the informal discussion that followed, I asked one of the active workers about him. The man explained that the stranger was a refugee from military service in Italy who had made his appearance at the clubroom one evening a short time before and had been introduced by one of the members who had known him as the son of a Socialist in Romagna. He was obviously starving, and Serrati, who was present, had welcomed the man and had fed him at the expense of the Party at the coöperative restaurant. He had not been able to find work and was still living as a vagrant.

"He sleeps under the bridge except when I can take him in and give him my bed in the daytime while I am at work," he went on. "At home he was supposed to be a school-teacher, but it is said that he drank too much, had a terrible disease, and was always getting into scrapes. He claims he is a Socialist, but he seems to know very little about Socialism. He talks more like an Anarchist. But he is in great need."

Another worker in the group, a stone mason, added, "My wife made him some underclothing from an old sheet. The next time he comes to a meeting, comrade, I will see that he is cleaner. All of us manage to get work, but he says he can't, that he is too sick."

I felt greatly disturbed at the young man's plight and after a while I went over to him where he was sitting alone at the back of the hall.

"Can I do anything for you?" I asked. "I hear you have no work."

His voice, as he answered, was almost hysterical, and he replied, without looking up, "Nothing can be done for me. I am sick, incapable of work or effort."

I scarcely knew what to say. Then he began to speak again, more quietly:

"I have no luck. A few weeks ago I had a chance to earn fifty francs, but I had to refuse it." (He uttered a vulgar blasphemy.) "A publisher in Milan offered me fifty francs to translate a pamphlet by Kautsky—'The Coming Revolution.' But I had to refuse. I know only a few common words of German."

"But I know German. I shall be glad to help you," I told him.

[43]

"You help me?" His voice grew hysterical again. "Why should you help me?"

"Why not? I am a Socialist. I happen to have grown up under privileged conditions with opportunities you were denied. Certainly it is my duty to repay——"

He was too weak to resist the offer and yet it was obvious that he disliked himself for yielding to it. As I held out my hand to shake his, he took it reluctantly.

"What is your name, comrade?"

"Benito Mussolini."

Little did I dream that night that I was embarking upon an association which ten years later was to have such bitter consequences; that, due in part to my aid and sympathy, the miserable vagrant of that Lausanne meeting was to assume a leading rôle in the movement to which I had given my life, and that he was to be guilty of the most infamous betrayal of modern times. But no one could have foreseen in this bewildered and neurotic youth of twenty the man who rules Italy today. For every Mussolini, redeemed from misery and despair by human solidarity at some critical moment, there are hundreds who, having found life worth living, have sacrificed that life to the struggle for social justice.

The work of translation did not last long, as the pamphlet was a small one. As we worked together on it I could see how much this sort of work meant to him, how it stimulated his ambition. It was obvious that he despised manual labor and I guessed that at least part of his wretchedness, his inability to adjust himself to life among the *émigrés*, was due to the fact that in order to exist in Switzerland he had had to choose between vagrancy and the most humble occupations. In spite of the violence of his hatred of all privilege, he did not consider himself a proletarian. His mother had been a school-teacher and he himself had taught for a brief time in an elementary school in Italy. He thought of himself as an "intellectual," a leader, and the contrast between this conception of himself and the humilities of his daily life had induced in him an exaggerated self-pity and sense of personal injustice.

As we worked together, I tried to make him feel that I was

his collaborator rather than his teacher, so that he would not feel dependent on me. His self-confidence increased from day to day, and as it did so he became more careful of his personal appearance and less hysterical in his manner.

I soon saw that he knew little of history, of economics, or of Socialist theory and that his mind was completely undisciplined. His father had been an Anarchist and in the '70's had belonged to the First International as a disciple of Bakunin; later he became a Socialist. Benito Mussolini had been raised among radicals in the most revolutionary province of Italy—Romagna. Not to have been either a Socialist or an Anarchist in Romagna would have meant to swim against the tide. For a worker to have been anything but a radical in that province might have required courage. Mussolini's radicalism and anti-clericalism were more the reflection of his early environment and his own rebellious egoism than the product of understanding and conviction. His hatred of oppression was not that impersonal hatred of a system shared by all revolutionaries. It sprang from his own sense of indignity and frustration, his passion to assert his own ego, and from a determination for personal revenge.

I came to understand these things about him gradually, of course.

As our collaboration on the Kautsky translation increased his self-confidence, elevating him for the moment from the status of a tramp to that of a "writer," he became more vocal and assertive at the discussions which took place nightly at the Italian Socialist Club. Though he had read nothing of Marx except the Communist Manifesto, he did not hesitate to argue violently both with the Socialist workers there and with the real "intellectuals" among the émigrés, some of whom had been Marxian scholars for many years. He had no faith in the political education of the masses and he expressed his contempt for such "gradualism" in loud and violent harangues.

"He is a Blanquist, not a Socialist," remarked one of the workers on one occasion and to the extent that Mussolini had any concept of a social program, this was undoubtedly correct. He liked to talk about "philosophy," but his philosophic views were always the reflection of the book he had happened to read

[45]

last. The writers who most appealed to his temperament were Nietzsche, Schopenhauer, Stirner—men who glorified the Will, the Ego, the act of the individual rather than of the mass. It was inevitable that he should be intoxicated with the theories of the French radical Blanqui who had conceived of revolution as a violent *coup d'état*, the seizure of power by a small group of revolutionary conspirators; and it is to the revolutionary adventurism of Blanqui, rather than to the revolutionary collectivism of Marx, that one must look for the key to Mussolini's subsequent career.

If I was more patient at this time with his bombastic individualism, his philosophic pretensions, than were the other Italian radicals, particularly the more hard-headed workers, it was probably that I understood—what they did not—that his egotism, his glorification of strength and physical courage, were the compensations for his own weakness, his longing for personal recognition and prestige. Once he was well in mind and body, I told myself, once he really felt himself the equal—rather than the inferior—of other men, once his personal bitterness was allayed by human understanding and sympathy, his assertiveness, his childish will-to-power and his intellectual confusion would pass away. He was, after all, very young; with study, with more experience in disciplined, organized movements, he might develop into an effective agitator for Socialism, a genuine revolutionist, rather than an emotional demagogue.

If Mussolini was ever sincere with any human being, I believe that he was with me. He talked a great deal about himself —about the bitterness of his childhood (though as he talked it seemed to me far less harsh than that of most Italian workers), about the suffering and privation he had endured since he had fled from Italy to avoid military service. He had sought work as a stone mason's assistant, he said, in all the large towns and cities, but the combination of his physical illness and police persecution had defeated his efforts. In spite of odd jobs as a butcher boy, a porter, a delivery boy, and in spite of the assistance he had received from comrades who were little better off than himself, he had known acute physical hunger for days at a time, he had been forced to beg alms from the hated bourgeoisie, and several times he had been arrested for vagrancy. A year before at Bern, he had participated in a strike of stone masons and had been expelled from the Canton as an "anarchist."

Whenever I met Mussolini I urged him to read, to study, and lent him pamphlets and books.

"It is not enough to be a rebel," I told him. "You cannot abolish injustice by merely raging against it. You cannot lead the workers intelligently unless you know something of the labour movement. You must understand its history—its failures as well as its successes and the reason for both."

Possibly because he knew something of my social background —a knowledge which aroused a snobbish pride in his association with a member of a class he affected to despise—and partly perhaps because I was a woman with whom he did not need to "prove" that he was the equal or superior of other men, he did not seem to resent either my advice or my rebukes even when he failed to act upon them. He needed some one to lean upon and his vanity would never have permitted him to lean upon a man. He made no attempt to hide from me his weakness. If he had done so I probably should have had less pity for him and he undoubtedly realized this. During all of our association I was drawn to him by the knowledge that I was the only human being with whom he was completely himself, with whom he was relieved from the strain of bluffing; and during the ten years that followed he never hesitated to take advantage of the sense of responsibility which this knowledge imposed upon me.

Once as we walked together to the station where I was to take the train to Geneva, he pointed to the public garden we were passing and related the following episode:

"Just after I came here I was living in the greatest misery. The comrades who had been able to help me were away or out of work. One day I passed this park, so wretched with hunger that I thought I could not live another day. I saw two Englishwomen sitting on a bench with their lunch—bread, cheese, eggs! I could not restrain myself. I threw myself upon one of the old witches and grabbed the food from her hands.

[47]

If they had made the slightest resistance I would have strangled them—strangled them, mind you——" He added a vulgar term. Then he stopped, his hands in his pockets, and began to laugh, his whole body swaying. "Don't you think it would have been better if I had killed those parasites? Why does not the hour of revenge arrive?"

I pointed out to him that the assassination of two women would not have solved the problem of human hunger, but he was not concerned with hunger as a social problem. He thought in terms of the satisfaction of his own needs—food and revenge.

I felt assured that if he once achieved a more normal life in Switzerland, earned enough to assure his bodily needs, regular meals, a place to live; if he no longer had to suffer the humiliation of being dependent upon the charity of his fellow radicals, he would become less agitated in mind and spirit.

I was making frequent trips at this time to various towns and cities, speaking for both the Italian and Swiss Socialists and organizing *émigré* groups. Wherever I went, I kept in mind Mussolini's need for employment. The response among the comrades in the towns in which he had already lived was not encouraging.

In Geneva, I visited the secretary of the Italian Socialist Club, Pietro Losio, a shoemaker. For Pietro, as for most of the Italian radicals, Socialism was not merely a political creed, it was a way of life; human solidarity not a conviction but a religion. His little shoe shop in Geneva was a magnet for the Italian *émigrés*. Whether one wanted one's shoes repaired, a Socialist pamphlet, a paper, bread and wine or advice in some moment of need, one went to Pietro's. If any one could understand and help me to aid Mussolini, it was Pietro.

He greeted me warmly and called to his wife in the kitchen behind the shop to prepare some food for me.

"I have come for only a few minutes, dear comrade; do not bother. I thought while I was here I would ask you if you knew of any work for this young Mussolini in Geneva——"

"Mussolini work? Ah, so he is able to work now," he laughed as he replied. "I must tell my wife that. She will not believe it. When he first came here he came to see us, he complained so much about his illness, his inability to find work, that I told him he could take his meals with us. But he cursed so much, his manner was so rough, so peculiar, Luigia decided she did not like our guest. 'I am happy to share what we have with the comrades,' she said, 'but I mistrust this man. He never looks in your eyes, he is so restless, so rude.' After that, a few of the comrades and I bought meal tickets for him at a cheap eating-house and soon after that he went away. I do not think there is anything for him in Geneva."

A few days later I received a letter from Lausanne telling me of an occurrence which took place at a lecture given by an Italian priest there. The Italians had decided that they must have some one present on this occasion their anti-clerical position to the priest's working-class audience, and because Mussolini was more eloquent on this subject than on any other, he had been chosen. He had agreed to accept if he was assured that a large section of the audience would come to his support if a conflict arose. I was familiar with his approach to the subject without reading the report of his remarks—"Religion is an immorality and a psychical disease. Those who are deeply religious are not normal," etc.

But at the beginning of his address he had asked some one in the audience to lend him a watch. Striking a dramatic attitude, he had proclaimed: "I will give God just five minutes to strike me dead. If he does not punish me in that time, he does not exist."

I immediately wrote him a letter, pointing out how superficial and foolish was such an approach.

He did not answer my letter, and when I returned to Lausanne I found that he was now speaking frequently for the radicals on anti-clericalism and anti-militarism. Whatever gifts he possessed as a speaker were better fitted to denunciation than to exposition and he was becoming an effective "soap-box" orator on these subjects. It was just as well that he confined himself to them at this time. I doubt if he could have given a coherent lecture on Socialist or Anarchist principles and tactics. Shortly after this he printed his first pamphlet—"God Does Not Exist"—at the expense of his radical friends. The preface of

[49]

the pamphlet ended with the proclamation, "Faithful, the Antichrist is born!"

I was back in Lugano when word came that the Swiss government had ordered Mussolini's expulsion from the country. I do not remember the particular incident that gave rise to this sudden decision. He had been expelled from several of the Swiss cantons because of the violence of his utterances on other occasions, but now it appeared the government had decided that he was a danger to its peace. They evidently took him more seriously than did his comrades. The Swiss radicals immediately began an agitation against the expulsion and the Socialist Deputy Wyss denounced the decision in the Grand Council at Geneva. Was Switzerland, the historic asylum of political exiles and military deserters, to return a humble refugee to the tyranny from which he had fled? The Minister of State replied that Mussolini had admitted he had entered the country on a forged passport, and the only result of the agitation was a change in the point of departure. Instead of being expelled at Chiasso on the Italian frontier, he was permitted to leave the country at the Austrian frontier.

Years later, Mussolini was to ascribe his departure from Switzerland at this time to "the yearnings for home which blossom in the hearts of all Italians. . . . The compulsory service of the army was calling me."

It was not to call for another year when the King issued a birthday decree of amnesty for political refugees and for all deserters who were willing to enter the army on their return.

I did not see Mussolini again until he passed through Lugano on his way back to Italy. He wrote me from Trento where he seemed to have made more friends among the patriotic irridentists, who were later to influence his career, than among the Socialists. In Austria, he wrote, he was achieving a certain success as a journalist and his letter glowed with self-confidence. When he wrote that he was planning to write a history of philosophy, I could not help but be amused. It was natural that a small measure of success and security, after the misery and defeat of his years in Switzerland, should go to his head. It would take time, I told myself, for Mussolini to achieve a normal balance.

I was still living in Lugano with Maria when he passed through on his return to Italy. Maria, I had learnt in the meanwhile, had disliked Mussolini intensely from the first time she had met him in Switzerland while on a propaganda tour.

"I never believed that any of his convictions were deeprooted," she told me. "He is too self-centred to care either about the cause or about other people."

"But remember his childhood, Maria," I argued. "He was never happy, he had nothing. And for years he has been sick and obsessed with a sense of inferiority. Even in comparison with the average worker his life has been wretched."

"You will see," Maria answered. However, on the day he arrived she agreed to cook the dinner, as she always did when we had company, because she was a much better cook than I.

When Mussolini appeared I was amazed to find that his sojourn in Trento had made so little difference in his appearance, or even in his point of view. As always in Switzerland, he seemed ravenously hungry and he told us that if we had not invited him to dinner he would have had nothing to eat that day.

"Who cooked this macaroni?" he asked as he gorged himself. "I bet you did, Maria."

"Maybe you would have preferred something else," Maria answered, contemptuously. "Chicken or truffles, but we, you see, are proletarians ——"

He looked up at her angrily. "And why not? *Porca Madonna!* Before I came here, I read the menu of the hotel—*boia d'un Signor!* I felt crazy. If you only knew what those swine eat and drink. If once in my life, I could ——"

Maria interrupted him furiously. "Why do you always talk about yourself, your appetites? I am afraid that if you had an opportunity to live like those people you would soon forget the masses. . . ."

There would have been a violent quarrel between them if I had not changed the subject. I was feeling keenly the disappointment of finding him unchanged. What had happened to the self-assurance he had shown in his letter? He was as unstable, as hysterical, as he had been in Lausanne. Perhaps the letter had been written to impress me.

As the time came for him to leave, Maria and I walked with him down to the pier. Not even the beauty of the lake in the moonlight, the solemnity of the mountains, could turn his attention from himself.

As we waited for the boat to leave, he waved his arm towards the restaurants and hotels along the pier. "Look! People eating, drinking, and enjoying themselves. And I will travel third class, eat miserable, cheap food. *Porca Madonna,* how I hate the rich! Why must I suffer this injustice? How long must we wait?"

I remembered the story he had told me of the two English-women in Lausanne.

5

I WAS IN LUGANO WHEN NEWS CAME OF THE
Russian Revolution of 1905, the general strike in St. Petersburg, the mutinies of Kronstadt and Sebastopol, the convocation
of the First Duma, and the counter-revolutionary terror and
pogroms which followed. The excitement among the Russian
émigrés scarcely exceeded that among the Italians. It is significant that the Italian masses—belonging to a supposedly backward country—showed a solidarity with their Russian comrades
which was unequalled by the workers of any other nation.

Most of my activity at this time was devoted to gaining sympathy and raising funds for the Russian revolutionaries. I travelled over all of Italy, speaking at hundreds of mass meetings in
the larger cities and to small groups in remote villages. Everywhere I was greeted with the wildest enthusiasm. One evening
as I was speaking in a great hall in Trieste, I dwelt at some
length upon the career and character of Maria Spiridonova, the

heroic revolutionist who had devoted her life to the cause of the Russian peasants. At this time political prisoners were supposed to be treated with a certain respect, and Maria's treatment at the hands of the Russian gendarmes had stirred the indignation of the world. When I spoke of the manner in which one of her guards had burnt Maria's hand with his lighted cigar, I was suddenly interrupted by a shout from the gallery, "*We* shall revenge!" The entire audience rose as a body in the most spontaneous demonstration I have ever witnessed. When I was finally able to conclude, and after we left the hall, we were joined by the thousands who had stood outside, unable to get in. For hours that night one could hear the crowds shouting in the streets: "Long live the Russian Revolution! Long live Socialism!"

(Since 1918, Maria Spiridonova has been incarcerated in a Russian institution, because of her opposition to the Bolsheviks, and her name has rarely been mentioned in the world press—but that is another story.)

This meeting was not exceptional. It was typical of hundreds held throughout Italy. In no other country was sympathy with the victims of Tsarism so widespread. After 1905, when Maxim Gorki, already one of the world's most famous literary figures, was delegated to raise funds in the United States for the Russian victims, his total collections amounted to one-third of what I obtained among the Italian workers and peasants who lived under conditions which would have seemed unbearable to most American workers. Gorki's mission was marked with sensational incidents. He was refused admission to a New York hotel where he attempted to register with the Russian actress, Andreyeva, with whom he had been living for some time, and American conservatives started a vicious scandal-mongering campaign against him. A relationship which was accepted as a matter of course in Europe placed too much strain upon the American bourgeois conscience. Even Mark Twain joined the chorus against him, a chorus which was answered by the many radicals and intellectuals who rallied to his defence.

The publicity involved in this incident made Gorki the target of newspaper interviewers in Europe, but when he returned to Italy, he succeeded in giving the correspondents the slip. Some of the frustrated journalists turned to me for help. One morning at Lugano I was visited by the representative of one of the great Italian dailies who peered about my bare room as though he expected to find the famous author hidden under my bed. I could not convince him that I knew nothing of Gorki's where-abouts. The following day a wild story appeared in the paper which gave the impression that I was hiding Gorki in a "secret villa." For weeks thereafter I was pursued by newspaper men. Later, when I visited Gorki at Capri, where he had bought a beautiful villa, we laughed heartily over my adventures with the journalists. Gorki later turned this villa into a radical school at which Lenin taught for a while.

To an invitation received during this period, I owe one of the deepest friendships I have known—that of Elia Musatti and his wife.

In Venice I was to deliver two lectures for the People's University—one dealing with revolutionary Russia, the other with the interdependence between the Russian labour movement and that of other countries. The first lecture was a great success with a predominantly middle-class audience. It was fashionable in those days to condemn Tsarist tyranny in much the same terms used today against Hitler. People who would not lift a finger to help the workers in their own countries and who fought against the mildest reforms, imagined that their hearts bled for unfortunate *moujiks* thousands of miles away.

The following day, when I dealt with conditions in Italy, the atmosphere became cool and hostile at once. A banquet had been arranged for that evening at which I was to be the guest of honour, but now many of those who had accepted invitations discovered that they had other engagements—much to the despair of the dean of the university.

This dean, incidentally, had a daughter who has been famous because of her intimate friendship with Mussolini and as his official biographer. She was married to a wealthy lawyer by the name of Sarfatti. She did not boast of this relationship to Mussolini as long as the latter was a poorly dressed "fanatic of the revolution." After Il Duce came to power, however, Madame

[55]

Sarfatti referred to it at every opportunity and her wealthy husband took no offence at the gossip surrounding it.

In pre-Fascist Italy, Madame Sarfatti's husband was the object of innumerable cartoons and satirical anecdotes in the radical press. As a member of the City Council of Milan, he had voted to impose a tax on meat brought into the city from neighbouring provinces where prices were lower. One day, as he entered the city, he was stopped by officials who examined his briefcase and discovered several pounds of beef among his legal papers. After that, our papers referred to him as the "Honourable Meat."

Among the Socialists who had been invited to attend the banquet in Venice was Elia Musatti and his wife. Musatti was the only son of a very wealthy Jewish family in Venice. He had become a Socialist while a law student in Rome and had married a gentile girl. This caused a break with his parents and he renounced all his rights as heir. The Musattis were the most devoted couple I have ever known and both consecrated their lives to the movement. Though a brilliant lawyer, Musatti earned little, as most of his time was spent defending those who had no money for fees and in political activity. My tactical views were identical with Musatti's and I later assisted him in the electoral campaigns which resulted in his election to Parliament. Because of his intransigence there, he became one of the most maligned men in Italy. Once when I was walking with his wife in Venice, a young student, evidently inflamed by stories in the press, spat at us.

Through my frequent visits with the Musattis in Venice I became well acquainted with that city whose beauty has inspired so many poets and artists. I soon learnt that life in Venice was not a matter of moonlight gondola rides and pigeon-feeding. Humid dwellings of undernourished families lined those romantic canals and faced out over those limpid lagoons. Women sat on balconies, not to flirt with passing gondoliers, but to catch the last gleams of light from those glorious sunsets, straining their eyes over intricate pearl-work from which they were barely able to eke out an existence. Rich women from other lands brought their children to Venice to enjoy its sun, but the mothers of the Venice slums were compelled to send their children into the gloomy tobacco factories from which, after a few years, these children would crawl home to die from the effects of nicotine poisoning.

These mothers, wrapped in black shawls, would come to meet me with torches when I spoke in their poorly illuminated districts. Thousands of people would gather, many of them in rags. An old table would be placed in their midst and I would mount it and begin speaking. Their eyes would begin to sparkle and shine. The trip home would become a triumphal procession, the whole crowd marching to my door with steady, confident tread.

Though Lugano on the Swiss-Italian border was my headquarters between 1904 and 1907, I spent almost as much time in Italy as in Switzerland. The bond of instinctive sympathy between myself and the Italians, which I had felt ever since my university days in Brussels, grew steadily stronger.

While the program of Italian Socialism was more or less identical with those of the other parties of the Second International, the spirit that dominated the Italian party was different. It was not predominantly political; it was rather a reflection of a common aspiration on the part of the Italian masses for a world which would guarantee justice and liberty. Elsewhere in Europe the movement had the same goal, but the day-by-day struggle for economic improvements and electoral successes tended to absorb more of the energies of the leaders and the rank and file.

I do not know of any country where love of liberty was so highly developed as in Italy. I mean an innate sense of human dignity which may co-exist with a high degree of economic and political enslavement. Revolutionary propaganda had developed this instinctive feeling into class consciousness. In no other country were the ruling classes so aware of the transient nature of their privileges.

In speaking to young and old in Italy—factory workers, peasants, or small landowners—one realized immediately that one's words did not fall upon barren soil. Some reminiscence of a common heritage seemed to dawn on these men and women as they listened. Often they came to Socialist or Anarchist meetings

[57]

out of curiosity, or because the priest had warned them against doing so, but they would become transformed after the first few words of the speaker. Their eyes would shine with enthusiasm and their work- and care-worn faces would reflect their comprehension. Even their posture would change, as though they were freed of a burden, and they would walk home arm-in-arm, singing revolutionary songs.

Proletarian institutions—workers and peasants unions, Socialist and Anarchist branches, coöperatives, people's houses, schools and libraries—began to spread in Italy towards the close of the nineteenth century and from then on they offered an education which completed or substituted for that of the official schools and the churches. The clergy began to lose its influence and was called on less frequently at births, weddings, deaths. Children were less frequently named for saints or war heroes, more frequently for those who had fought for liberation. Most of the Italian workers understood the rôle of the Church in preaching humility, and it was not difficult for them to throw off the chains of superstition. Contrary to what is usually thought of the Italian masses, they are not credulous. Once they begin to doubt, they continue to do so. There has always been a sceptical and ironic curiosity among Italians, and iconoclasts attract them. Their attachment to Church traditions has been more superstitious than religious, and they rarely view the clergy with that veneration which one finds among the Irish believers, for example, or used to find among orthodox peasants in old Russia.

Though misery and fear, fear of being yet more wretched, make the Italian peasant appear humble, there is in his soul the seed of rebellion. He is receptive to a propaganda which reveals the absurdity of a social system which practises, "Those who work do not eat; those who eat can afford not to work."

All of this explains a phenomenon unknown in other countries before the war: peasants and small landowners joining the Socialist movement, organizing strong agricultural coöperatives and passing resolutions for the abolition of private property, even as early as 1901. (The convention at which this resolution was passed was attended by representatives of 145,000 organized peasants and landowners.) Those who know the usual hostility of peasants and farmers to revolutionary ideas can understand the enormous difference between the movement in Italy and that of other European countries where the class organization of agricultural workers has hardly been approached even yet, though they continue to threaten the status and gains of the industrial workers.

The relative proximity of town and country in Italy created close contacts between the agricultural and industrial workers, thus facilitating the spread of Socialist propaganda. On market days or on days of political demonstrations the peasants would come to town, mix with the industrial workers, and be subjected to the same influences. They came to understand the community of interest between themselves and their fellow workers in the cities.

Another factor which had a profound influence upon the development of Italian Socialism was the attitude of the returning *émigrés*. Workers, peasants, small land- and shop-owners were often forced to look for work in other countries. They would compare the conditions in these countries with those of poverty-stricken Italy and they realized why they had been forced to emigrate. They came to understand the ties which existed between themselves and the workers of other nationalities and to understand that it was a disgrace for them to act as "blacklegs" or "scabs." This is the most effective training in internationalism—to work in the same factory, to undergo the same exploitation, to face the same problems with workers of other nationalities. When a concept of labour's solidarity has been developed through such experience, it cannot be easily irradicated.

The returning emigrants contributed largely to the growing electoral victories of Italian Socialism. Not only would many of them come home to vote (the government was required to pay their expenses), but they also made every effort to induce their countrymen to support the Socialists. Since most of these returning workers belonged to peasant families, they were able to influence even the more backward peasant voters.

The basic premises of the Socialist gospel were familiar in Italy long before its industrial development had reached a stage

[59]

where an organized movement became possible. The intellectual precursors of Socialism, even when engaged in so-called patriotic movements, such as the struggle for national unity, would, like Garibaldi, point out that Socialism was "the future of humanity." The keen minds and the sense of solidarity with the oppressed of such men as Campanella, Filippo Buonarotti, Ferrari, Pisacane, led them to anticipate the ultimate development of the efforts in which they were engaged. Most of these men had renounced wealth or privilege to live according to their principles and to share the lot of those for whom they fought.

The reciprocal attraction between the newly awakened masses and these intellectuals who endorsed their cause created an atmosphere of sound and fertile idealism which reached all strata of the urban and rural populations, so that at the beginning of the present century Socialism as a gospel was almost as widespread in a backward country like Italy as in such a modern country as Germany and certainly far more popular than in England. The academic world in Italy was probably more influenced by Marxism than that of any other country.

In Russia for nearly a century the revolutionary movement was led by men and women from the more thoughtful sections of the aristocracy and bourgeoisie and the prestige these pioneers brought to the movement extended its influence far beyond the groups for whom they were fighting. So it was in Italy, though here these revolutionists were less numerous and endured far less persecution. They gave to the Party a moral prestige which made it an important factor in the life of the country. So long as the workers alone were dissatisfied with their conditions, it was possible for many people to maintain that the exploited demanded their rights merely because they were greedy or ignorant. But when intellectuals whose character and intelligence were far above the average espoused their cause, the enemies of the movement had to acknowledge that something other than greed and ignorance inspired the revolutionary movement.

After economic conditions in Italy had improved, thanks largely to the organizational work of the Socialists and their parliamentary struggles, a new Italy seemed to be born within the confines of a capitalist monarchy. New ways of living, new educa-

[60]

tional methods, and new standards of ethics were created. New slogans began to adorn the walls of workers and peasant dwellings, such as: "You are small because you kneel; rise and you will be big!" "Our country is the entire world, our creed is liberty," went one of the most popular songs of this new-born Italy. Mothers would sing it to their babies and children would echo it at play.

The test to which the Italian workers were to be subjected by war and Fascism gave them an opportunity to prove the strength of their faith and solidarity, as well as the superiority of Socialist education in Italy. With the advent of the World War the same faith which united them to their fellow Italians continued to bind them to their fellow workers in other countries, even those who were supposed to be their enemies.

Future historians trying to interpret the history of the labour movement from a purely theoretical viewpoint will have difficulty explaining why the "backward" Italian and Spanish workers have responded to the test of struggle against war and Fascism better than the workers of a highly developed country like Germany. They will miss, in all probability, the importance of the psychological factor. Before the test of war and Fascism, one measured the strength of the labour movement by the membership of its trade unions and political parties. Though the organization of labour is one of the most important factors in the development of a revolutionary movement, it is not the only one, and its importance may vary with differences in the social background of that movement and of each historical period.

As a Socialist worker I devoted to the Italian movement more than a decade of intense activity. I was editor of and contributor to numerous papers, a member of the Party's Central Committee, and signed dozens of articles and appeals. But never on a single occasion did I feel a stranger in the country. There was little chauvinism in Italy before the war, and no one ever raised the cry of "alien agitator." Russian revolutionists had always been active in the Italian labour movement. (For a while, before the spread of Marxism, Michael Bakunin had directed the powerful Anarchist movement there.) Foreign agitators might be persecuted in Italy, along with native Italians, because of

[61]

their radicalism, but never because of their foreign birth. Any action against foreigners as such would have met with ridicule and hostility from all sections of the population.

The storm of protest that swept Italy at the bloody reprisals directed against the Russian revolutionaries after the 1905 uprising did not die down. When the conservative press announced that the Tsar was planning to visit Rome, the indignant workers staged protest meetings and street demonstrations, while Socialist deputies took the floor to stress their hostility. Thousands of shrill whistles carved with the effigy of Nicholas II were distributed, and it was planned that from the moment the Tsar set foot in Italy, the shrill notes of these whistles would be dinned into his ears. The official visit to Rome was cancelled and instead the Tsar conferred with the Italian King at the latter's remote country residence near the border.

In 1907, the Socialists in Parliament took action to block any assistance to the Russian government. Members of other radical parties joined with them, and in order to give the widest possible publicity to their hostility to the Russian régime a special convention was called in Milan, then the scene of a great international exposition.

I came to the convention, not as a delegate, but as a spectator, and I arrived at the hall on the afternoon on which the Socialist and Republican resolution against Tsarist despotism was to be presented to the public. Turati, one of the most popular men in Italy, was speaking as I entered. I was startled when he suddenly stopped short in what seemed to be the middle of his speech and said: "No more words of mine. We have with us a representative of oppressed Russia—Angelica Balabanoff."

I was lifted up by strong arms and carried forward to the platform, where I faced thousands of upturned faces. I *had* to speak. I remember saying: "If instead of sending to this exhibition the handiwork of oppressed and undernourished peasants, Russia would send the skeletons of starved farmers and the skulls of tortured revolutionaries, the public would get a more accurate idea of Tsarist Russia."

The response was like a deep echo of the sufferings I sought to

[62]

transmit. The following day the democratic *Secolo* dedicated an editorial to this speech of mine and declared that public opinion in Italy would echo the protest I had voiced at this meeting. This pledge was kept. The fact that the Bolsheviks, as soon as they achieved power, forgot the moral and material support they had received from the Italian masses was for me one of the first proofs of the perversion of the revolutionary spirit in Russia.

It was at this meeting that I first met Filippo Turati. The son of a prosperous functionary of northern Italy, he was one of the most brilliant men of his time, equally able in the fields of criminology, education, and literature. His first work on *"Crime and the Social Question,"* published when he was quite young, attracted international attention. His attempts to create schools and libraries for adults established him as one of the pioneers in the field of adult education. For many years he edited and wrote for a scientific review, *Critica Sociale*. Almost every article and essay to which he signed his name deserves inclusion in an anthology. He disliked to be reminded of the poems of his youth, but everyone in Italy knows that he was the author of the "Workers' Hymn," one of the most beautiful and inspiring of revolutionary songs.

One of the first Marxists in Italy and a personal friend of Engels, Turati had participated in the revolutionary movement long before the Italian Socialist Party, of which he was a founder, was created. His approach was often misinterpreted in other countries because it was so typically Italian. Many Italian intellectuals like to appear sceptical of theoretical axioms even if they are not. This attitude is natural among a people belonging to an old civilization upon whom a faith has been imposed for centuries. Realizing how relative truth may be, they exaggerate their heresy, whether religious or scientific.

Thus it was that Turati came to be considered a theoretical sceptic and even an opportunist. While he belonged to the Right Wing of the Party, he hated dogma and demagogy to such a degree that he leaned over backward to be fair to political opponents of his own party. How many paradoxes of his have become famous through misinterpretation by less scrupulous politicos to both the left and the right of him!

[63]

After the rise of Fascism, the Black Shirts sang obscene songs under his window, and those "regenerators of civilization" pledged themselves to tear out his beard and make it into shoe brushes. Though his life was in constant danger, Turati was reluctant to leave Italy. Only the pressure of his friends induced him to do so. In France, he dedicated himself to the anti-Fascist struggle, but without roots in his beloved Italy he wasted away.

Two other Socialist leaders whom I came to know well at this time were Claudio Treves and Costantino Lazzari. Treves was a lawyer, a member of a wealthy family, who had renounced his career to become a militant Socialist and the most brilliant journalist in modern Italy. Though probably superior to Turati as a Marxist scholar, he considered himself a disciple of the older man. The final triumph of Fascism killed him in exile. He died a few hours after having commemorated, in Paris, the death of Matteotti.

Lazzari was a "self-made" Socialist and one of the founders of the first Italian labour party in the '80's. Unlike so many people who are led to the Socialist movement by intuition and experience rather than by theoretical study, he never wavered between Socialism and other radical doctrines, between syndicalism and reformism. There was something adamant in his consistency. When the Fascists reintroduced capital punishment, he spoke and voted against it in Parliament. Despite the fact that he was then seventy years of age, he was thrown out of the Chamber and brutally beaten. He died soon after from the injuries he received.

At the opposite pole from these men was the brilliant but illogical and undependable Arturo Labriola, a remarkable orator and facile writer. Though he had begun his career as a Marxist, Labriola had already swung to that extreme, anti-political syndicalism which was later to cause his expulsion from the Party. At this time, already under the influence of Sorel and other French syndicalist writers, he was denouncing the Socialist leaders as "middle-class opportunists." During the World War Labriola became a violent advocate of Italian intervention and a member of the government. His post-war career has been equally contradictory. After the Fascist triumph he left Italy and became a member of the Social Democracy he had denounced. Finally he returned to Fascist Italy, presumably as a convert to Fascism. He now collaborates in editing an organ of the Italian government in France. This paper was formerly an anti-Fascist satiric weekly and it is now staffed almost exclusively by former radicals who have followed the example of Mussolini.

6

ALTHOUGH I WAS A MEMBER OF THE ITALIAN, rather than of the Russian, Socialist organization during this period, I worked in close contact with the leaders of the Russian Marxist movement both in Switzerland and in Italy. Plekhanoff was living in Nervi, on the Italian Riviera, because of his poor health, and my meeting with him there marked the beginning of a collaboration that was to last until the World War. Plekhanoff's personal life was as much an inspiration to me as his books had been during my university days in Brussels. His years of exile were years of illness, poverty, and personal tragedy during which it never occurred to him to put his brilliant intellectual gifts at the disposal of the bourgeois world. His first child, like Marx's son, had died as a result of the privations the family was forced to undergo and it was not until his wife—a girl he had known as a young revolutionary in Russia—had finished her medical studies and had become a well-known physician that they were able to experience some measure of material security. Though Plekhanoff's manner gave the impression of cold intellectuality—in relation with women, an almost formal chivalry—he had a very passionate temperament and was an affectionate and devoted father and husband. In 1914 I was to discover how completely he could be dominated by his emotions.

With most of the Russian revolutionary leaders and students in Switzerland at this time, Geneva was actually the capital of the Russian movement. Each faction of that movement—Mensheviks, Bolsheviks, Socialist Revolutionaries, Bundists—had its own press, its own organization, and its own group of enthusiastic supporters—including certain "progressive" industrialists and wealthy intellectuals. The life of any political movement in exile is inevitably far more introverted than that of a movement functioning in its own native background under normal circumstances and in daily contact with the masses. In exile, the personal equation becomes exaggerated, differences ripen more easily into dissension and the intellectuals play a far more dominant rôle. The life of the Russian exiles during this period, like that of the European exiles in London after 1848, and like that of the Italian and German exiles today, was a tense and stormy one, marked by political controversies and competition for both moral and financial support. In spite of this fact an enormous amount of agitation in behalf of the Russian movement was carried on in western Europe, and impressive support was won throughout the world. At a time when the excesses of Russian absolutism were shocking democratic opinion in Europe and America, the Russian exiles could command a hearing in upper-class circles not accorded their Socialist comrades of other lands. It was even more fashionable to be a Friend of Russian Freedom in the early years of the century than it is to be a Friend of Soviet Russia in 1938.

At this time, as in the past, Switzerland served as a physical symbol of the slogan: "Proletarians of all countries unite!" For more than half a century the little patriarchal republic had been the refuge of political dissenters from Germany and Austria as well as backward Russia. Experienced in social struggles and trained in revolutionary theory since the collapse of the First International, these refugees had brought the seeds of revolutionary organization into a country with a weak industrial development. It was these outsiders, mostly the Germans and Austrians, who had urged the Swiss workers to organize and who had developed its trade unions and Socialist organizations. The French section of the Swiss workers, more closely tied by language and tradition to a less industrialized nation, remained under the influence of the communo-anarchist Bakunin. The Russian refugees had represented a group apart, with a predominance of intellectuals, who were never absorbed into the life of the Swiss labour movement. Not all of them were revolutionists, as even the liberals in Russia had suffered persecution and espionage that drove them abroad. And in addition, there were many girls who had left Russia as I did, to find opportunities for freedom, service, and education that were denied them at home.

Many of the younger Russians and the intellectuals who came to Western Europe attended the universities not so much to learn a profession as to prepare themselves for revolutionary activity among the peasants and workers upon their return home. Because of this fact they were not able to affiliate officially, or at least openly, with the various revolutionary parties, an act which would immediately bring them to the attention of the authorities. Instead, they organized or joined "groups of supporters" (much like the numerous Communist Party periphery groups today) which raised money for the official party, sold its literature, and rendered many other services. I was a member of one of these Marxist groups. Chicherin, later Soviet Commissar for Foreign Affairs, was the secretary of the Russian Marxist university students in western Europe.

The life of the Russians was differentiated from that of the other foreign students by its physical austerity and its preoccupation with science and politics. In fact, political discussion was considered the inevitable complement of scientific study as well as its inspiration. Food and shelter were quite secondary considerations, while outward appearance was completely ignored. Even those who could afford to live and dress in comfort or fashion, scorned to live better than the masses they intended to

[68]

serve. The girls, in particular, accentuated their contempt for externals by dressing as plainly—even as unbecomingly—as possible, so eager were they to differentiate themselves from the parasitic women of the ruling classes. Those who had more helped to provide for those who had less or nothing at all, among their fellow students, and also for the expense of the illegal literature of the groups to which they belonged. Devoted disciples of the various political refugees whose position of leadership had been won by revolutionary experience and intellectual superiority, they lived, spiritually and intellectually, in Russia rather than in Switzerland.

It was at the meetings conducted by the various student groups at this time that I first met many of the Russian revolutionary leaders—including the Mensheviks, Martov and Axelrod, the Bolsheviks, Lenin and Zinoviev. In 1906, at a meeting called by the Swiss Socialists to commemorate the death of Ferdinand Lassalle, I spoke on the same platform with Leon Trotsky, who was living in Vienna at this time. Martov was the theoretical leader of the Mensheviks and the most brilliant writer and journalist in their group. Axelrod, who with Plekhanoff had organized the first revolutionary industrial unions in Russia, was now devoting his days to the practical work of the movement, while at night he eked out a precarious existence manufacturing that cultured "buttermilk" which several years later was to become a therapeutic fad.

I suppose it is a common temptation for writers, in dealing with an illustrious figure whom they met first in a period of obscurity to pretend that they realized at first sight that here was a Man of Destiny, and it is difficult not to modify one's first, spontaneous judgment of such a man in the light of his later fame. To be honest I must admit that I cannot remember just when and where I first met Lenin, though I believe it was at a meeting in Bern. I already knew who he was and the position he represented, but he made no personal, physical impression upon me at the time. Lenin had no exterior characteristics that would lead one to single him out among the revolutionary figures of his day—in fact, of all the Russian revolutionary leaders, he seemed, externally, the most colourless. Nor did his speeches at this time impress me, either by their manner or by their content. Trotsky, whom I met later, was a far more brilliant and effective orator, though certain of his mannerisms and his general self-consciousness were to irritate me at times. Later, and particularly at the Zimmerwald conferences after 1914, where I had an opportunity to know and observe him more closely, I realized how shrewd and incisive was Lenin's mind. But though he was a master polemicist—and frequently an unscrupulous one—he had none of the characteristics of a demagogue. It was in this latter capacity that Zinoviev served him so well. At Zimmerwald, and later in Soviet Russia, Lenin's approach to tactical problems, like his approach to life itself, seemed to me very often a primitive one. I have often wondered since if this impression was correct—whether he was inherently primitive in his intellectual and emotional makeup or had so trained himself to concentrate his attention upon one problem, or even one aspect of a problem, as to convey that impression. This concentration and ruthless singleness of purpose were undoubtedly the secret of his success—or if one may use the word—his genius.

Since its organization in Minsk in 1898, the Social Democratic Party had been the party of Russian Marxism, with its base in the growing industrial populations of the cities and larger towns. Unlike the Socialist Revolutionary Party, based largely upon the aspirations of the peasantry and whose leaders were for the most part humanitarian rather than intellectual rebels from the Russian upper class, the Social Democrats objured terrorism and placed their hope of Russia's emancipation upon the growing class consciousness and mass activity of the new proletariat.

When the fifth Congress of the party was called in 1907, I was elected to attend as a fraternal delegate from the Russian organization of university students. The Congress was to be the largest and most significant gathering in the history of the Party and was to include a delegation from the Bund, a federation of Jewish workers of Russia, Poland and Lithuania. The Polish Social Democratic Party was also to be represented, and among its delegates was Rosa Luxemburg, who functioned in both the Polish and German movements.

[70]

The Congress was scheduled to take place in Copenhagen, but at the very last moment, due to the opposition of the monarchy, permission to meet there was denied. The Danish King was the brother of the Dowager Tsarina, widow of Alexander III. The delegates from Russia were already on their way to Denmark, and as they were travelling illegally, without luggage, and for the most part without funds, the situation was a serious one. Russian congresses, unlike those of other nationalities, often last for weeks, and the housing and feeding of more than 300 delegates during this period, to say nothing of their travelling expenses, enlarged by the complication of shifting the Congress to London, presented a monumental problem. It was an insoluble one without additional help from some of the stronger parties, and at this moment I received a wire from the organizers of the Congress to go to Berlin to seek the financial assistance of the powerful German Social Democracy.

I finally arrived in London with a substantial check signed by Paul Singer, the treasurer of the German Party, sufficient, I hoped, to keep the more needy of the delegates going for several weeks. Many of the Russian delegates had already arrived, and among them was a group from the Caucasus whose wild appearance, accentuated by their huge sheepskin *shapkas*, had created a sensation in the London streets. Much to my indignation, I discovered that the delegates from Russia had been housed in a former "barracks" by the English authorities, where they were kept under constant supervision between sessions of the Congress.

When I went to visit them at these barracks, I had an intimation of what the tone of the Congress would be. Never having attended a Russian convention before, I had failed to realize how seriously my compatriots took their factional alignments. The first sentence that greeted me when I finally gained admittance to the barracks was neither a salutation nor a welcome, but the question, "To which faction do you belong?"

Strangely enough, the Congress was held in a church. It was called the Fraternity Church and the congregation was probably composed of Christian Socialists or pacifists vaguely sympathetic to the Russian cause, who would undoubtedly have been profoundly shocked had they attended some of the sessions and understood some of the debates. They evidently had not anticipated the length of our convention when they had consented to our use of the place, and during the weeks that followed, the most passionate theoretical debates would be interrupted by the announcement, usually from one of the London *émigrés*: "Comrades, the Board of the Fraternity Church advises us that we can have use of this building for only two more days." As we had no money with which to pay for another building, a compromise was finally reached whereby the Russians would vacate for a day or an evening, while church services were being held.

I had attended the stormy and dramatic conventions of the Italian Party, the impressive gatherings of the German Social Democrats and the memorable sessions of the Executive Committee of the Second International where the various tendencies within the movement expressed themselves in brilliant verbal clashes or in well-ordered debate. In all of these groups one had a sense of sufficient unity on certain fundamental concepts to provide an effective working alliance against a common enemy.

At the Russian Congress one felt no such assurance of fundamental unity. Though the organizational split between the Bolsheviks and Mensheviks had been healed in Stockholm the year before, and the final and irrevocable break between them was not to take place for another five years, the Congress was dominated from its opening session by an all-absorbing, almost fanatical, spirit of factionalism that seemed capable of rending it apart at almost any moment. In spite of the preoccupation with factional strategy, the bitterness and even the dishonesty of some of the arguments—particularly those employed by the Bolsheviks—the general theoretical and scientific level of the discussion was higher than in any gathering of revolutionaries I have ever attended. The speeches of the leaders lasted for hours (the Congress itself was to last for six weeks), and when they were dealing with theoretical issues and historical analogies, one forgot that this was a political convention. It might have been a gathering of academicians, or a prolonged scientific debate. It never occurred to the Russians that these lengthy theoretical discussions might be subordinated—as they frequently were among other revolutionists—to practical and tactical matters, or that their prolonged polemics represented a waste of time. It was axiomatic to them that all revolutionary activity must be preceded and guided by complete theoretical clarification, and if they carried this conviction to a somewhat absurd extreme in their congresses, it was due not so much to the peculiarities of the Russian intellectual temperament as to the peculiar conditions in which the Russian movement functioned. The movement being illegal, and to a large extent an *émigré* one, its leaders were cut off from practical activity and responsibility among the more backward rank and file. Unlike the leaders of the western labour movement, their time and energies were dedicated to study of social, philosophic, and economic theories which they had little opportunity to apply. Even those immediate and practical problems such as were raised by the report of the Social Democratic representatives in the Duma, were treated in relation to a prolonged and brilliant discussion of the class relationships in Russia between the bourgeoisie, the industrial workers, and the peasantry.

All the Social Democratic titans of revolutionary Russia were present—from the extreme right to the extreme left—Tseretelli, Plekhanoff, Axelrod, Deutsch, Martov, Trotsky, Lenin, Zinoviev, Rosa Luxemburg for Poland, and even Gorki who came as a visitor rather than a delegate.

The opening sessions of the Congress were to be occupied, as usual, with the election of officers and the Præsidium, a presiding committee composed of representatives of the various factions which arranges the order of business and whose control is a highly strategic matter. Everyone knew in advance who the contending candidates for chairman would be—Plekhanoff for the Mensheviks, Lenin for the Bolsheviks. But the election of the chairman and the choice of the speaker to inaugurate the Congress provoked a debate that covered practically every issue with which the Congress itself was to deal.

The struggle over this decision waged for over a week with a ferocity which I felt sure must have exhausted the entire stock of polemics as well as the strength of the delegates themselves, even though most of these had participated merely in the cheering and heckling.

When it became clear that the convention would drag on indefinitely, the problem of financing it arose again. Gorki, who at this time was the most Left Wing of Bolsheviks as well as the most famous revolutionary novelist in the world, was our best guarantee of success. He was added to the Finance Committee composed of one Bolshevik, one Menshevik, and myself.

Both Gorki and his second wife, the actress Maria Andreyeva, were the Bolsheviks' most fertile source of financial support and of contact with the wealthy and sympathetic bourgeoisie in Russia as well as England. The Party Congress had received wide publicity in the liberal English press, and its leaders had been invited to the homes of the more "radical" and adventurous sympathizers, where they were expected to titillate drawing-room audiences with tales of persecution in Darkest Russia.

I remember that Charney Vladeck, now leading spokesman for the American Labour Party, was present at the Congress under the political name of Lassalle, given to him because of his oratorical capacity. Several of the would-be hostesses evidently took him for the original Ferdinand Lassalle whose life and death—in the romantic duel over Helene von Dönniges—had been fictionalized by George Meredith. In addition to the wealthy dilettantes there were many sincere and clear-headed friends of the Russian masses in the literary, journalistic, and radical world of London—friends of an older generation of Russian exiles who had come to London in the '80's—but we could not look to these for financial aid. It was decided by our Committee that we might be able to borrow sufficient money from some of the rich liberals to continue the Congress if Gorki, our best-known member, would sign the note. Gorki at first agreed to do so, and then, after he had been pulled aside into a whispered conference with some of the Bolshevik leaders, he informed us that he would sign only if the Party Central Committee that was to be elected in the course of the Congress would consist of Bolsheviks.

We were finally able to borrow a part of the necessary sum from a liberal industrialist who had invited ten or twelve of the

[74]

Russian leaders to his home, and who was most vociferous at this time in his sympathy for the Russian Revolution. After dinner we were obliged to stroll through his picture gallery and exclaim at his masterpieces. It was in front of one of these that Gorki paused and remarked in Russian, "How terrible!"

Our host looked to Plekhanoff to translate the remarks of his celebrated guest and I felt a sudden panic for the fate of our loan. There was no ripple in Plekhanoff's urbanity as he saved the day. "Comrade Gorki has merely exclaimed, 'How remarkable!'" he assured our host.

Two days after the October Revolution in 1917 I received, in Stockholm, a letter from our friend of 1907, demanding full and immediate repayment of the loan.

To the counter-revolutionary reaction in Russia which was arousing the liberal and revolutionary forces throughout the world to protest, there was added at this time some of the worst of the anti-Jewish pogroms. If I had accepted all the invitations I received in this period to speak on the Russian situation, I should have addressed three or four meetings a night. One I received from the Torinese labour movement, on my return from London, I was happy to accept. The audience would consist largely of workers from the modern, highly organized factories of this district and would represent the most advanced and disciplined section of the Italian labour movement. Greetings were telegraphed to the meeting from labour organizations throughout the country, as well as from many of the outstanding liberal and revolutionary intellectuals—writers, scientists, university professors.

By the time I arrived with the Committee in charge at the Camera del Lavoro where the meeting was to be held, we found it impossible to get inside. The hall was already overcrowded and thousands stood outside. We finally succeeded in getting in through a back door, but throughout the meeting the street cars were forced to suspend service because they could not pass through the street. The meeting ended with resolutions of solidarity and sympathy, endless cheers for the heroes of the Revolution and the victims of the Jewish pogroms.

I rushed from the lecture-hall to my hotel, as I had to leave early the next morning for Lausanne. At the hotel I found a note from Professor Cesare Lombroso apologizing for not having been able to attend the meeting and asking me to come to see him that evening. "You will do me a great honour," he wrote me. "I am not well enough to come to you."

I was deeply moved by this invitation from the famous scholar to whom my generation owed so much, and I hurried over to his house. He opened the door for me himself and ushered me into the room in which were gathered a number of writers and scholars, as well as members of his family, as this was Lombroso's *jour fixe*. Among those whom I met there were Lombroso's son-in-law, Guglielmo Ferrero and his daughters, both of them writers. The conversation had already centred on Russian Tsarism, the perspective of the revolutionary parties, and the gathering immediately turned to me with questions on these subjects. The situation was not unlike others I was to face many years later, in regard to Italy and Germany.

The discussion became more or less of a monologue. Whenever the other guests began to speak on the subject, Lombroso would interrupt them and suggest that I be permitted to go on. During that visit I had an opportunity to realize anew the thoroughly Socialistic spirit prevailing among the Italian intellectuals of that time. I remembered having read the results of a "referendum" conducted by a radical magazine among the best-known writers, artists, scientists, and teachers only a short time before. Most of them had declared their faith in Socialism as the only hope for humanity's future. In no other country in Europe, possibly, except Russia, were there so many outstanding figures in the world of art and science who were members or sympathizers of the Socialist movement—besides Lombroso and Ferrero, there were Chiaruggi, the embryologist, Catelli, the physicist, Sanarelli, the discoverer of the yellow fever germ; DeAmicis, the most widely read of the Italian novelists, the poets, Graf, Guerrini, Pascoli.

Involuntarily, I compared the atmosphere here at the Lombroso household with the German academic milieu. What world-famous German scientists would invite a Socialist "agitator" to his *jour fixe* and would any German academic gathering have spent an entire evening discussing revolution and labour problems? The difference existed only, of course, in the academic and intellectual world.

On the following evening I spoke in Lausanne where the Italian stone masons had gone on strike. I was to speak in French that evening in order to arouse support among the French-Swiss population and explain to them the reasons for the strike. The next day I was to speak in Italian in order to encourage the strikers and their families. Secret agents were particularly active in Switzerland at this time and the Swiss authorities themselves were even more nervous than usual about the Russian and Italian "agitators" within their borders. When I left my hotel for the meeting, the porter called me back. I had forgotten to register. The French trade-union official who accompanied me warned me at once that I must take unusual precautions on this visit because of the apprehension of the authorities.

It was the time when the King of Italy had been invited by the Swiss government to inaugurate the opening of the famous Simplon tunnel between the two countries. The work had been done by Italian immigrants, many of whom had been killed—some blown to bits by dynamite, some suffocated, while others died of exhaustion. In my speech that evening I suggested that the "democratic" Swiss government might be expected to honour the real builders of the tunnel—the Italian workers—on this occasion, rather than the Italian King. Instead, these Italian workers were treated by the Swiss as an inferior species, to be crowded into special waiting-rooms and trains at the railway stations—in much the same manner that the Negro workers were segregated in the American South.

When the meeting was over the union men warned me that I would probably be arrested and one of them suggested that I spend the night at his house instead of at the hotel. I refused, but we had gone only a few blocks when we were stopped.

"Are you Madame Balabanoff?" I was asked by a respectable-looking gentleman in civilian clothes. When I admitted the fact he went on:

[77]

"Will you please follow me to the police station? You are under arrest."

At the police station I was measured, finger-printed, photographed, and, to my astonishment, accused of having registered under a false name. Not being able to decipher my hurriedly written signature, the police had thrown in this additional charge for good measure—but my name had been printed on thousands of leaflets and posters used to advertise the meeting in the past few days, which made the charge ridiculous.

"You are expelled from the Canton Vaud and must leave immediately," the magistrate informed me. "You will be accompanied to the frontier of the canton."

I was less indignant than amused. I had received only that morning an invitation from a Russian friend in Bern to attend a *Wetcherinka*, a party given by Russian refugees and students and which I had wanted very much to attend as I had had to decline so many such invitations because my evenings were mostly dedicated to political activity. The following evening, however, thanks to the Swiss authorities, I was able to enjoy myself at the *Wetcherinka* in Bern.

7

THE LAST CONGRESS OF THE FIRST INTERNA-
tional, organized by Marx and Engels, met in a small café
at The Hague in 1872. When the sixth Congress of the Second
International met in 1907, the meeting took place in the largest
auditorium in Stuttgart with one thousand delegates and a
crowd of fifty thousand attending the public demonstration with
which it opened. A German city had been chosen for the Congress, as a challenge to the German autocrats and as a demonstration of our strength. The strength of pre-war Socialism had
been growing steadily year after year, and in 1907, while women
and a large section of the workers were still disfranchised, the
parties affiliated with the International commanded nearly ten
million votes. Even Japan and India were represented at Stuttgart. Most of the older delegates there had known prison and
exile. A hundred were members of parliaments. One of them
alone represented a million workers.

I had come to the Congress as an observer rather than as a delegate, but the language difficulties involved in the debates and discussions, particularly in the commissions and subcommittees, soon involved me in the rôle of translator. The regular sessions were preceded by a convention of the women from the various countries to consider problems of particular interest to workingwomen, and at the request of Clara Zetkin I translated all of the discussions at this meeting. Here, the most heated debate arose between the Austrian Socialists and those of other countries on the subject of woman suffrage. In clerical Austria, where the male workers were still fighting for a direct and secret vote, they hesitated to prejudice their case by a struggle for universal suffrage. They suggested a compromise which would have postponed that struggle until after male suffrage was won. This viewpoint, of which the Austrian women approved, was vigorously criticized by Clara Zetkin and the majority of delegates.

Of the five leading issues dealt with by the Congress itself, that of war and militarism was by far the most important and gave rise to the most brilliant and passionate debate, with all the shining lights of the movement participating—Bebel, Victor Adler, Jaurès, Guesde, young Liebknecht, Volmar, Vaillant, Hervé. Already the colonial competition in Africa seemed to carry the threat of another war. All the delegates were passionately opposed to all increase in armaments, but the debate revolved around the methods of preventing or ending an international conflict. The French leaders, though differing widely in approach and temperament, insisted that the war resolution should lay down concrete proposals and methods to this end—a general strike, a military strike, or, according to Hervé, a general insurrection. Bebel and Victor Adler, representing the overwhelming majority of the German and Austrian Social Democrats, were opposed to the inclusion of such specific recommendations on the basis that they would provide a weapon to the governments with which to outlaw or suppress the Socialist parties and their press.

"We Germans are not fond of empty threats," said Victor Adler, "but we are prepared to go further than our promises."

Bebel's attitude towards the general strike in particular was already well known. He considered it a prelude or accompaniment of revolution itself, to be used only when the masses were in a revolutionary—not merely dissatisfied—state of mind. "Such strikes are not artificially organized by workmen's associations," he said. "They are provoked by events." In the German party Bebel's position had been opposed by Luxemburg, Mehring, and young Liebknecht from the Left and by Volmar from the Right.

The clash between the two main viewpoints on this issue culminated in an attack made by Gustav Hervé upon all his opponents. Hervé was at this time the most bitter anti-nationalist and anti-patriot in Europe. When the war broke out in 1914, like so many others of his temperament, he became a violent nationalist. The superficiality and vindictiveness of his speech at Stuttgart met with general disapproval.

The deadlock on the war resolution, in the Congress and its committees, lasted nearly five days in spite of the efforts of Vandervelde, a specialist in finding solutions, to effect a compromise. Finally a subcommittee of which Lenin, Rosa Luxemburg, and Martov were members, drafted an amendment which was incorporated into Bebel's resolution. It read:

"If war threatens to break out, it is the duty of the working class and its representatives to make every effort to prevent it. Should war come, notwithstanding these efforts, it is the duty of the workers and their representatives to intervene to bring about a speedy end to the war and to take advantage of the economic and political crisis to hasten the transformation of the capitalist society into a Socialist society.

This resolution, which was reaffirmed by two subsequent congresses, did not exclude such measures as were advocated by the French, nor did it offer any pretext for action by the German authorities.

Though the war resolution was passed unanimously and with great enthusiasm, the germs of internal factional alignments were already present. Lenin, who was one of the sixty Russian delegates to the Congress, did not participate in any of the public discussions, but he influenced the work of some of its subcommittees, indirectly, by advising more active delegates like

[81]

Luxemburg and Liebknecht. It was here that he first attempted to form an extreme Left group in the International, composed of those delegates to whom the Second International did not seem sufficiently revolutionary. But though Luxemburg, Liebknecht, and some of the Dutch delegates met and exchanged views with him, no organized group was formed.

Though the German government had found it advisable to tolerate the Congress in the most liberal province of Hohenzollern Germany, an incident occurred which showed that the authorities were watching proceedings carefully. During the discussions, Harry Quelch of England, speaking of the diplomats then gathered at The Hague to "stop war," referred to the meeting as a "thieves' supper." An hour after his speech was published in the local papers he received an order to leave Germany at once. In spite of our protests, he was forced to leave after an impromptu supper was given in his honour. During the remaining sessions, his chair was covered with flowers.

It was at Stuttgart that I first heard Jean Jaurès, the man who had fought side by side with Clemenceau in the Dreyfus case and had later overwhelmed "the Tiger" in some of the most significant debates ever to take place in the French Chamber. In Paris, when it was known that Jaurès was to speak at the Chamber, thousands of Frenchmen struggled for admission to the galleries. And yet the incomparable power of the man did not lie merely in his gifts as an orator. Jaurès was as adroit and brilliant a tactician and parliamentarian as he was a speaker. He possessed to a matchless degree the gift of identifying himself with the mood and character of his audience—whether a mass demonstration, a legislative gathering, or a congress of Socialists. At no time did he abandon his high standard. His influence was wider—and more feared in reactionary circles—than that of any other man in France. Personally he was the most genial and warm-hearted of men.

I realized later that at Stuttgart, Jaurès was distinguished from the other speakers by the prophetic nature of his insight. He seemed to foresee the political situations which would develop in the future, and in a passionate address, in which his whole body seemed to participate, he tried to convey to his audience, and to

[82]

the workers outside, the seriousness of these developments. The attitude of most of us towards the growing war danger was an abstract one—like that of radicals today who have had no experience with Fascism. The attitude of Jaurès was not abstract, and therefore his speeches, re-read later, seemed like prophecies as well as exhortations.

At the opposite pole from Jaurès in temperament, approach, and physical appearance was Jules Guesde, the scholarly, intellectual French Marxist. Though a member of the Chamber of Deputies, Guesde was far more interested in theory than in practical politics, and in that field he was considered the most intransigent and doctrinaire of Marxists. He opposed the idea of the general strike against war for the following reason: a general strike would be most effective in those advanced nations where the workers were the best organized and most class conscious and had made the most gains. In time of war a general strike would leave those nations and labour movements at the mercy of countries in which labour was weak and the strike ineffective.

When we listened to this austere warning from this most orthodox of Marxists, we did not dream that in less than a decade he would be a member of the French War Cabinet.

August Bebel was, of course, the outstanding figure at Stuttgart as at all International congresses up to the time of his death. With William Liebknecht he had built the German Social Democracy, and since Liebknecht's death, he had been its unquestioned leader. In 1907 he was one of the most powerful figures in Europe. Theodore Mommsen, the German historian, once said: "Everybody in Germany knows that with brains like those of Bebel it would be possible to furnish forth a dozen noblemen from the east of the Elbe in a fashion that would make them shine among their peers." But when this German saddler had first been elected to the Reichstag he had been ridiculed by his political opponents because of his rough speech and occasional grammatical errors. His brilliant debates with Bismarck soon changed their tune. Bebel was soon recognized as the ablest speaker and parliamentarian in Germany. His book, *Woman and Socialism*, written while he was imprisoned for having voted against war credits during the Franco-Prussian War, became a source of inspiration for millions of workingwomen.

No man in the pre-war revolutionary and labour movement ever achieved the prestige of Bebel or was so loved by workers throughout the world; but the worship accorded Bebel had in it nothing of that hysterical and grovelling quality which characterizes the cult of the post-war "beloved leaders." It was a product of deep affection, admiration and comradeship and at no time did its object lose his simplicity and essential humility.

I remember an incident that happened in my early and more obscure years in the international movement. I happened to be travelling to a meeting of the Executive of the Socialist International on the same train with Bebel and Paul Singer, the treasurer of the German party and a former capitalist who had renounced his business to work for Socialism. As members of the Reichstag, they travelled free in first, but when they discovered that I was in a second-class carriage, they insisted on joining me and then invited me to lunch. Both were apologetic because they had been travelling in more comfort than I. Just as we were leaving the dining-car, Bebel excused himself and said that he would join us in a few minutes. When he returned he was beaming with joy.

"Socialism penetrates everywhere," he said. "While we were eating, the waiter hinted that he would like to speak with me. When we were alone, he told me that he had just become converted to our movement."

This man who had fought for half a century in behalf of labour, and who was the most successful and famous figure in an international movement, was overjoyed to have found one more convert in a dining-car. When the train stopped, he stepped off jauntily like a young man.

Later, at Jena in 1911, when the Moroccan situation threatened to precipitate a Franco-German conflict, I heard Bebel analyse that situation and then impress upon his followers the implications of the Stuttgart resolution. He spoke like a father to his children. "Children, children," he cried, "you do not know what war really means!"

One of the richest and most varied personalities in the International was Victor Adler, leader of the Austrian party. His was probably the widest range of interest and knowledge of any individual in the movement. His personality fascinated even those who disagreed, as I did, with his tactical position. Adler had been a successful physician before he had decided to devote all of his time to the labour movement and since that time he had practically created the Austrian Socialist Party and a new school of labour journalism. His passion for music and his critical appreciation of the drama were well known to his co-workers. He would sometimes slip out of a meeting which seemed to him unimportant to "keep an appointment" with Beethoven's Ninth Symphony. A beautiful portrait of Eleanora Duse, the unique interpreter of human sorrow, hung in his living-room.

At Stuttgart I was impressed as I had never been before by the difference between the leading Continental and British Socialists. So many of us approached the problems of the movement from a theoretical and intellectual viewpoint. The English leaders, however, symbolized by the miner, Hardie, were for the most part workers themselves, active in their own labour unions, essentially practical and impatient of generalizations. When Hardie spoke, one felt at once that here was a man who was voicing directly the desires and aspirations of huge masses of exploited people, and that he was speaking from the depths of his own, as well as their, experience. He did not speak often at international congresses, but when he did, his sincerity and hard-headed intelligence, coloured by a deeply ethical feeling, made a profound impression.

The Congress had stressed the need for creating an international youth movement to unite Socialist and labour youth organizations in the various countries, particularly for the fight against militarism. During the sessions, Karl Liebknecht, who had already been imprisoned for anti-militarist activity, approached me and said: "I have made a rough draft for a youth International. Will you help me to elaborate it?"

When the Congress adjourned, about twenty of us remained and met in a small hall to launch this project. Among them, in addition to Liebknecht and myself, were Henriette Roland-Holst from Holland, Danneberg from Vienna, and Henri de Man from Belgium. De Man was then a gifted young Left-winger and an ardent anti-militarist. Working together as translators at various international gatherings, we became very good friends. When the World War broke out, his anti-militarism, like that of so many others, became transformed and now he is a member of the Belgian government. Liebknecht's development was exactly the opposite. Karl was already the most popular of the younger German Socialists and a leader of the Party's Left Wing. Intellectual brilliance might have been expected of the son of William Liebknecht, but it is not at all common for the children of great revolutionaries to follow in their fathers' political footsteps. With his passionate, restless, and exuberant temperament, Karl was the image of his father. Even in that comparatively quiet time it seemed that here was a man destined not to "die in bed." He not only accepted any service and responsibility requested of him, but he seemed always to be looking for new work and activity.

At conventions we usually spent much time together, between and after sessions, at the cafés where the Germans would sit to enjoy their coffee or beer while reading an infinite variety of newspapers. Karl's pockets were always bursting with papers of every kind. As we worked and talked together in Stuttgart of war and revolution, our words had no specific application. I did not dream that word of Karl's horrible death twelve years later would reach me in the first Workers' Republic.

By 1912 the Tripolitan and Balkan wars made imperialist conflict a reality and the threat of world war imminent. The International Congress held in Basle in that year was intended primarily as a demonstration against this threat and a preparation for specific action should the Balkan conflict spread. Here Jaurès introduced into the Stuttgart resolution references to the revolutionary uprisings which had followed the Franco-Prussian War and the Russo-Japanese conflict. The agenda contained only one topic—war and international Socialism. The tension was acute as we anticipated a calamity and wondered whether or not the working-class vanguard in the countries affected would be able to deal with the situation and whether the masses would

[86]

follow our slogans. Bebel was right when he had told us that we of the younger generations at this time knew so little of the reality of war.

The climax of the Congress was a public meeting held in the cathedral at Basle. This was not a political assembly. It was a great popular demonstration in which almost the whole population took part, most of it unable to get inside the cathedral, so that some of our speakers had to address a vast audience outside. The fact that we were able to hold this meeting in a cathedral was an indication of our strength and of popular sentiment at that time. When Bebel and Jaurès, representing the French and German workers, appeared before that great audience, they seemed to be serving notice upon their respective governments and upon the world that war between these two nations would never be tolerated.

Agnini, one of our oldest Italian deputies, and myself had been delegated from the Italian party, and when Agnini appeared as a spokesman for Italian Socialism's opposition to war which had been demonstrated during the Tripolitan adventure, his speech was wildly applauded even before I could translate it. After I had translated it successively into French, German, and English, the entire audience, including the press representatives and visitors, arose from their seats and cheered. It was not until Bebel stepped forward and embraced me that I realized that the applause was for me.

"Comrade Balabanoff," he said, "in hearing you I felt that I was listening to and seeing a living incarnation of the International."

At that time in America the lives of two Italian syndicalists were in danger—Ettore and Giovannitti, leaders of the Lawrence strike. As a member of the Executive Committee representing Italy, I submitted a resolution protesting against the reactionary prosecution of their case. It called upon working-class groups throughout the world to echo this protest. The resolution, signed by the best-known delegates to the Basle Congress, was cabled to the United States. I remember the emotion and apprehension with which we awaited the outcome of the trial.

When word finally came that the men were freed, we were overjoyed. Who would have believed at that time that the Sacco-
Vanzetti tragedy would be possible?

Bebel died the following year. It was Mussolini who brought
me the news in Milan. He seemed almost as upset as I was at this
irreparable loss. Years later, thousands of Bebel's disciples in
Italy were persecuted and humiliated by this man who wrote
such a moving commemorative article at this time for *Avanti*.

I was delegated to represent the Italian party at Bebel's
funeral and I left Milan immediately for Zürich. Arriving there
early in the morning, I rushed to a florist's to purchase an offering of red roses, of which Bebel had been so fond. A young man
and I were the only customers in the shop and he too bought
red roses.

After he had gone out, the florist asked me: "Do you know
who that was? He is the grandson of August Bebel."

After the death of his beloved wife, Bebel had lavished all his
tenderness and affection on this young man, the child of his only
daughter, whose husband, a physician, had died for science as
the result of medical experiments.

When I arrived at the People's House where Bebel's body lay
in state, the door of the hall had not yet been opened to the
public, but Oscar Cohn, one of the most generous and noble
men I have ever met, now dead in exile, permitted me to enter.
Mine were the first flowers to bank the coffin, but three days
later, when the funeral took place, thousands of wreaths and
great bunches of red flowers had been added to my offering. As I
stood beside his body, my feeling that Bebel had earned the
right to rest was stronger than my personal grief. It was as
though I foresaw the tragedy that was soon to overtake our movement and humanity in general and was relieved that he might
be spared the knowledge of this tragedy.

Thousands of workers, school children, Socialists from various
countries passed his coffin in those three days. There was scarcely
time for them to drop their flowers and glance at him because of
the thousands pressing behind them. Among them were old men

[88]

and women in worn clothes, the old men holding their crumpled hats in their hands, the women wiping their eyes with a corner of their aprons. I heard one mother repeating to her children: "Look at him for the last time; he was our father, now we are orphans."

8

THE HISTORY OF THE ITALIAN LABOUR MOVE-
ment in ten years preceding the World War was one of
almost constant violent struggle—strikes, demonstrations,
clashes with the police in the cities, with the landlords and local
authorities in the agricultural districts. In the latter, the Socialists and Anarchists, though bitterly opposed to each other under
ordinary circumstances, were often lined up against the Republicans, composed for the most part of the small landowners and
merchants.

These struggles were particularly violent in Romagna, that
most revolutionary of provinces, where practically everyone
except the clergy and the members of the ruling classes was a
Socialist, an Anarchist or a Republican.

In 1910, after his return to Romagna, Mussolini had become
editor of the weekly party paper at Forli—*Lotta di Classe*. It was
one of the numerous Socialist weeklies published in Italy, and

neither the paper nor its editor attracted much attention outside of Romagna during the next year or two. The paper reflected the confusion and violence of Mussolini's own temperament, oscillating between a superficial variety of Marxism and an extreme anarchistic approach. At one moment its editor would be chiding the "reformists" in his own party for timidity and voicing the most anti-parliamentary sentiments; at another moment he would be launching an attack upon the Syndicalists. When the famous bombing of the Colon Theatre took place in Buenos Aires in 1910, it was typical of Mussolini that he defended this act of terrorism, even though the Anarchists themselves disclaimed responsibility.

"Thiers never had any pity for the partisans of the Commune," he wrote in *Lotta di Classe*, "yet one sees Socialists moved by the victims of the Colon Theatre. This one-sided sensibility of the Socialists shows to what extent Christianity is still alive in their souls. It is Christianity which has given us this morbid, hysterical, and effeminate pity."

A year later, after the assassination of Stolypin in Russia, he wrote: "The Russia of the proletarians is in festival and awaits the day when dynamite shall pulverize the bones of the Little Father whose hands are red with blood."

He had been arrested several times for brief periods, since his return to Forli, and when the Tripolitan War broke out, he was sentenced to five months in prison because of his participation in an anti-war riot. At this time he launched a violent attack upon the ex-Socialist, later Nationalist, Monicelli, which is particularly interesting in the light of Mussolini's own subsequent actions, and the later attempts of his Fascist apologists to give the impression that Mussolini had been a patriotic "Tripolitan."

"Cartilaginous spines like his do not resist the shocks of Socialist crises," he wrote. "The banks of the Rubicon swarm with men who want to sell themselves—Heralds blow your trumpets, it is the liquidation of the season's end—consciences and tissues are elastic."

It was during one of the most violent internal struggles in Romagna that I received the following message from Mussolini:

[91]

Carissima, we need you here. We have to organize a meeting which should be an enormous success and have wide repercussions. It must be like a bomb which shakes the entire population and which will inspire them for the First of May demonstration. Only you can instil such enthusiasm. You must come. Please don't refuse.

The Romagna situation had by this time attracted the attention of all Italy. Between the Socialist trade unions and agricultural coöperatives, supported by the Anarchists, and the authorities, supported by the Republicans, daily clashes were taking place. And in view of the fiery temperament of the Romagnoli in general, any excess might be expected.

May 1st was celebrated in Italy in the most widespread and impressive fashion. The peasants and workers, even the white-collared and professional workers, looked upon May 1st as their own distinctive holiday. Because of the influence of the Socialists even upon unorganized masses, the celebration was unanimous, and in the towns governed by Socialists, the schools and municipal institutions closed. It was a day of spring in the hearts and minds of the masses, as in nature. The workers paraded to demonstrate their strength and display their solidarity, and in the meetings that followed, they also summarized their own accomplishment and weaknesses, the distance they had travelled towards their goal, the tasks that remained to be fulfilled.

As International Labor Day was observed in the smallest towns and villages, the party speakers were in great demand. Local organizations began early in the spring to invite the speakers whom they considered best or most beloved, so that the most able of the Party leaders always received ten times as many invitations as they could possibly accept. I hated to refuse these invitations, and to simplify matters I usually tried to choose a location in which the towns were sufficiently close together to enable me to make four or five addresses during the day. This was the situation when I received Mussolini's invitation to Romagna. I accepted the invitation, therefore, with the understanding that I would speak on April 30th and leave the same day in order to fulfil another engagement on May 1st in a distant province.

At a small station about half an hour before I arrived in

Forli, Mussolini and another man entered my compartment. After we had exchanged greetings, the former spoke of a lecture he had delivered the previous evening. "How was it?" I inquired. "Was the audience interested?"

Mussolini laughed ironically and left it to his companion to answer me.

"Well," said the latter, "he spoke for an hour and a half and so fast that the first half-hour I was barely able to follow him; in the second half it became too difficult; and at the end I had to hold my eyes wide open in order not to fall asleep."

Mussolini was now laughing so hard that his whole body was heaving and shaking. "Such a bluff, such fun!" he said.

This was a trick of his with which I was already familiar. Let people laugh at him, find him crazy—he did not care so long as they noticed him and thought him original.

During the remainder of the journey he referred repeatedly to the serious situation which had developed in Forli because the hostility and frequent riots between the Socialists and the Republicans had caused the authorities to intervene. This meant the possible arrest of leaders and organizers in order to prevent the May Day demonstration.

"Maybe we shall have to call off your speech," he said.

"I don't think we should break the promise we made to the people when we announced our meeting," I replied.

At Forli, Mussolini's apprehension increased. He tried to influence me through other Socialists to renounce the meeting, but I refused to do so.

When the time came for me to speak, we proceeded to a large square. It was thronged with thousands of peasants and workers with their wives and children—many of whom had come from miles away to hear me and to participate in the demonstration planned for the morrow. The Republicans gathered near by. In fact, practically all the people in Forli had been mobilized by their respective political parties. The enormous crowd was attracted to the meeting not only to hear a speech on the Paris Commune, but because riots seemed likely, and those whose sympathies were with us wanted to be on hand to do their duty if necessary. The situation was tense and exceedingly dangerous.

The Republicans, on their side, seemed anxious to provoke trouble. They shouted and tried in numerous ways to disrupt the meeting. I had scarcely begun to speak when Mussolini rushed to me and whispered in my ear that we must get away immediately. A Republican had killed a Socialist in a street near by. Further bloodshed seemed certain.

I knew that if I interrupted my speech at such a moment, it would mean panic and bloodshed, so I increased my efforts to gain the attention of my audience and succeeded.

When the meeting ended, the police authorities, fearing an attempt on our lives, provided a coach for Mussolini and me to drive away in. Two *carbinieri* were to sit with us and four others were to accompany us in another coach. Mussolini's excitement exceeded all bounds. Which coach should we enter in order to escape safely? Would the first or second one be most likely to be bombed?

The information the police had received was correct: there was a plot to assassinate us. A bullet struck one of the *carbinieri* who was in the first coach. Mussolini, who sat beside me in the second, shrank down in his seat, trembling and cursing. Long after we were clear of the crowd he was still shaking.

"I don't feel like going home now," he said. "Those damn yellows [Republicans] are certainly waiting for me. I would rather go with you to the station. There will be so many police there they will not dare to attack me."

As we neared the station he began to plead with me not to leave. "Riots and very serious ones are inevitable," he whined. "Please don't go. Who knows what can happen tomorrow? I cannot bear the responsibility alone."

At the station a cyclist came with the information that the local authorities had been ordered by the government to forbid the demonstration planned for the following day. Mussolini quieted down immediately.

I understood later that his insistence on my coming to Forli in the first place, and upon my remaining there, had been a manoeuvre. The conflict between the two political factions had become so critical, and Mussolini's violent speeches had provoked so much hatred, that a clash seemed inevitable and he

[94]

wanted to dodge the responsibility for what might happen. In case of bloodshed, the blame would be laid upon my speech. Should the Party have criticized the attitude of the leadership in this locality, it would be easy for Mussolini to shift the blame onto my shoulders.

When the Tripolitan War broke out in 1911 the tide of anti-militarism in Italy, stimulated by the Socialists, was running high. The Party officially opposed the war, its representatives in Parliament and in lesser legislative bodies spoke against it, anti-war meetings were held throughout the country, and *Avanti* carried on an energetic campaign against imperialism in general and this program of colonial conquest in particular.

A few of the Socialist leaders, however, men like Bissolati, Bonomi, and Cabrini, who had belonged to the reformist wing of the Party, took the position that Socialism being possible only in industrially advanced nations, imperialistic expansion into backward communities carried with it the germs of a more mature capitalism and in that way hastened the development of Socialism. This reasoning led them to temper their opposition to war. The rank and file of the Party, however, was overwhelmingly opposed to the war and violent demonstrations against it—such as the one in Forli, where the railroad ties were torn up to prevent the movement of troops—took place in the more revolutionary centres. Mussolini was practically alone, however, in advocating physical sabotage and violence, and he was imprisoned for five months after the Forli affair. He had also advocated that the women lie down on the railroad tracks so that the trains carrying troops for Africa could not run.

Shortly after the dissension over the war issue, another situation arose which caused additional resentment among the Party members against Bissolati and Cabrini in particular. After an attempt to assassinate the King and Queen, in March, 1912, both these deputies personally congratulated the monarchs upon their escape.

As a result of this growing dissatisfaction with some of the reformist deputies an extraordinary convention of the Party was called at Reggio Emilia in July, 1912.

When the gathering convened, it was evident that the Left Wing, to which I belonged and which had bitterly opposed the Tripolitan venture, would have a majority. The Left Wing of the Italian Party was then comparable to the "orthodox Marxists" of Germany who opposed the Bernstein "revisionists." The slogan of the revisionists was: "The movement is all; the goal is nothing." While not opposing reforms or immediate demands, the Left Wing in both Germany and Italy, stressed the socialist *goal*.

We decided that at the convention we would introduce a very brief resolution demanding the expulsion of Bissolati, Cabrini, Bonomi, and Podrecca from the Party. The acceptance of this resolution, striking directly at an important section of the Party leadership, would constitute a general victory for the Left. It would also place the responsibility of the Party completely in our hands.

"Whom shall we designate to submit this?" asked one of the members of our caucus.

"It doesn't matter," said another. "It speaks for itself and has merely to be read. Who does the reading is not important."

"I suggest Comrade Bacci," said a delegate.

"Oh no, that would be foolish," said a comrade from Romagna. "Bacci will be one of our speakers in a discussion where we want an impressive name. Why shouldn't we appoint Mussolini?"

"Mussolini?" inquired a delegate. "Who is he? Why should we appoint him?"

As a matter of fact, Mussolini was little known at that time outside of his native Romagna, from which he had come as a delegate. His name had only occasionally been mentioned in the columns of *Avanti*.

"Why not appoint him?" asked the Romagnard delegate who had made the original suggestion. "We Romagnoli have fought against the war more strenuously than others. Not only with words, but with deeds! Let one who fomented revolt against war and was put in gaol for it voice our protest against deputies who forget they represent revolutionary labour."

"Let's not waste time," declared an elderly delegate. "What

difference does it make? The comrade suggests Mussolini. Let him take the floor, whether he is known or unknown."

The next day at the convention Mussolini appeared on the platform with a piece of paper which he nervously twisted in his hands while most of the delegates looked at him with curiosity. They had never seen him before.

In submitting the brief resolution which was approved by a great majority of the delegates, Mussolini, in relation to the Bissolati and Cabrini episode, said: "Why be moved and weep before the King—merely for the King? Why this hysterical, excessive sensibility over crowned heads? What is a king, anyway, if not by definition the useless citizen? Socialists cannot afford to associate themselves with mourning and prayers, or with festivals belonging to monarchy."

The approval of our resolution meant, as I have pointed out, the triumph of the Left Wing over the Right. Until then we had been the rank-and-file opposition. Now we were to lead the Party, the most influential party of the country. With our victory came great responsibilities. The first difficulty was to explain to our membership, as well as to the public in general, why we had expelled from the Party four of its best-known members, some of them its founders.

It was not difficult to foresee that the bourgeois press would take advantage of the split, exaggerating its importance, laying stress upon the great value of the men we had expelled. They would try to insinuate that futile personal motives had determined our attitude. And we knew, too, that a part of the rank and file would be accessible to those arguments and would think we should have been more conciliatory.

A statement had to be made immediately by some authoritative member of our group whom nobody would believe to be moved by personal rancour or ambition. The choice fell on me. I can't remember a single occasion in my life when I have been so aware of the responsibility I was assuming. I knew whom we were going to lose and how difficult it is to interpret decisions dictated only by principles.

"Only a Party like ours," said I in my speech, "which is rooted in a mass movement, whose future is intimately linked to the fate of the masses, can expel from its midst men like these whom we are going to part with today and who may be followed by others—men whom other parties would be honoured to have in their ranks. But such is the fate of those who join a movement like ours. When the masses disapprove of us we have to go. Maybe such will be the fate of those of us who expel you today, or perhaps life will be merciful enough to spare us."

When my speech was over I was congratulated not only by those on whose behalf I had spoken, but by the defeated minority as well. I believe everyone understood how painful this duty was to me. I neither felt nor behaved like a victor.

I asked my comrades to allow me not to join them at lunch. I wanted to be alone. A few minutes after I had left them and was going to my hotel, Bissolati crossed the street.

"Would you allow me to shake hands with you? May I call you once more, for the last time, 'Comrade'?" he said, with a sorrowful expression in his eyes.

"If you care to do so after my speech," I replied, surprised.

Not more than two years after we had expelled Bissolati, we were obliged to expel—for far graver reasons—the one who had introduced our resolution—Benito Mussolini.

In both cases Italian Socialism proved its consistency with its internationalist ideals.

At the close of the convention we had to appoint a new Executive Committee. It was customary that the Executive Committee be composed of delegates representing each province of Italy. I was elected for the first time on this occasion, as were Mussolini and other members of the Left Wing. There was difficulty in selecting a new staff for the Party's central organ, *Avanti*. As the offices of *Avanti* had been tentatively transferred to Milan, comrades whose homes and work were in other localities could not be nominated.

"I have a suggestion," said Lazzari, our venerated secretary, in one of the successive meetings of our Executive Committee. "Let's nominate one of our younger comrades—Mussolini, for instance. Why should the older ones always be selected? Besides, the whole Executive is responsible for our central organ and it is not important who is to be in Milan and considered its editor."

The idea did not displease us. Only one member of the new Executive objected. "I am a little afraid of Mussolini's temperament," he declared. "He is too egocentric."

Upon hearing this objection, Mussolini, who had not spoken until then, said in an irritated tone: "Leave me alone. I have not the slightest intention of accepting the appointment. I am not capable of handling the job. I have not an adequate Marxist background and I don't want the responsibility."

"If the Party decides you are needed and if you are a true revolutionist, you will accept," insisted Lazzari.

Others then urged the appointment. Mussolini brooded in silence. I knew him sufficiently well to understand what was going on in his mind. Tempted and flattered as he was by the proposal, he hesitated because of the responsibility involved. The matter was still undecided when we adjourned for lunch. Mussolini and I lunched together. I tried to induce him to accept the proposal of the Executive, but his mind was apparently made up and he declared point-blank that he would not consider accepting. Upon the reconvening of the Executive Committee, however, his first words were: "Well, I agree. But there is one condition: Comrade Balabanoff has to join the staff as co-editor."

I understood immediately the motivation behind this strange conduct. He did not want to renounce the honour which had been offered him nor did he want the responsibility. He knew that as a member of the *Avanti* staff I would help him, in fact that I would assume complete responsibility when things went wrong, but that I would not attempt to make personal capital from our successes. He knew also that, though I might help him, I would not move to Milan merely on his behalf; but if the Executive requested it, I—as a disciplined member of the Party—would comply. Hence this manœuvring.

The first thing Mussolini asked me to do after we became editors of *Avanti* was to write to the former editor, the late Claudio Treves, to the effect that he was no longer a member of the editorial staff, his post having been taken by myself. I was indignant at this, for even if I had considered myself able to substitute for Treves—which I did not—I would not have accepted an appointment to displace him. Besides, the Executive had decided unanimously to keep Treves because of his exceptional journalistic ability.

"Why did you not object to Treves' nomination when we were discussing it at the Executive meeting?" I asked Mussolini.

Though he would not answer, the reason for his unfair move was clear to me. Treves was one of the most brilliant journalists in Italy and Mussolini was afraid that Treves' contributions would emphasize his own deficiencies. To avoid this and also to avoid unpleasantness, he tried to induce me to write the letter.

Whenever Mussolini was called upon to face an unpleasant situation, to refuse an article, to dismiss a collaborator, encounter the anger of those to whom he had made promises which he had broken, he would ask me to substitute for him. Whenever a controversial article had to be written, he would ask me to write it. Whenever *Avanti* readers disapproved of an editorial, he would call upon me to defend it before the Executive or he would make a point of being absent from the meeting and I had to do it.

In my whole political life I have never met any one who made such continual demands upon my compassion as did Mussolini. He would ask me directly for assistance or I would sense somehow that he was afraid of a situation and would take care of it myself. I helped him because the interests of the Party required it.

At the beginning of this period of collaboration with Mussolini at Milan he discovered that we were living on the same street a few doors from each other. When the paper had gone to press, Mussolini would often say: "Please wait for me, comrade. Let us go home together."

I used to come to the office early in the morning, whereas Mussolini, who had to wait for the first copy of the paper each night, came late. I preferred, therefore, to leave before he did, but I came to realize that he was afraid of walking home alone at night, and despite my exhaustion at the end of a long day I usually humoured him by waiting.

"What are you afraid of?" I asked him one night as we were walking home through the deserted streets.

"Afraid of?" he repeated, halting in his tracks and looking about him with eyes that appeared to be filled with terror. "I am afraid of trees, of dogs, of the sky as well as of my shadow. Yes, my own shadow!" At this point he seemed to recover himself somewhat, shrugged his shoulders, and laughed sardonically. "I am afraid of everything, of everybody and—of myself."

One night he stopped before some trees and said, "These are the trees on which we shall hang the reformists, Turati and Prampolini."

"And where shall we be hanged," I asked, "when the working class shall disapprove of us?"

Often Mussolini would prolong our walk by stopping. Mistrusting everyone and being afraid that his utterances would later be used against him, he was very monosyllabic with everybody but me. All that he accumulated during the day he would pour out to me on our walk home. He made sarcastic thrusts against both himself and others.

"Have you read Valera's last article?" he would ask me, alluding to an eccentric editor of a weekly periodical. "He is crazy." Then he would add in a sardonic tone, "I bet my article on the same subject will be crazier." And he would pause to see what my reaction would be to his extravagance.

Sometimes he would tell me of his intention to write something much more "frightful," more hair-raising, than the short stories of Edgar Allan Poe.

"When I first read Poe in the libraries of Trento and Lausanne," he said, "I thought I would go mad immediately, I was so frightened. I would never read him in the evening. Terrible!" And he would stop once more, adding, after an interval, "I have begun to write in the same way, too, but my volume of stories shall be called *Perversion*."

"You know," and this would be his conclusion so often that it became a kind of *leit-motif*: "I am crazy. What madhouse will take me in when I go completely insane? I do not know, but mad I am," and he would laugh sarcastically.

"Of course you are," I would answer. "But leave Poe alone

and don't talk continually about your craziness. You just boast about it. Is it so interesting?"

On a later occasion he referred to our former comrade and colleague, the above-mentioned Monicelli, who had once been a member of the *Avanti* staff under the editorship of Enrico Ferri, but who had become a Nationalist and left the Party at the time of the Tripolitan War. Monicelli had recently gone insane, and Mussolini, who had attacked him most violently for his desertion of the Party, now seemed glad to find the solution of the psychological puzzle in Monicelli's subsequent commitment to an asylum. In alluding to this, in a letter he wrote me while I was in Germany, Mussolini reverted to his long-since-familiar theme: he, too, would end up in a madhouse and Monicelli had only preceded him.

"I quite agree with you," I answered him. "Monicelli has only preceded you, but I hope you will not follow his steps in deserting the labour movement before you are committed."

"And mind you," I added, following the line of thought his allusion had evoked, "you may be sure I shall be the only person who will visit you in the madhouse. You are so selfish, so self-centred that you have not a single friend in the world."

At that time, because he no longer lived among peasants in the provinces or among illiterate emigrants who considered him superior, Mussolini seemed to me more than ever aware of his inferiority and to be suffering more because of it. He sought to gain notoriety—regardless of how or of what kind. Whatever attracted attention to his personality pleased him. Even disparaging remarks made him happy, provided somebody, somewhere, noticed him as an individual.

Once when the Futurist movement, led by Marinetti, was creating an international furor, Mussolini asked me: "Have you seen how your compatriots treated Marinetti in Moscow?" When I shook my head, he continued: "As soon as he appeared on the stage to deliver his lecture, the audience began to scream, to howl, and to throw rotten tomatoes at him. Isn't it beautiful? How I envy him! I should like to have been in his place."

9

DURING AN UNEMPLOYMENT DEMONSTRATION in Milan a mason had been killed by police. Tragedies such as this were not uncommon in Italy during these years, but whenever they occurred a wave of revolutionary protest swept the country. The circumstances surrounding this particular killing, however, were exceptional, and radical and liberal opinions were more outraged than usual.

The victim was not a revolutionist—not even a member of a trade union. He was a simple young man without any class consciousness whatsoever. Moreover he was deeply religious. Before leaving his family on that fatal morning (he had merely wanted to see what the demonstration was about) he had told his wife not to forget to put oil into the lamp which burned in their home day and night before the image of the Virgin Mary. He had insisted upon this, though his wife told him she would have to buy oil and they had only a few centesimi between themselves and starvation.

[103]

All Italian labour organizations, following the example of the Executive of the Socialist Party, published vehement manifestos calling for a general strike in Milan on the day of the funeral. Mussolini, however, criticized our manifesto as not being strongly enough worded.

"How tragic the destiny of this innocuous worker!" I said. "To be assassinated in such a savage manner without knowing why or wherefore! If he had been one of our comrades, he would have known that he was dying for an ideal. But he relied on God, on the Virgin Mary, on miracles, to obtain work. He was not even aware of his situation. What a contrast between his life and death!"

"Yes, indeed, the contrast is very striking," said Mussolini. "You must write an article on the subject."

The funeral became a mass demonstration of a most revolutionary character. Solidarity with the dead, his family and his class; anger, hatred, revenge against those responsible for the tragedy; the ardent desire to support the struggle against all social injustice and inequality—all these emotions drew thousands into the streets. The general strike was complete; factories, mills shut down, transportation paralyzed, stores closed. Even the higher-class shops and restaurants were forced to suspend business.

By the time the funeral procession was under way the crowd was in a fiery mood. Immediately following the coffin were the relatives of the slain man. Behind them were the representatives of the various political parties and trade unions. I was among these. During a pause in the procession I heard some one shout: "Come on, Benito. Here's Comrade Balabanoff. Don't be afraid. We'll make way for you."

Through an opening in the crowd appeared Mussolini, breathing hard, his face contracted and his eyes bulging.

"What is the matter?" I exclaimed.

"Something terrible," he said, excitedly. "I won't assume responsibility. The relatives of the dead man want a priest to come to the cemetery for the ceremony."

"Why are you excited?" I asked, trying to calm him. "It is

quite natural that the relatives of this man, who was such a devout Catholic, should want a religious burial."

"What do I care for such idiots as these backward people with their gods and their priests? Let them go to the devil, all of them," he shouted.

"There is nothing to get so excited about," I told him. "Let the priest come and do what the relatives want him to do."

"What do you mean? Do you think this crowd will tolerate such a thing?"

"I'm sure it will," I replied.

"Very well, then," Mussolini said, angrily. "But you must take the responsibility upon yourself. I don't want to be lynched by this mob. I know what their mood is and I will not take blame for what happens."

"I assume the entire responsibility," I said. "I do not consider it courageous to act against what obviously would have been the wishes of the dead man. Since we are such an enormous majority, it would be cowardly to impose our will upon a few poor and superstitious relatives. We are strong enough not to do it. Let us be generous. I am sure our comrades will understand and approve. They will help us to convince the others."

During my memorial speech at the cemetery I told the aroused audience why we should permit the priest to officiate. There was not a single protest or sign of disapproval. The crowd left the cemetery in perfect order without disturbing the priest. The following day all newspaper reports on the funeral commented on the perfect discipline, quoted my speech, pointed out that, due to our tolerance, a tragic riot had been avoided, and complimented the Socialists on their moral and political integrity.

I was working at my desk when Mussolini, having perused the morning papers, asked me in an irritated tone, "Have you read what the papers say about your speech?"

"No," I answered, truthfully, for I had not yet read the reports. "It is not important."

"Well," he continued, unable to conceal his bad humour, "if I were you I would not be so indifferent. It is always a bad sign when our enemies praise us. Mind you, they praise you too much."

"I sincerely hope our enemies never have other reasons to praise you than they have in praising me," I replied.

This was the first time, I believe, that Mussolini looked on me as a rival.

At about four o'clock each afternoon Mussolini would leave for a doctor's office. Though extremely reticent in his relations with most of his comrades, never removing the mask by which he tried to hide his emotions and thoughts, Mussolini utilized every opportunity to speak of his affliction. This was one of the ways he used to attract attention and gain sympathy. He considered it very original to boast of something which most people would have concealed. Regardless of what guests were in our office, on leaving for the doctor's he would tell where he was going, and why. Upon his return he would complain loudly of his pain and would remain in a very excitable mood for hours.

Irritated by this manner of obtaining attention, I interrupted him once while several other people were present. "Why repeat always the same thing?" I asked him. "Even if the subject were interesting, it would become monotonous. Can't you go to a specialist and be done with it?"

"You are right," he said. "I will go to a specialist."

About six o'clock the next afternoon my attention was attracted by something unusual—a coach stopping at the door of the *Avanti* office. The man who got out and entered our editorial-room was Mussolini, but I scarcely recognized him; he seemed to have become old and bent. He was trembling, his face was pallid, his eyes full of terror. Each word he uttered seemed to cause him unbearable pain. He threw himself into an armchair, hid his face in the palms of his hands, and began to sob. Though accustomed to his hysterical outbursts, I realized that this time it was something other than his usual nervous attack.

"What is the matter with you?" I asked. "Why are you crying?"

He raised his head and looked at me with a horrified expression. "Don't you feel, don't you smell?" he moaned. "Don't you smell an antiseptic?"

"Antiseptic?"

"Yes. And fancy, this damn doctor took some of my blood.

[106]

Before he did so he used an antiseptic. Now I smell it every-where—everywhere. It persecutes me!"

I tried to calm him, assuring him that he would soon be rid of the painful impression and advised him to go home for dinner.

"I am afraid of this odour," he continued. "I am afraid of everything."

He left finally after making me promise that I would be there at nine o'clock when he returned. In the interval I paid a visit to the specialist, a comrade whom I knew.

"You don't need to tell me what he is suffering from," I said to the doctor. "I know. But tell me, is his case so serious? Maybe the Executive can afford to send him to a sanatorium. He has no means of his own. And his poor wife, when she finds out he is so ill! I pity her more than him. She is an illiterate peasant woman who had courage enough to follow him to Milan in spite of his irresponsibility."

"Comrade," he replied, "as medical chief of the clinic I have thousands of patients every year. Believe me when I tell you that I have never seen such a coward as Mussolini."

When Mussolini returned to the office he was accompanied by a very humble-appearing woman and an undernourished, poorly-dressed little girl. He introduced them, "My comrade Rachel and our daughter Edda." It was the first and only time his family visited our headquarters. It was nasty weather—pouring rain, cold, piercing wind, and both mother and child were dressed inadequately and the child was shivering. I realized that he had brought his wife and child with him only because he was afraid to be alone, and this aroused such indignation in me that I could scarcely bear to look at him.

For days thereafter, shortly before four o'clock in the after-noon, he would moan and hide his face in his hands.

"Now what is the matter?" I would ask.

"Don't you smell it—that disinfectant!" he would cry. "Look! It is four o'clock."

I finally resorted to the stratagem of setting the hands of the clock ahead. When he would start his groaning, I would say: "Look at the time. Four o'clock has passed. It is almost five."

He would immediately raise his head, his eyes shining with

relief and joy. "If that's so, I'm ready for work," he would say, smiling. "Would you kindly let me have a cup of tea?"

One morning two young workers from Romagna, compatriots of Mussolini, came to the office. They were obviously very perturbed.

"What is it, comrades?" I asked.

"We must see Benito at once," they said.

"He will be here shortly, but can't you tell me what is troubling you?"

They explained excitedly that one of the Romagna comrades who was living in Milan had been killed the night before. Mussolini came in before they had finished their story.

"What brings you to Milan?" Mussolini asked. *"Porca Madonna!* Is there trouble again with the Republicans? Those damned Republicans! Unless we exterminate them ———"

"No, Benito, it's not that," one of the young men replied. "You remember Ruggero of Forlì. He has been murdered here in Milan and by a Romagnolo, too, but not because of politics. Jealousy, a woman, you know."

"A woman!" exclaimed Mussolini. "Is it worth while to die for a woman? Aren't there enough of them?"

"Look here, Benito, we came here to ask your help," said the other young man.

"Help? What have I to do with such business? Women, jealousy, death! Leave me alone."

"Listen, Benito," said the young man who had just spoken, "we appeal to your spirit of solidarity. We are Romagnoli, aren't we? The man who has been killed was a playmate and friend of yours. You remember him. His father, 'Uncle Beppe,' as we used to call him, was a close friend of your father. As soon as he got the terrible news, he asked us to come here at once to arrange the funeral. He is old now and too weak to travel. He does not want his son buried like a dog in a common grave as they do with unknown people here in Milan. 'Go to Benito,' he told us; 'he will help you.'"

"What the devil can I do? I can't resuscitate Ruggero, can I?"

"It is not a question of resuscitation," replied the youth. "We simply want you to come to the morgue with us."

[108]

"To the morgue!" Mussolini screamed.

"Yes. The corpse must be identified by some one who knew him and whom the police know if it is to be buried as the father wishes."

Mussolini looked at me with an imploring expression. Finally he told the two men that he would go with them that afternoon. As soon as they left, he asked me to go in his stead.

"Why didn't you tell them the truth at once?" I asked him. "Why always lie? You're afraid to go to the morgue and yet you, as a revolutionist, expect other people to die and yourself to kill if necessary. You, a revolutionist!"

"Yes," the words burst from him, "I am afraid. What have I to do with corpses? But please do me this favour. I have promised, but—you are courageous; you don't mind, but I—I can't, I can't."

Another day Mussolini entered the office with a particularly gloomy and downcast air.

"Now what is it?" I asked.

"Giulletti has announced that he is coming to see me tonight."

Giulletti was the energetic, impetuous, and undisciplined leader of the Italian Federation of Maritime Workers. The organization jealously guarded its own autonomy and remained separate and apart from other working-class organizations. Politically, Giulletti called himself an "independent" Socialist, which meant he did not actually belong to, or accept the discipline of, the Socialist Party. But whenever this organization called strikes—which it did with great frequency—it sent detailed news reports and long propaganda articles to *Avanti* and other Socialist papers. We published as much of this material as possible; but naturally we could not always print every word of it. Other labour news was important, too, and our space was limited.

Recently I had received a telegram addressed to *Avanti* from Giulletti which had displeased me and created in me a feeling of distrust. It read: "Please publish all we send on maritime movement. Shall be thankful to your paper. Am sending money."

Did Giulletti think we were to be bribed? It was our editorial duty to help all the struggles of the working class. We were not there to receive money for special favours to any one section of that class, to sell the columns of *Avanti* to the highest bidder.

Mussolini seemed to share my indignation on this point and he supported me when I proposed to the Executive Committee that any money received from Giulletti be returned immediately.

I could not understand now why Mussolini should be so terrified at the prospect of a visit from this man. When I questioned him, he explained his attitude as follows: "You have never seen Giulletti. That's why you don't understand. He's the strongest man in the movement—I mean physically strong—and he is always surrounded by strong men—rough sailors who are ready to fight for him."

"Are you afraid he will beat you?" I asked, in surprise.

"Well, I wouldn't like to be on bad terms with him if I can help it. I shall tell the porter to say that I'm out when he calls. He wants us, as members of the Executive, to sign a statement requesting withdrawal by the entire Executive of a decision which reflects upon him personally. He is in the wrong. Why should the Executive reverse its action?"

"Why don't you tell him this to his face tonight?" I asked. "But if you're afraid, I'll do it."

"Excellent," Mussolini exclaimed. "You can receive him in one of our small rooms while I shall wait here until he has gone."

When Giulletti arrived, I received him and told him without any preliminaries that it would be impossible for us, as members of the Executive, to comply with his request.

"What a pity Mussolini is not here and I can't see *him*," he said, after trying in vain to sway me.

"You are mistaken if you think Mussolini would help you," I replied. "The Executive discussed this matter thoroughly and we are unanimous in our opinion. Mussolini, even more than the others, is firmly convinced that you were in the wrong. Why should you expect him to yield?"

When Giulletti finally left after much argument, Mussolini came out of hiding. "How splendid that you did not yield," he said. "It would have been a real shame. Such an insolent demand! How right you were to refuse the money he wanted to send to the Party! Of course it is not easy to deal with such an obstinate and violent man. He is a true Romagnolo."

About eleven o'clock next morning, Giulletti was again announced by the porter. He entered the room breezily. "I came to greet you again, Comrade Angelica," he said. "I admire you. You are not an easy one to persuade and are exactly the kind of militant worker the Party needs. Bravo! I am happy to have met you. Last night you were so firm, probably because of that telegram of mine. If this telegram had not been received by you ——"

"Well," I interrupted, "that is all past. You have seen the Executive unanimously rejects your offer. A revolutionary party is not like others. You must remember that. But tell me, why didn't you leave this morning as you had planned?"

"I changed my mind. I did not want to leave without having obtained at least one signature. Having gotten that, I am in no hurry. I may as well stay on for a few days."

"What do you mean? What signature are you talking about? Who gave you a signature?"

"Mussolini."

"Mussolini! You are joking. You have not even seen him."

"I called upon him this morning at his home."

"And he gave you his signature?"

"How could he refuse? You know there is such solidarity between Romagnoli."

During the Tripolitan War, a young Anarchist soldier named Masetti had shot and wounded his colonel in the barracks at Bologna. Fearful of executing the assailant because of the widespread anti-militarist spirit, the authorities had declared him insane. There had been continuous popular demands for his release ever since.

Finally, June 7, 1914, was chosen as the day for a great popular demonstration in behalf of Masetti—a demonstration in which even the Republicans were to take part. It was agreed that if there were any acts of repression on the part of the police, a general strike would be called immediately. At one of the meetings at Ancona, three strikers were killed by police. The general strike was declared and spread rapidly throughout Italy. It became so menacing that it seemed to some that Italy was on the verge of revolution. The week between June 7th and 14th saw the most violent disturbances in Italy since 1870 and the period was to be known thereafter as Red Week. During this period, while every resource of the Party was thrown behind the strike, Mussolini was in his element. One would have thought, from his accounts in *Avanti*, that he was in the very thick of the fray—instead of issuing fiery editorials from his office. When the strike was called off at the end of the week by the Confederation of Labour, Mussolini denounced the labour leaders for this "act of treason."

10

THE FIFTIETH ANNIVERSARY OF THE SECOND
International was to have been celebrated at the coming
Congress in Vienna towards the end of August, 1914. Preparations for the Congress had been going on in an atmosphere of
increasing tenseness and solemnity. The delegates from every
nation were to meet and reaffirm the solidarity of the international labour movement and its unflinching opposition to the
growing threat of war. Two years before, when the storm in the
Balkans had threatened to engulf Europe, the solidarity of
workers, as personified in the clasped hands of their Socialist
leaders in Basle, maintained a united front of opposition to the
war-mongers. Once more, in Vienna in 1914, these spokesmen of
the revolutionary labour movement would warn the rulers of the
world that the workers would refuse to shed their blood in any
war but one—the battle for their own emancipation.

The affiliated parties of the International represented millions
of men and women in every nation of the world, and among

these were the most advanced and articulate workers, the most influential leaders of labour, many of the ablest journalists and the foremost intellectuals of the day. Its leaders sat in parliaments and in trade-union councils. Its hundreds of newspapers were the daily fare of the European masses, animated by a common faith. This faith had been for years the most serious obstacle to the designs of the imperialists. Once again it would be reaffirmed in a manner calculated to serve notice to the exploiters and war-makers that their days were numbered.

Thus we believed and for this we planned.

But at the end of a few mad days in July, what we had long declared was inevitable under capitalism actually happened. Europe was headed for a precipice. Instead of thousands of jubilant Socialists meeting in gay Vienna, about twenty of us—members of the Executive—gathered in a small hall of the People's House in Brussels on a gloomy, rainy day. It was July 28th, five days after Austria's ultimatum to Serbia and four days before Germany declared war on Russia.

I have already related how the summons to this emergency meeting reached me in Tuscany and described my trip to Brussels. I came to the hall direct from the station, weary and bedraggled from my journey, which had included a ride in a baggage-coach.

As yet, only Austria and Serbia were involved, but all of us realized that unless the conflict were stopped or isolated, the whole of Europe would be set ablaze. The Executive must act immediately to put into effect the anti-war program adopted by the previous Congress. We must make plans, act boldly but wisely, measuring our strength accurately against the strength of war-mongers, counteracting with our propaganda the flood of militarist propaganda that was already engulfing the press. I knew the will of my Party and of the Italian masses and I knew that I could speak unequivocally in their behalf.

Though most of the Executive remained unconvinced throughout our deliberations that war between Austria and Serbia meant a general international war (when news of the Russian ultimatum reached us, the Russian representatives in-

[114]

terpreted it as an invention of the press), the meeting was permeated from the outset by a tragic sense of despair. Our feeling of hopelessness and frustration mounted steadily as we listened to the speeches.

The speech of Victor Adler, who came from a country already at war, was awaited anxiously by all of us. What did this brilliant man, this experienced politician, expect the workers of his country to do? What effect had the outbreak of the war had upon them? His report was a bitter disappointment to those of us who retained hope of the masses rising against the war. This man, who was more at home in world politics than any other member of the Executive and who certainly knew more than any of the rest of us about conditions in his own country, failed to utter a single word that would indicate that we could hope for any uprising on the part of the Austrian masses. His judgment seemed sound, his expression was poised. But he made no effort to conceal his deep pessimism. The passivity of the workers was taken for granted!

In despair, we turned to the German and French representatives. Did their appraisal of the situation coincide with Adler's? The attitude of Hugo Haase, the chairman of the German Social Democratic Party, was most symbolic and pathetic. Usually calm, he was now too restless to sit still; his mood alternated between hope and despair. He spoke of the great mass demonstrations against the war which his party was organizing throughout Germany. His words were corroborated by telegrams from his homeland, one of which told of a great mass meeting in Berlin attended by 70,000. During most of his speech Haase seemed to be talking directly at Jaurès as if he were eager to prove to the great French Socialist that the German workers did not want war and that they anticipated the same attitude on the part of their French comrades. After war was declared, Haase was one of the fourteen German deputies who voted against the war credits. In 1919 he was wounded by a nationalist and died a month later.

In retrospect, Jean Jaurès and Rosa Luxemburg seem to me the only delegates who, like Adler, realized fully the inevitability of the World War and the horrors it entailed. Jaurès gave the

[115]

impression of a man who, having lost all hope of a normal solution of the crisis, relied upon a miracle. Keir Hardie, who, with Bruce Glasier, represented Great Britain, referred in a quiet and positive manner to the general strike which he and others in the movement had advocated as a means of preventing war. He expressed the opinion that if war were declared in England, the trade unions would at once call a general strike! The majority of the Executive indicated by their attitude that they did not share his confidence in this matter.

When I took the floor and called attention to the fact that previous international gatherings had considered the general strike as a primary means of averting war, Adler and Jules Guesde looked at me as if they thought I were crazy. The former made it clear that he would look upon any attempt to precipitate such a strike at that moment as utopian and dangerous. Guesde took the position that a general strike in war time would be a direct menace to the Socialist movement. "The slogan of a general strike would be effective only in countries where Socialism is strongest," he declared, "and thus the military victory of the backward nations over the progressive ones would be facilitated." The other delegates paid no attention to my words. As a recommendation for specific action, the Executive contented itself with calling for an intensification of anti-war demonstrations throughout Europe.

One of the tasks of the meeting was to decide where the International Congress would be held since Vienna was now out of the question. Luxemburg and Jaurès were charged with this task. They chose Paris, emphasizing that the Congress should be preceded and followed by great mass meetings to impress the European governments with the workers' hostility to the war. Of course, the Congress never took place. Before it could be convened, war had spread over most of Europe. And before Jaurès could even report to his compatriots the decisions of the Brussels meeting he was struck down by an assassin's bullet in Paris.

I happened to be in the same room with Jaurès in the People's House when he was working on the last manifesto he was ever to write. He had been appointed to draw up an appeal to the workers of the world to demonstrate their mass solidarity in order to prevent the coming *débâcle*. Most of the delegates had gone to dinner, but Jaurès remained to write this appeal and to prepare his speech for the mass meeting which was to be held that night in the Cirque Royal. I remained with him, but in order not to disturb him I had taken a chair some distance from his desk. I knew, too, that he was suffering from a severe headache. Suddenly a delegate noted for his lack of tact entered the room, and sitting down beside Jaurès, began talking to him. Noting Jaurès' glance of despair, I tried to induce the man to leave, but to no avail. He continued to talk.

The streets leading to the Cirque Royal were so crowded that evening that we had difficulty pushing our way through. The great hall was packed to the doors at an early hour. The great majority of the Belgians who attended the gathering, or who waited in the adjacent streets to take part in the street demonstration that was to follow, had not the remotest idea of what was hanging over them.

It is no exaggeration to say that the Cirque Royal shook at the end of Jaurès' magnificent speech. Jaurès himself was quivering, so intense was his emotion, his apprehension, his eagerness to avert somehow the coming conflict. Never had he spoken with such fervour as on this the last time in his life he was to address an international audience.

A few minutes after the close of the meeting, thousands of workers were swinging through the streets of Brussels, intoxicated with the enthusiasm engendered by the revolutionary songs they were singing. The slogans: "Down with war; long live peace!", "Long live International Socialism!" echoed for hours throughout the city and its suburbs.

A few days later crowds animated by another fervour marched those streets shouting for war.

The catastrophe developed so much more rapidly than we had expected that the Italian and Swiss delegates, who made a trip to Antwerp at the end of the meeting, were almost caught in Belgium at the beginning of the war. The train we entered at Antwerp for our respective countries was the last normal train leaving Belgium.

The next morning, when we were breakfasting at Basle, two members of the Central Committee of the German Party rushed by us, obviously excited.

"Now there is no doubt about the war spreading to France and Germany," said one of our delegates. "I spoke with the German comrades a few moments ago. They came here to put in safe-keeping the money of the German Party."

"And what about its spirit?" I asked.

The next day, stopping at Bern on my way to Italy, I read on a street corner that Jaurès had been assassinated by an exalted French nationalist. I was so stunned I could scarcely realize the meaning of this loss. That same day I received a telegram summoning me to an extraordinary meeting of the Italian Executive in Milan.

On July 29th, while we were meeting in Brussels, the Italian Socialist Party had issued its anti-war manifesto. It read in part:

It is to the interest of the proletariat of all nations to impede, circumscribe and limit as much as possible the armed conflict, useful only for the triumph of militarism and of the parasitic enterprises of the bourgeoisie.

You, proletarians of Italy, who in the painful period of crisis and unemployment have given proof of your class consciousness, of your spirit of sacrifice, must now be ready to prevent Italy from being dragged down into the abyss of this terrible adventure.

Among the signers of this proclamation was Benito Mussolini, editor of *Avanti*, member of the Executive and of the City Council of Milan.

The Milan meeting was called to reaffirm the position taken in this manifesto. All Italian working-class organizations were invited to send fraternal delegates. Even the Syndicalist unions, which in normal times fought us bitterly, responded.

When one of the Syndicalist delegates remarked that it would be more difficult to oppose the war if the Italian government decided to assist the Allied powers, I moved that this viewpoint should be declared incompatible with the Party's position, as our opposition to war could not be influenced by the choice of the ruling class. My motion was passed unanimously.

[118]

That the Party Executive should go on record for Italian neutrality was a foregone conclusion. During the discussion, however, Mussolini, who had expressed himself in favour of absolute neutrality, came up to me, stated that he would have to leave the meeting before the discussion was ended, and asked me to vote for him. No one could foresee at that time what action Italy would take. Mussolini's withdrawal provided him with a possible loophole. He could always claim that if he had remained and had heard all the discussion, he might have voted differently.

At that time it was not only the working class of Italy that opposed the war. The great majority of the Italian people in general were for neutrality. Mussolini, who always followed the stream, ran true to form in this matter. He repeated all the slogans of the Party, branded those who failed to accept them as "traitors" and "renegades." While most of us were attempting to analyse for the workers the origin and meaning of the war, he was hurling epithets and attempting to prove that he was more revolutionary than the Party.

What little pro-war sentiment existed in Italy at this time was divided. Some of the conservatives, functioning through the Nationalist Party under Federzoni—who later became Mussolini's henchman—favoured entry on the side of Austria and Germany. There was some agitation among the Freemasons, small business elements and turbulent youth for joining the Allies. In the general anti-war atmosphere, however, few dared openly to agitate against peace. The only way in which to involve Italy on the side of the Allies was to make the war against Germany appear to be a *revolutionary* war. For this, the Allies needed a demagogue who knew his revolutionary phraseology and who could talk the language of the masses. Such a man was to be discovered in the person of Benito Mussolini.

One circumstance gave an impetus to war propaganda in Italy and rendered our position more difficult. This was the attitude of the German and Austrian Social Democrats—an attitude echoed, of course, by the French and English parties. While we were urging the workers to stand by their internationalist pledges, the papers announced that our German comrades had voted war credits and had given up or "postponed" their struggle to overthrow capitalism. We had no way of knowing at that time that there was any anti-war opposition whatever within the German and Austrian parties. The information on this subject, and upon the anti-war group in France and in the British Independent Labour Party came later. On August 5, 1914, the Austrian Socialists had announced that if their Parliament were in session, they too would have voted the war credits. This article, entitled "The German People's Historic Day," was, I believe, the psychological origin of Fascism. Bissolati, no longer a member of the Party, wrote in a democratic paper that the International, being based upon reciprocity, no longer existed—as the collapse of the German Social Democracy meant the end of the Second International. He concluded that therefore the Italian Socialists must support the war for "Democracy."

About this time I received an urgent letter from Plekhanoff asking me to visit him in Geneva. I had no sooner arrived there when he asked me, abruptly, "What is your and your Party's attitude towards the war?"

The question amazed me. Surely, Plekhanoff, the great Marxist, must know that the answer was implicit in his own philosophy and mine.

"We will do our utmost to prevent Italy from entering the war and to end the war as soon as possible," I said. "As far as I am concerned, I shall naturally do all in my power to assist the Party."

His eyes flashed angrily. "So you would prevent Italy from entering the war. How about Belgium? Where is your love for Russia?"

"What do you mean—my love for Russia? Must my attitude towards war change because Russia is involved? Would other imperialist governments not act as Germany has done in Belgium if it were necessary to gain their ends? Wasn't it you who taught me the real causes of war? Didn't you warn us that this slaughter was being prepared and that we must oppose it?"

"So far as I am concerned," he answered, "if I were not old and sick I would join the army. To bayonet your German comrades would give me great pleasure."

"*My* German comrades! Are they not yours as well? Who, if

[120]

not you, taught us to understand and appreciate German philosophy, German Socialism—Hegel, Marx, Engels?"

That evening I left Geneva and hurried back to Milan. Never, in all my life, have I travelled with such a heavy heart.

As soon as the war was under way, attempts to influence us in behalf of intervention came from both sides. Not all of these attempts were inspired directly by the warring governments themselves. Some were made by misguided radicals who—like Plekhanoff—had been carried away by the war fever and honestly believed that they were supporting a sacred cause. In other cases—and this was to be true of Mussolini's—the warring nations were prepared to buy up any Italian leader who might prove to be corruptible, using as their agents, whenever possible, those social patriots in their own countries who had succumbed to the war propaganda and who were now serving their governments.

Mussolini was still thundering against the war in *Avanti*. He had just written in an editorial: "We mean to remain faithful to our Socialist and International ideas to their very foundation. The storm may attack us but it shall not break our faith."

But by September there were rumours afloat that in private conversations with some of his friends he had indicated that he was ready to abandon neutrality. He denied these rumours indignantly. The Sudecum episode which occurred about this time indicated that Mussolini had not yet made up his mind which way to jump.

Sudecum was a German Social Democrat and member of the Reichstag. I was surprised when Mussolini informed me that he was coming to see us. When Sudecum arrived, accompanied by Claudio Treves, former editor of *Avanti,* I shook hands with him and continued to read some foreign proofs. But Mussolini, habitually rude to Right-Wingers, was very cordial to Sudecum. I was astonished to hear him ask Sudecum for an interview for *Avanti.*

"I shall ask Comrade Balabanoff to translate it," he added.

Sudecum immediately drew from his pocket several sheets of paper on which the interview had already been written. It was harmless enough—calling attention to the horrors of militarism and war. But it ended with an assertion which I considered ridiculous, a statement that the Kaiser had tried to preserve peace, but that he and the German government had been the victims of Allied aggression. After I had translated this document, I knew that there would be objections to it from the members of our Party, so I insisted that it be read by Mussolini before publication and that it be accompanied by some editorial comment. We were to meet with the author after dinner to go over the whole document with him. After dinner we waited for hours in the office, but Mussolini did not return. I refused to give the copy to the printers, as I realized now that he was trying to shift the responsibility for publishing the interview (which I disapproved of) onto my shoulders. When midnight came and we could wait no longer, I substituted another article. After we had gone to press, Mussolini arrived. He was finally forced to write the commentary for publication with the interview the following day. We were all surprised at the moderation and gentleness of his criticism—he who was usually so harsh and implacable.

A few days later, the "scandal" broke. The press of the Allied countries published a "revelation." The Italian Socialists had been in contact with a German agent who had come to Italy to win their support. The attack grew more virulent daily. When Sudecum went to Rome to speak with the Party Executive, the Party, knowing that the news of this visit would be distorted, published a verbatim account of the meeting. By this time, however, those under the influence of the jingoist press did not want to know the truth. Very soon I was denounced as the person responsible for Sudecum's visit to Italy.

In 1914 the European governments were still fearful of working-class opinion and particularly of Socialist and Internationalist sentiment. Because of this, the military and diplomatic manœuvres leading up to and accompanying the outbreak of the war had been conducted with the utmost secrecy. It was thus possible to make the Germans believe that Germany had gone to war because it was attacked by barbarous Russia; the French, English, and Belgians that their respective countries were defending civilization from Prussian militarism, to persuade the smaller nations that they must fight for their independence, and the world in general that this was a war to end all wars.

In order to save what was left of our international movement and to counteract among the workers of the warring and neutral nations the propaganda of the jingo press, the Italian Socialists proposed an informal international conference at Lugano for September 27th. The Swiss Socialists supported our call. Though the Lugano conference was to have little immediate effect, it was to act as an impetus to the Zimmerwald movement in the following year.

Mussolini was to have gone to Lugano as one of the delegates, but at the last moment he pleaded that he was not well enough to go. It had been agreed that there should be no announcement of the conference, in view of the fact that it was certain to be misrepresented by the press and if possible prevented. But on my arrival at Lugano, where I had gone ahead to make preparations, I was besieged by newspaper men with questions about the meeting. I then discovered that the first page of *Avanti* that morning carried the news of the conference.

Though I was perplexed, I did not yet doubt Mussolini's honesty. There must have been some misunderstanding, I thought. Later I discovered that Mussolini was already in contact with the interventionists and was merely working with us to allay suspicion until his plans matured.

As the pressure of the Allies for Italian intervention, backed up by the propaganda of the armament and other big-business interests, became more insistent, the atmosphere in Italy became more hostile to us. And yet, the attacks and insinuations launched against us did nothing to diminish our prestige among the workers and other groups under our influence. The Party itself remained adamant in its opposition to intervention. Because the rank and file was behind us, it was impossible for the emissaries of the belligerents to split the Party. The numerous Allied agents, particularly from France, who were arriving at this time, and some of whom claimed to speak in behalf of the French workers, knew better than to approach the Party Executive. They conferred with former leaders like Bissolati, who had been honestly converted to the "democratic" slogans of the war, but it was impossible to impress the Italian masses through converts who had already lost their influence.

It was necessary to find a man who was still in "good standing" but who could be corrupted. Mussolini fulfilled these requirements. He was editor of the Party paper which was read by a majority of the workers throughout Italy. Because of this, it was believed that he must exert an enormous personal influence and that his change of front would carry with it an important section of working-class opinion. Through his personal friends who had already embraced the Allied cause and who in the beginning probably acted as intermediaries between Mussolini and the Allied agents, they learnt all they needed to know about his weakness and ambition. Mussolini was chosen because his patrons needed a man with revolutionary traditions who was without scruples.

At the moment when the attacks upon us had reached a climax, a conservative newspaper in Bologna, *Il Resto del Carlino*, published a statement to the effect that a certain member of our Executive, in private conversation, had said:

"Don't be afraid of the Socialists; you can be certain that when the government decides to support the Allies, the Socialists will assent."

At first, we believed Mussolini's assertion that this was just another calumny; but after the statement had been reaffirmed the Party members demanded an investigation. An extraordinary meeting of the Executive was called. Mussolini and I travelled to the meeting in the same train compartment. During the journey he spoke only of the attacks which had been made upon *me*.

"Don't concern yourself about them," he said. "Our adversaries are capable of anything."

Just then another member of the Executive entered the compartment. Ignoring Mussolini, he said to me:

"Have you read this morning's *Avanti?*"

"Not yet," I replied.

"And Mussolini has not spoken about his article?"

I took the paper and read it for myself. In an editorial Mussolini had more than confirmed every "slander." He had written in favour of Italian intervention and, worse, had ascribed this attitude to the Party as well. When I had finished the article I turned to him.

"The man who wrote this has no place in the Socialist Party. He belongs at the front or in a madhouse."

"The whole Executive will approve and follow my lead," he replied.

Mussolini had known that he would not be able to face the Executive and defend his article. He knew that at the first attempt to justify his new position he would betray himself for what he was—a traitor. He was afraid, not only of us, but of himself. We might appeal to his conscience, his past pledges, his sense of duty, and so stir up sentiments or apprehensions which he was trying to suppress. Being too weak to answer our arguments or to resist the temptation of money and power, he had created a *fait accompli*—a situation which could not be cancelled. This constituted his defence against his own weakness. Taking advantage of the fact that he had been left alone in the office of *Avanti*, he had published an article advocating what he had formerly denounced—Italy's participation in the war. Once he had done this, it was no longer necessary to fight his own vacillating will. It left us no alternative for our final decision.

At that time we did not suspect that he had been corrupted. We thought that he had not been able to resist the wave of jingoist sentiment that was sweeping the country, that he had followed the example of so many radical intellectuals. We agreed that he could no longer remain editor of *Avanti* or a member of the Executive.

It is not true—as has been asserted—that Mussolini resigned from *Avanti* and then tried to explain to us his new position. During that whole meeting he never uttered a single word of explanation, even when he was urged to do so.

"How could you do it, Benito?" our chairman, Bacci, asked. "Why didn't you talk with me about it? You saw me every day."

"Why didn't you resign when you realized that you were not in agreement with the Party policy?" asked Lazzari.

A delegate from Turin said: "I am a simple worker, therefore maybe I don't understand. Can this be the same Mussolini who aroused the Romagna peasants and workers against the African War?"

It was my turn to speak. "I warn you that you are betraying your class and the Party which redeemed you from moral and physical misery. You are betraying the faith which has made a man and a revolutionist of you, which has given you dignity and ideals."

He still kept his eyes turned from us.

"Comrades," I went on, "before we part I should like to have a temporary allowance made for Mussolini. Until he finds something else to do, we should provide for his family."

Then he spoke for the first time. "I don't want your allowance," he interrupted, angrily. "I'll find work as a stone mason. Five francs a day are enough for me. Of one thing you may be sure. I shall never speak or write a word against the Party. I would rather break my pen and cut out my own tongue. Whatever action you take," he added, pathetically, "I shall remain true to Socialism. You may deprive me of my membership card but you will never be able to tear Socialism out of my heart—it is too deeply rooted."

When he spoke thus he had in his pocket the contract for a sum of money to found his own daily paper—*Il Popolo D'Italia* —in which he was to attack the Party with the utmost bitterness. That paper is now the official organ of the Italian government.

Even more contemptible than the rôle he played at the Executive session was his behaviour when he was summoned before the Socialist branch in Milan to which he belonged. Hundreds of workers and intellectuals had come to the meeting to hear Mussolini's defence of his position and the explanation of his abuse of power as editor of *Avanti*.

Instead of replying to the questions which were on the lips and in the minds of his audience, Mussolini, in order to gain sympathy, tried to pretend that he had had no hearing from the Executive.

"Even a bourgeois tribunal gives the accused a chance to defend himself," he said to the audience who had come to hear this defence. Then he tried to divert the attention of the audience, which was losing patience with his irrelevant remarks, by a meaningless phrase:

"You persecute me because you love me," he shouted.

From that time on his audience grew stormier until Serrati had to rise and ask them to hear Mussolini without interruption. Mussolini tried one more subterfuge. He repeated the remarks he had made to the Executive about being faithful to the Socialism which was rooted so deeply in his heart.

"If you proclaim that I am unworthy—" he began.

The reply was a roar of "Yes!" from the audience. He left the hall in a rage.

The newspapers were still publishing items about this scene when Mussolini's new organ appeared. Under the masthead were two slogans: "He who has steel has bread"—a quotation from Blanqui; and Napoleon's, "The Revolution is an idea that has found bayonets." One of the first issues carried a cartoon of a man trampling upon a red banner. The original of this cartoon was later displayed in the window of the most fashionable tailor in Milan.

Everyone knew, when *Il Popolo D'Italia* appeared, that Mussolini's "conversion" had a financial basis, and in Italy it was generally understood that the money came from the Allies and the Italian industrialists. The question most frequently heard at this time was, "Who paid?"

Shortly after the appearance of the new organ, Marcel Cachin, one of the French government envoys who had come to Italy to propagandize among the radicals for Italian intervention, hailed this new triumph of Allied propaganda in the French Chamber of Deputies. Cachin had worked through Naldi, the editor of *Resto del Carlino*, an agency of Allied propaganda in Italy, to "convert" the editor of *Avanti* to the Allied cause. Mussolini's condition of capitulation had been a paper of his own. The full story was not to be told until 1926, during the famous trial in Paris of a young anti-Fascist, Bonomini, who had shot an associate of Mussolini. It was then stated that the first payment had

[127]

been 15,000 francs, and that this was followed by regular payments of 10,000 francs.

With the desertion of Mussolini, Giacinto Serrati, who had been a member of the Executive since 1912, became editor of *Avanti*. More than any other individual, Serrati was responsible for the rôle of Italian Socialism during and immediately after the World War. It is difficult to imagine a man more reluctant to assume the rôle of leadership or one who could fill that rôle more courageously and consistently under such trying conditions. After Italy entered the war we suffered the handicap of a revolutionary anti-war party disorganized by persecution and censorship. Because of the difficulties under which the Party functioned—it was often impossible to hold meetings—Serrati was obliged to assume responsibility for the attitude of the Party and for the greater part of the labour movement, to make decisions of the utmost importance. As a result of his position he was the object of continuous and unscrupulous campaigns of vilification—particularly on the part of *Il Popolo D'Italia*. By attacking those who had known and helped him in former years, Mussolini satisfied his desire for revenge on those who were the living witnesses of his own corruption.

Few men suffered as much for their convictions during and after the war as Serrati. Lenin and Trotsky were to achieve the immunity of success. In the United States, though Debs was imprisoned, he did not bear the brunt of daily attack accorded a man who was the active leader of his party and the editor of its daily paper. Serrati had to fight on every front. Because of his attachment to the movement, his hostility to flattery, and his animosity to every kind of compromise, Serrati was considered by superficial observers a cold and passionless man. In reality he had the spirit of a cavalier. In his youth he had listened to the sailors and olive-oil makers in his native Oneglia discuss a new gospel of social justice. He had renounced the career which his family had prepared for him and joined the Socialist Party. During the next ten years, under the most reactionary régime of the pre-Fascist period, he had been gaoled again and again. He was finally deported, and in 1902 he became editor of an Italian weekly, *Proletari*, in the United States. Thanks to his energy and devotion and the enthusiasm he succeeded in arousing among the Italian immigrants, the paper became a daily. As its editor, devoting to it all of his time and energy, Serrati received ten dollars a week.

The quality of Serrati's character was illustrated by his attitude towards an opportunity which was given us, after Mussolini's expulsion, to expose an eloquent episode in the latter's personal life. By this time the story of Irene Desler has been told in some detail. After living with Mussolini for two years prior to 1915, she and her son—Mussolini's acknowledged child—were deserted by him. A native of Trento, still under Austrian rule, she was imprisoned soon after this, and in 1917 she was incarcerated in a concentration camp—probably under pressure from Mussolini, because she knew or suspected too much about his negotiations with the French government agents. After her desertion by Mussolini she came to *Avanti* and offered to tell the whole story of his treatment of her and his son, particularly after the change in his financial circumstances. Though Serrati thus had an opportunity to expose this episode long before it was generally known, he refused to do so.

11

THE ATTEMPT OF THE ITALIAN AND SWISS SO-
cialists to draw together at Lugano in September, 1914,
the remnants of the International and to carry on the struggle
against the war was followed in the spring of 1915 by international conferences of the women's and youth sections of the
movement. When I received a letter from Clara Zetkin asking
me to help her arrange a conference at which representatives of
workingwomen in the warring and neutral countries could
demonstrate their hostility to the war, I gladly agreed and met
her at Lugano to discuss the matter. Clara had been so affected
by the failure of the German Social Democracy, to which she
had dedicated the best years of her life, that I felt she would
never recover from the shock. After a few days of discussion and
planning, it was agreed to call the conference in Bern during
Easter week. Then she went on to Holland and I returned to
Bern.

The Bolshevik women who were living as exiles in Switzerland—among them Krupskaya, the wife of Lenin, and Lilina, wife of Zinoviev—showed great interest in the plans for the meeting. Naturally, Russia would be represented by delegates residing abroad. In view of the complications of travel at that time, we were gratified to have delegates from Germany, France, England, and Italy, as well as the neutral countries. This was the first undeniable proof that the war had not destroyed the links of international solidarity among the Socialists. Dr. Marian Philips and Margaret Bondfield spoke in behalf of the English women in the Socialist and organized-labour movements, and of their encouragement when the news of the conference—inspired by German women like Clara Zetkin—had been brought to them. One of the most striking personalities at the meeting was Louise Saumoneau, a French delegate. She had been a seamstress who, by study after her long working-hours, had become a school-teacher. There were few women in the organized-labour movement of France at this time, and Louise had been the most courageous of these Socialist and Syndicalist women. She had already been gaoled for her anti-war and revolutionary leaflets.

Our conference had two tasks to perform: to publicize the fact that in spite of the vetoes of their governments and the opposition of the labour leaders, women had met and worked together for peace and for Socialism; our second task was to formulate slogans for this struggle and to publish a leaflet for women to whom the reaction to the war marked a first approach to social problems, to explain the causes and consequences of the war and the manner in which they could be abolished.

Our appeal to them began: "Where are your husbands, your brothers, your sons? Why must they destroy one another and all that they have created? Who benefits by this bloody nightmare? Only a minority of war profiteers. . . . Since the men cannot speak, you must. Workingwomen of the warring countries, unite!"

The convention was in itself a moral victory, but one circumstance endangered the whole situation and threatened to destroy that unanimity which was necessary for moral effect. The absence of one signature on our manifesto—an absence which would be exploited by the nationalist press—would be sufficient to convince the general public that "the Internationalists cannot agree among themselves." In the face of this situation the Bolshevik women, working under Lenin's direction, introduced a resolution which was irrelevant to the specific purpose of our meeting and which the majority could not sign. It called for an immediate organizational break with the majorities in the existing Socialist and Labour parties and for the formation of a new International. It also called for the transformation of the war into a civil war.

The majority of the delegates did not oppose this resolution because it was too "radical" or because they approved of the Second International. Most of them wished to remain members of their respective parties at this time in order to influence the rank and file. Nor could they make decisions which committed the parties to which they still belonged to a specific action of such far-reaching importance. The main difference between the two groups lay in their psychological approach. The majority of us were eager to impress upon the masses that something effective could be done immediately. Lenin, through the Bolshevik women, was concerned with a political, factional problem affecting the future of the political movement itself. In November, 1914, he had already raised the slogan of "Long live the Third International!" in the Bolshevik organ published in Switzerland.

That occasion first revealed to me one of Lenin's characteristics which I came to understand fully only after the October Revolution. As long as he was an *émigré*, the leader of a small factional minority, I could never grasp why he was so concerned about the number of votes cast for various resolutions at international gatherings and Executive meetings, or why he wasted so much time polemicizing for a certain viewpoint among delegates whom he could not possibly convert. I was particularly surprised to find him behaving in such fashion during the war, when the general tragedy was so overwhelming and our movement so weakened that the purely theoretical decisions of an insignificant minority of intellectuals seemed of so little importance. In Russia, where I had an opportunity to observe him more closely, I was amazed to find that even during the most serious and dangerous periods, he would devote the same time and energy trying to impress a few foreign delegates whose influence was insignificant. Lenin considered every individual and every social event from the viewpoint of the revolutionary strategist. His whole life was a matter of strategy and every word he uttered in public had a polemic intent. Every incident and trend was a link in the chain of social cause and effect, to be taken advantage of for theoretical or practical purposes. Realizing, no doubt, the general insignificance of the support of a few *émigrés*, he nevertheless would carry on the struggle for his resolutions or his viewpoint for hours or days—if only for the purpose of having them and his polemics introduced into the annals of the Socialist conventions and meetings. He was concerned always with their historical importance. Even after the Russian Revolution had endowed him with tremendous power and responsibility, much of his thought and energy were absorbed by the old internal factional disputes between the Bolsheviks and the Mensheviks.

At the Women's Congress in Bern, although the Bolsheviks were fully aware of the importance of basic unity, they would not make the slightest concession. Again and again Clara Zetkin appealed to them to withdraw their resolution. She was quite ill, and those of us who knew that only her tremendous will power was keeping her going at this time were fearful of the serious effect of this struggle upon her health. After the discussion had lasted for hours without result, Clara, completely exhausted, suggested that there be an intermission. During this interval she withdrew with the Bolshevik delegates and Lenin into a separate room. Here Lenin finally agreed to a compromise. The Bolsheviks would vote for the majority resolution, providing theirs would appear in the official report of the convention. The long deadlock was overcome and the convention ended successfully. When I went to Clara Zetkin's room I found that she had had a bad heart attack and, thinking that she was dying, she was calling for her sons in Germany.

A few weeks later the scene which took place at the Women's Congress repeated itself at the Youth Congress, also held in Bern. Here it created an even more discouraging impression upon those of us who had witnessed it before. The example of the Women's Congress had encouraged the Socialist youth organizations, including many of the prospective soldiers of the next three years, to a similar demonstration. Such a gathering was more difficult and dangerous for those who participated. And· yet a number of young Socialists from the warring countries contrived to attend. Here the disciples of Lenin submitted their same amendment and the same deadlock took place. While the enervating discussion was going on I met Lenin in the restaurant of the People's House, sitting in the very place from which he had directed his followers a few weeks before. I asked, ironically:

"Vladimir Ilyitch, did you come here for tea or for the resolution?"

He answered me with an annoyed glance.

Again, the same compromise solution was finally adopted.

The Italian Party decided to intensify its efforts for an international gathering of Socialists from all the warring and neutral countries. One of its most popular deputies, Morgari, was delegated to approach the leaders of the shattered International. The attitude of its chairman, Vandervelde, then a member of the Belgian government, was typical. "So long as German soldiers are in Belgium, no talk of peace is possible," he said, and admitted that he considered the International the hostage of the Allies.

It soon became clear that we could defend the honour of internationalism only by demonstrating that the failure of our movement was not general, that in every warring country heroic individuals and minorities had remained true to their faith. In order to aid in this development and to send *Avanti* authentic news from a neutral centre, I had moved to Switzerland. Here I received the first news of Karl Liebknecht's anti-war declaration in the Reichstag in December, 1914, and *Avanti* was the first paper to publish it.

A few years before, a modern People's House had been built in Bern by the labour organizations. It included a hotel in which I lived and which now became the unofficial headquarters of our international peace efforts. Most of the foreign radicals who came to Switzerland, including those who had to come illegally, gathered here, eager for news from other countries. Those who visited me in Bern were not official delegates, but individuals tormented by the failure of their parties and risking their liberty to bring word from groups of German, Austrian, and French Socialists who had not abandoned their principles; who brought us word of what war meant for those in the trenches and behind them; who were trying to get in touch with their comrades in other countries in the hope of creating an international movement against the war. Their hostility towards their respective governments and towards their own former leaders was overwhelming, and I noted that the German Socialists among them would often be more lenient in their attitude towards the French "social patriots," the French more inclined to extenuate the failures of the German official leaders, than their own. Though this atttiude led to erroneous conclusions, I appreciated it as an effort to combat the general avalanche of nationalist jingoism.

The necessity of establishing a regular relationship and common action between the representatives of the various anti-war tendencies became more and more evident. The initiative for the creation of such a nucleus came largely from Robert Grimm, an active and intelligent Swiss journalist and Socialist leader. The paper which he edited, *Berner Tagwacht,* contained all publishable information of the war opposition in the various countries. On his frequent visits to Bern, Morgari encouraged this movement.

The arrangements for a conference of anti-war Socialists were shrouded in secrecy. When the conference opened in the small Swiss town of Zimmerwald on September 5, 1915, with delegates from Germany, France, Italy, Russia, Poland, Hungary, Holland, Switzerland, Sweden, Norway, Rumania and Bulgaria (the English delegates were unable to secure passports), even many of our friends were surprised. The participation of delegates from the warring countries was evidence of a high degree of courage and determination since association with "the enemy" to discuss war issues could be construed as "treason."

The determining factor in the war at that moment was the relation between France and Germany, and the solidarity of our

[135]

movement depended largely upon the collaboration for peace action of the delegates from these two countries. As soon as the representatives of these "irreconcilable" peoples had an opportunity to meet and discuss the situation, their attitude proved how artificial and blasphemous was the whole campaign of nationalist hatred. This fact alone would have justified the Zimmerwald movement even if it had not achieved the resurrection of international Socialism at a time when the Second International was shattered and the masses had lost faith.

The work at Zimmerwald began with a statement signed by the German and French delegates. It was Ledebour and Hofman, representing Germany, and Merrheim and Bourderon, representing France, who suggested that they sign a declaration to the effect that "this war is not our war," and pledge themselves to work for peace without annexations, a peace which would help to dissipate national hatreds. The suggestion was greeted by prolonged cheers. During the elaboration of this document and while I was translating the discussion, I was deeply impressed by the fact that it was the German delegates who insisted that the immediate evacuation of Belgium should be among our first demands. In addition to this declaration it was necessary to formulate a program upon which all the delegates could agree and which would be applicable to conditions, and understood by the workers, in all countries.

The Russian delegation included representatives from the Bolsheviks, Mensheviks, and Social Revolutionists. Of the thirty-five delegates at the conference, Lenin commanded eight, including the Swiss, Platten. This Bolshevik bloc later referred to themselves as "the Zimmerwald Left."

Our majority statement condemned the war as imperialist on both sides, repudiated the voting of the war credits, and called for a struggle against war and for Socialism. But the Bolsheviks insisted, as they had at the Women's and Youth Congress, upon their resolution which called for open "civil war," an immediate break with the Second International and the organization of a Third. In the end it was they who suggested the same compromise—probably because of the fact that in the inner "fractional" meetings with delegates whom he had hoped to win over,

[136]

Lenin had been less successful than he had hoped. (The discussion with the French delegate, Merrheim, alone, had lasted eight hours.)

The manifesto, which finally passed unanimously, asserted: "The war-makers lie when they assert that the war would liberate oppressed nations and serve democracy. In reality, they are burying the liberty of their own nations as well as the independence of other peoples. . . . To you, men and women of labour, to all those who suffer by and for war, we say: 'Above the frontiers, above the battlefields and devastated countries, Proletarians of the World, unite!' "

The hope that our appeal would make some impression upon the masses in the warring countries, the sense of having accomplished a difficult and complicated task—an international gathering in war time—brought a sense of relaxation and relief to all of us. The Conference appointed an executive of four members: Robert Grimm and Charles Naine of the Swiss party, Morgari and myself of the Italian party. The headquarters of the movement were established at Bern and its Executive Committee was called International Socialist Committee (I.S.C.).

In a preface to a book on the Zimmerwald movement, written for the Archives of History of the Socialist and Labour Movement and published in Germany in 1928, I pointed out that in "the interval from the end of July until March, 1919 (creation of the Third International) there was no *international* Socialist movement, except those parties, groups, and individuals who joined the Zimmerwald movement and whose mouthpiece was the International Socialist Committee in Bern." If it were not for this movement, historians might assert that the war had annihilated not only the organizations, but the very essence of working-class internationalism. For decades, organized labour in Europe had pledged itself to oppose and resist war. When war between Austria and Serbia was declared, these pledges were repeated at huge meetings called by Socialists throughout the world. Then suddenly the contents and tone of most of the labour papers changed, war credits were voted, the comrades of yesterday became the "enemies" of today. To understand the bewilderment and confusion of those men and women to whom

[137]

internationalism had been a guiding star, it is necessary to recall the panic over real and imaginary invasions, the mental chaos induced by the elaborate machinery of nationalist propaganda, and the isolation of each national group from the others by rigid censorship. In the very midst of this confusion and propaganda the voice of Zimmerwald proclaimed: "We representatives of Socialist parties, of trade unions, of minorities, of various warring and neutral countries have gathered to reëstablish the international relationship of the workers, to appeal to their reason, and to summon them to fight for peace. This is the fight for freedom, for fraternization, for Socialism!"

It is impossible to determine the exact influence of these words launched at a time when the jingoist fever was at its climax. The manifesto was signed by Socialists and Syndicalists well known in their respective countries, and this example of their courage and sense of responsibility could not help but fan the embers of internationalist sentiment and determination wherever their words were read.

Early in 1916 it became apparent that there was little hope for an early end to the World War. The conflict had reached a deadlock, with each government decided to fight to the bitter end. The patience and endurance of the victims proved greater than either the supporters or adversaries of the war had imagined. An increasing realization among labour groups that there must be some international move against the war was reflected in the growth and activity of the Zimmerwald movement. Our attempt to coördinate the efforts of single individuals and groups became more difficult as censorship and suppression became more rigid.

The time had come, however, when the followers of Zimmerwald were sufficiently numerous to assume an open attitude in the various parliaments. We tried to call meetings of different parliamentary groups who agreed with our platform to induce them to make identical declarations based upon that platform, and to demand immediate peace without annexations. The Italian Socialists had anticipated this decision and not only in the Chamber of Deputies, but also in the hundreds of county and municipal councils, they had made the Zimmerwald manifesto familiar to the masses as well as to the conservatives and militarists. But in other European countries where the Zimmerwald followers represented a minority, their efforts were disavowed by the majority representatives of their parties. This was particularly the case in such decisive countries as Germany and France. In Germany, during 1916, a growing number of Socialist deputies, led by Karl Liebknecht and Otto Rühle, opposed the voting of the war credits and their leaders were expelled from the Party's parliamentary fraction. Early in the year the first organized division took place in the German Social Democracy between the pro- and anti-war Socialists. But the attitude of the anti-war representatives lost much of its effectiveness so long as it was not reciprocated in other countries.

We decided to call a second Zimmerwald conference with as many parliamentary representatives as possible present as delegates. It was held at Kienthal, a small town hidden in the Swiss Alps, on April 24, 1916.

Forty-three delegates came from Germany, France, Italy, Russia, Poland, Serbia, Lettnia, Latvia, and several neutral countries. Among the French delegates were three members of the Chamber of Deputies—Paul Brizon, Raffin Dugens, and Alexandre Blanc. These three "pilgrims of Kienthal," as they came to be called, deserve a place in history for the courage they displayed. Even those Frenchmen who once denounced them as "traitors" have spoken of them with respect. It was my task to bring together and interpret the discussions between the French and German delegates, and it was important to interpret not only their words, but also the spirit which animated them, to create an atmosphere of friendship, and to avoid any misunderstandings. This was not easy, as the delegates differed so widely in age and background. This was the first time the three French deputies had ever attended an international conference, and Brizon's speech in particular seemed commonplace and even frivolous to many of the experienced Marxists. His later work in the committee sessions, and particularly his consistent presentation of the Zimmerwald position when he and his fellow delegates refused to vote the war credits, proved that his manner of speech was not a true reflection of his inner sentiment.

After emphasizing that the war must necessarily bring defeat to the peoples on both sides and calling for immediate peace without annexation, our statement continued:

"Your governments and press have told you that the war must be continued in order to abolish militarism. Don't be misled. A nation's militarism can be abolished only by its own people.

"They tell you that the war must be extended in order that it should be the last war. This is also false. Never has any war abolished war. On the contrary, it arouses the desire for revenge.

"Lasting peace can result only from victorious Socialism!"

Other, more controversial problems had to be approached. The Bolshevik supporters who had constituted themselves as a "Left Wing group," urged again the immediate formation of a new International. As the events of the past seven months had disillusioned many who had formerly believed that the Second International would be able to function, the Bolshevik resolution received more support at Kienthal than at Zimmerwald. This could not be considered a victory for the Bolshevik conception of a new International. As always, they were eager to create a minority movement, whereas most of us aimed to win over as many workers as possible and create a mass movement.

I had served the Zimmerwald movement from its beginnings, attending all its meetings and informal gatherings. Knowing the heroism and the individual difficulties involved in the movement, the specific resolutions and factional controversies which arose within it seemed to me of secondary importance. This attitude of mine has been fortified by the later development of the radical parties and by the tactics of the Russian Bolsheviks—now Communists. I have always believed that the emancipation of labour must be achieved primarily by awakening and educating the masses to a consciousness of their human and social rights, whereas the Bolsheviks have maintained that the transformation of the social system must be accomplished by a comparatively small minority, under the command of a still smaller minority. To these minorities, factional differences and the resolutions which express them, naturally assume enormous importance. Our goal is the same, but the approach is different.

As the war continued, various utopian schemes and projects had been suggested to restore peace, most of them designed to conciliate the imperialist aims of the various governments, while also reconciling to those aims the workers who opposed the war. Our Kienthal meeting warned against these attempts and illusions and emphasized that militarism and war have their roots in conditions which must themselves be eliminated.

The conference ended in the early hours of May 1, 1916. Though I had been working steadily for forty-eight hours, I suggested that we await the sunrise of International Labour Day—the symbol of working-class unity.

12

I WAS IN ZÜRICH, RECOVERING FROM A SEVERE
attack of influenza, when I received word of the first
Russian Revolution of 1917. When an event takes place to which
one has looked forward for the major part of one's life, it has
already become too familiar to evoke surprise. The abdication
of the Tsar, the overthrow of the Russian absolutism, had seemed
inevitable for so long there was probably less outer display of
excitement among the Russian *émigrés* at this time than among
the non-Russian radicals and humanitarians. In the face of this
realization of our long-cherished dream, we felt a kind of shyness
with each other. We were not accustomed to displaying our intimate feelings, because for years these feelings had been subordinated to one purpose—our work for the cause; and as even
our most intimate emotions were related to this work, an outsider would probably have considered us almost indifferent in
this moment of historic triumph on the march towards our
final goal.

After the first few moments of deep emotion at the news from Russia, I thought: this is just a beginning. What is to be done now? How can I take my place in the ranks of the revolution? When I got in touch with the other Russian radicals in Zürich, I found them absorbed by the same thought. All were eager to return to Russia as soon as possible, all were preoccupied with the concrete steps by which this purpose might be achieved.

In the midst of these plans and problems long and violent discussions were going on among the various groups of *émigrés*, representing the different political tendencies. Now that the Tsar was overthrown, what would happen next? Could or should Russia follow the normal political development of Western Europe, or should a more complete revolutionary program be pushed at once? What of the war? Could the demoralized Russian armies be expected to continue fighting a war that had been launched by their oppressors? The discussions and polemics were carried on not only in meetings and at lectures, but wherever two or three of the exiles gathered together.

I attended a meeting called by the Bolshevik group in Zürich at which Lenin was to speak. It took place in a small dark hall of the People's House which was the headquarters of the city's Socialist and Labour movement. I had heard him speak a number of times during the war and I knew in a general way what his approach would be. No one in that small hall, or out of it, at that time had the remotest suspicion that seven months later the undistinguished figure who addressed us that evening would be the undisputed leader of a successful social revolution and the master of Russia's fate. In the years since our first meeting I had seen him for the most part at conventions and conferences where he had been engaged in fierce polemics with men in whose wisdom I had had far more faith. He had remained for me the spokesman of a small group of Russian revolutionaries, mostly intellectuals, rather than the leader and representative of any section of the working class itself. For this reason, probably, and for others which I have already described, I had failed to appreciate the power of his mind.

One sentence in the speech he delivered that evening was to recur to me many times in the months that followed, as it has many times since: "Unless the Russian Revolution develops into a second and successful Paris Commune, reaction and war will suffocate it."

I had been trained, like most Marxists, to expect the social revolution to be inaugurated in one of the highly industrialized, vanguard countries, and at the time Lenin's analysis of the Russian events seemed to me almost utopian. Later, after I had returned to Russia itself, I was to accept this analysis completely. I have never doubted since that if the revolutionaries—including many of the Mensheviks and Left Social Revolutionaries—had not convinced the peasants, workers, and soldiers of the need for a more far-reaching, Socialist revolution in Russia, Tsarism or some similar form of autocracy would have been restored.

Most of the revolutionary *émigrés*, including myself, began to lay plans for our return by way of the Allied or neutral countries. It did not occur to us at first—when all the "democracies" of Western Europe were hailing the new democracy of their Russian ally—that any obstacles would be placed in our way. It soon became apparent, however, that the Allied Foreign Offices had no intention either of facilitating or permitting our repatriation. More aware of what was actually happening in Russia than we were and fearful of what was to come, they were convinced that the return to Russia of a large group of revolutionary internationalists would mean an intensification of peace propaganda at a time when the Provisional Government was already finding it difficult to continue with the war.

In the face of this situation, it was Martov, the Left-Menshevik leader, who made a suggestion to which the non-Bolsheviks among us agreed unanimously: that the Russian government should propose to Germany the exchange of German war-prisoners in Russia for the Russian *émigrés* in Western Europe, the latter to be permitted to cross Germany on their way home. The arrangement implied no compromise or favour on the part of either government, but in spite of its reasonableness, our request was to meet with continuous delay and evasion on the part of both the Russian and German authorities.

In the meanwhile the Bolshevik leaders, headed by Lenin, had made arrangements for a separate return within two weeks after the Revolution. I realized later that this was a strategic manœuvre on the part of Lenin. His presence in Russia before the arrival of the Menshevik leaders would put him in an advantageous position and enable him to build up his influence among the revolutionaries there before the latter arrived. He was determined, therefore, to get into Russia immediately under any circumstances. Through Fritz Platten, secretary of the Swiss Socialist Party and an adherent of the Zimmerwald Left, arrangements were made with the German embassy to permit Lenin, Zinoviev, Radek (who had belonged to the Polish and German Socialist Parties and who had never been in Russia before) and about twenty other Bolsheviks to cross Germany immediately in an "extra-territorial" train. Anticipating the charges that were certain to be made by the Allies as a result of this arrangement, Lenin, who ordinarily was indifferent to public opinion, requested French members of the Zimmerwald group to make a public statement to the effect that they approved his travelling through Germany in the interest of the Revolution.

Several weeks after the departure of the Bolsheviks, the committee which had been set up by the *émigrés* heard from Robert Grimm, Swiss Socialist deputy and secretary of the Zimmerwald Commission who had gone on ahead to arrange for our repatriation, that the plan proposed by Martov was making no headway. The Provisional Government in Russia was ready to provide the necessary funds for the return of the Russians in Switzerland, if we could get permission from the German government to cross the German territory between Switzerland and Sweden. By this time there were more than 200 *émigrés* waiting in Zürich, some of whom had come there from France and England. Our eagerness to return to Russia was intensified by our desire for peace. It was Martov who had formulated in a masterly slogan what we all knew to be true:

"Should the Revolution fail to put an end to the war—the war will kill the Revolution."

Unquestionably the German government—which in 1917, after America's entry into the world conflict, was eager for an early peace on the best possible terms for itself—was willing to facilitate our departure with that end in view. But whatever their motivations in permitting us to cross Germany at this time, the Russian radicals were concerned not with Germany's ends, but with their own—the salvation of the Russian Revolution and of the European working class.

Through the mediation of the Swiss Socialists, the arrangements were finally made. The trains on which we were to cross Germany into Sweden were not sealed, as a stupid legend affirms, but we would not be permitted to leave the train while on German territory and we were pledged to make no attempt to speak with German citizens when it stopped at the various stations *en route.*

Among the leaders in our group who gathered at the Zürich station on the day of our departure, early in June, were Martov and Axelrod, Lunarcharsky and Sokolnikoff. The latter two were to become Bolsheviks in Russia, and after the October Revolution, Lunarcharsky became Commissar of Public Instruction while Sokolnikoff was to serve as ambassador to England. The *émigrés* were accompanied by their families, including the children who had been born in exile and to whom this journey back to Russia was a gay and glorious adventure.

As I was the only one among the *émigrés* who had taken an active part in the European labour movement, most of the large crowd of sympathizers who came to the station laden with flowers had come to bid me good-bye. My grief at leaving these friends and comrades with whom I had worked for years and to whom I had spoken so often in French, German, and Italian, was alleviated by our common enthusiasm for the goal of my journey—free revolutionary, republican Russia to which, as the representative of Zimmerwald, I would bring a pledge of solidarity from its friends in Western Europe.

The trip across Germany to Stockholm in the third-class carriages, crowded with men, women, and children, was marked by intense enthusiasm and continuous discussion of the problems and possibilities ahead. At Stockholm, Robert Grimm joined our party with the hope that in Finland his own efforts to enter Russia might prove more successful. Grimm had left Bern for Russia while Martov's plan was still being discussed. As a Swiss neutral it had not occurred to us that he would experience any difficulty in getting to Russia, but we had not reckoned with the power of Allied propaganda or its pressure upon the Provisional Government. The charges of pro-Germanism which had been launched against the internationalists with the Zimmerwald movement from the beginning of the war were now revived in the Allied press and directed with particular fury against Grimm. As a result of these charges, Grimm had been denied permission to enter Russia by the Miliukov Ministry. He had remained in Stockholm, attempting to establish there a new basis for the Zimmerwald propaganda.

It was in Finland, the day before we reached the Russian border, that we received word that two members of the Social Democratic Party, Tseretelli and Skobelev, and one Socialist Revolutionist, Chernov, who had participated in the Zimmerwald movement since 1915, had entered the Coalition Government. Though our group included several factions, most of us were internationalists, opposed to the continuation of the war and to the participation of revolutionists in the government which was conducting the war. The controversies and discussions which arose over this issue continued throughout the entire last night of our journey. In addition there were heated arguments about who should speak in behalf of our delegation when we were finally welcomed in Moscow. We had already sent a telegram to Chernov, the Socialist Revolutionist who had entered the Cabinet, demanding that Grimm be permitted to enter Russia with us and we anticipated a favourable reply as soon as we reached the frontier. In the meanwhile, factions had caucused, votes had been taken, and the train had become a miniature convention-hall, while the crying children, unable to sleep in the midst of this conflict, had added to the general confusion.

The day before, a Georgian Socialist in our party had protested that I must not enter Russia without the banner of Zimmerwald; and when the train stopped at one of the Finnish stations, he had rushed out to get a stick or branch which might serve as the standard for a banner. We then attached a red scarf to the stick, and on it I had outlined in embroidery: "Long live Zimmerwald; Long live the Russian Revolution." I entered our revolutionary Holy Land bearing this home-made banner.

As we came to a stop at the Finnish-Russian frontier, we were surprised to see a crowd of soldiers and citizens gathered on the platform to greet us. We had not expected any kind of demonstration until we arrived in Petrograd, and as the strains of the "Internationale" reached our ears we wept for joy. We were returning to a land in which, only a year before, that song had been sung in secret by persecuted revolutionaries; now it had become the hymn of an entire nation released from bondage. A miracle had occurred.

The day was grey and sodden and the monotonous grey uniforms of the soldiers were scarcely distinguishable against the sky, but the few red banners illuminated the entire scene for us. As we climbed down to the platform the crowd surged forward, still singing the "Internationale" but it seemed to me that they sang it more like a prayer than a hymn of triumph or a call to battle. Except for a few of the younger people whose excitement and enthusiasm were marked by their lifted heads and sparkling eyes, I got the impression of a certain bewildered helplessness, as though they had come here not so much to demonstrate their victory as to appeal to us for aid. There was something particularly touching in the expressions of the older men and women in the crowd. They seemed to be saying, "Help us, brethren, help us"—as though we, who were returning to participate in the building of a new world, had brought with us from the old that promise of aid and security of which they were so sadly in need. It was as though they had been caught in the midst of a battle that was not yet ended, the purpose of which they were not quite sure, and I had a feeling that they needed our assurance far more than we needed theirs. At that moment Lenin's prophecy in Zürich came to my mind. Unless the Revolution was amplified to give bread, peace, and full equality to these people, they would remain what they had been—slaves.

The returning *émigré* leaders were asked to address the crowd, and when one of them suggested that I, too, should do so, I shrank back.

"I feel too small, too insignificant," I objected.

Some of the soldiers who stood near-by took my remark literally, thinking that I referred to my size.

"Come then, we will help you," they answered, and before I could utter another word they lifted me up on their shoulders above the crowd. It was from this height that I delivered my first speech in the country I had left as a voluntary exile just twenty years before.

In Petrograd, we were welcomed by a much more impressive demonstration, at which Chernov, as a member of the Duma and the Cabinet, greeted us in the name of the government. He was answered by Grimm and Lunarcharsky, who naturally made no reference at this time to our disapproval of the step he had taken.

To my amazement, one of my brothers came to the railway station to meet me. Ever since I had become active in the revolutionary movement, I had been careful not to involve the members of my family in my life abroad in order to spare them any suspicion or persecution on the part of the Russian authorities. I had met my eldest sister, Anna, on several occasions when she had come for a holiday to some of the fashionable resorts in Germany and Switzerland, but since the war I had not even corresponded with her directly, for fear that letters from a Zimmerwald member might bring suspicion of "treason" upon the entire family. The war had also put an end to the allowance I had received from my family.

I had not informed any of my relatives of my return to Petrograd, but they had seen the announcement in the newspapers and now Anna had sent my brother to meet me and bring me to her house. I had known before I came to Russia how difficult living conditions would be—due to the shortage of food and housing, but I had been determined that in Free Russia I would share the hardships of the workers and accept nothing from my wealthy relatives. However, my brother was so upset at my reluctance to stay with my sister that I finally agreed to go there for a few days. Anna was the eldest of the family and I the youngest, and, like her children, I had called her mamma. Even though she had never shared or even understood my attitudes and ambitions, we had been very fond of each other. I found it hard to refuse this request; a few days at her house would not matter—

then I would find my own living quarters and proceed with whatever work there was for me to do. Leaving most of my luggage at the station and taking only a small handbag, we drove to my sister's house.

We had scarcely embraced each other after the years of separation when I noticed her agitation. At first I thought it was due to the general strain and uncertainty under which all the Russian bourgeoisie was living at this time of general demoralization when no one knew or could even guess what the next week might bring. I soon realized, however, that something more than the general situation was the cause of Anna's concern. The agitations of the Bolsheviks for the extension of the Revolution, their attacks upon the Provisional Government, had already aroused a counter-offensive against them in the bourgeois and liberal press, and this offensive naturally included in its scope all the Russian internationalists who were opposed to the continuation of the war. The word "Bolshevik" was already becoming synonymous, in the Russian press, with "bandit" and "German agent." And when Anna showed me clippings in which I was labelled a Bolshevik and one of the most effective adversaries of the World War, I understood immediately the reason for her agitation.

"Are you really a Bolshevik?" she asked in a troubled voice. "That means a fight against the new government as well as the old—more bloodshed, more persecutions. Even if you were a Menshevik or belonged to one of the other groups, it would not be so bad. But a Bolshevik—where will you go, how will you find shelter?"

I understood quite readily that she was afraid to offer shelter to a Bolshevik, even if I had been willing to accept it, and that her concern for me was struggling with her fear. While I was not a member of the Bolshevik group, like many of the other internationalists, I shared their general attitude towards the war and towards the Revolution. I did not want to reassure my sister by differentiating myself from them, and knowing that our break had better be decisive, I answered, "Yes, I am a Bolshevik."

When my brother called the next day and I explained that I wanted to leave Anna's house at once, he assured me that it might take weeks for me to find a room in which to live. With the rapid disorganization of the army, thousands of soldiers were pouring into the cities and with the breakdown of the railway service, thousands from the adjacent country were also moving in. Even the returning *émigrés* belonging to the dominant parties in the government found it difficult to obtain shelter. The quarters of the upper classes were not yet taken over, as they would be after October, and my brother was still in possession of a comfortable flat. His family was away at this time, and at his insistence I decided to stay with him until I could find my place in the new scheme of things.

The economic and social chaos which seemed to dominate the whole of Russia in this period and which was much more acute in the cities than in the country districts, was not due solely, or even for the most part, to the Revolution itself. In fact, in the first two months following the Revolution both the internal situation and the morale of the army had been considerably improved, in spite of the inevitable confusions attendant upon such a vast political change. The situation in the summer and autumn of 1917 was merely the culmination of a process of breakdown which had begun in 1915 under the corrupt bureaucracy, including Tsarist officials under German influence.

Though the first Revolution had halted this process, by the middle of 1917 it had begun again—this time encouraged by the propertied classes, especially the big industrialists, who, satisfied by the overthrow of the feudal oligarchy, felt that the Revolution had now gone far enough—in fact, too far. Even the Kerensky government, which sought nothing more at this time than a certain reformed and enlightened capitalism, was under constant threat and pressure from the Right, and to make this pressure more effective and particularly to smash the power of the Soviets, shop committees, and army committees, a new campaign of sabotage began. Factories were closed, transportation was disorganized, internal doubt and discouragement deliberately provoked. Though the industrialists had counted upon these measures to check revolutionary enthusiasm and any further "experimentation," their weapon proved to be a two-edged sword.

The shortage of food and the general disorganization which made life so difficult had the desired effect upon large sections of the small trading class and even upon the average man in the street. "Was it not better before?" many of them argued; or, "In what way has the Revolution helped us? We cannot eat ballots and proclamations"; or, "What we need is a strong man—an authority; the government just talks."

Among the workers and the more enlightened peasants who realized the important achievements of the March Revolution, there was uneasiness, too. But their dissatisfaction and their questions took another direction. "We have freedom but no bread. Where are our sons? Why does the war continue and for what are we fighting? When the soldiers come back from the front, what do they find at home but the same starvation? How long can this situation last? What about the land that was promised us? We are tired of waiting; we have waited long enough."

Lenin's slogan of "Peace and bread" was the most effective synthesis of the spirit that dominated the masses. Something had to be done.

In the summer of 1917, the complexion of the Revolution was already rapidly changing as the government, under Allied pressure, grew more determined to pursue the war in some fashion and to consolidate the Revolution on a political basis, while the workers in the cities—and even a large section of the peasantry under the more radical Social Revolutionists—moved steadily towards the Left. Though the old Imperial Duma was still the nominal governing body of the country, actual power was being steadily absorbed by the central committees of the Soviets, coöperatives, unions, and army committees, elected by the dozens of All-Russian congresses held in Petrograd during the spring and summer months. Some of these organizations had been in existence since the Revolution of 1905. Others, like the army committees, had been organized after March by the soldiers at the front to combat the influence of the Tsarist officers and to democratize the army.

As these central committees and the organizations they represented played an increasingly dominant rôle, it was towards these that the various revolutionary groups directed their propaganda and their struggle for control. A number of these organizations— such as the workers' and peasants' coöperative movement with its twelve million members—were now dominated by the Mensheviks and the Socialist Revolutionaries; the Peasants' Soviets were almost wholly under the influence of the latter, while the Bolshevik influence was already penetrating the Petrograd unions and the army and navy committees.

The March Revolution had failed to solve the basic problems of peace, land and workers' control of industry, and it became increasingly obvious that long before the calling of a Constituent Assembly—announced to take place in December—an attempt at their solution would be made by the masses themselves. Though the Right Wing Mensheviks and Socialist Revolutionists were participating in and supporting the Kerensky Ministry, the Menshevik Internationalists, led by Martov, and the Left Social Revolutionaries (who in October were to split off from the parent body and support the Bolshevik program) were already agitating for more decisive action to bring about peace. The propertied classes, both conservative and liberal, were less concerned with peace than with the growing revolutionary aggression at home. They would make no gestures that would offend their western Allies, whose aid might yet be needed to defend them from the Russian masses.

Soon after the February Revolution the Soviets had issued a proclamation to the effect that "the time had come to begin a resolute struggle with the predatory aspirations of the governments of all countries, for the people to take the matter of war and peace into their own hands." Later, on May 15th, the Petrograd Soviet, then under the domination of the Mensheviks and Socialist Revolutionists, had issued an "Appeal to the Socialists of All Countries," and the famous "Peace Terms of the Russian People"—peace without annexation or indemnities, on the basis of self-determination of peoples. The appeal also initiated a proposal for an international conference of Socialist parties and factions of all countries.

Shortly before this a neutral Committee of Dutch and Scandinavian Socialists had issued a similar call for an international congress to take place in Stockholm, and preliminary conversations with the party leaders in the Allied and Central Powers had already begun. They were to continue throughout the summer after the two movements for a conference, one neutral, the other Russian, had merged. The movement, strangely enough, came to be encouraged by some of those very social patriots who had been sent to Russia by their own governments, soon after the Revolution, to urge their comrades, and the Russian masses generally, to fight with the Allies to the bitter end. (Among these emissaries were Arthur Henderson of England, Marcel Cachin—whose rôle in Mussolini's betrayal I have already mentioned—and Albert Thomas of France, Vandervelde and de Man of Belgium, and Arturo Labriola, the former fiery Syndicalist of Italy, now a Monarchist member of the Italian government.) Once in Russia, where they were exposed to the war weariness and the internationalist sentiment of the Russian people, they had realized the hopelessness of their mission. Returning to their own parties, some of them had begun to advocate participation in the Stockholm Conference as a necessary gesture towards peace.

The Zimmerwald Commission had been asked by representatives of the Russian Workers' and Peasants' Soviets to participate in the preliminary preparations for the Stockholm Congress, and while still in Stockholm, Grimm had suggested a Zimmerwald Conference to decide this issue. In Russia, at the April meeting of the Bolshevik Party, Lenin had already called for a break with the Zimmerwald "Center" and for the immediate organization of the Third International.

"We ought to remain in Zimmerwald," he declared, "only to gather information." Zinoviev had introduced a resolution which stated that the Zimmerwald majority were "Centrists" and urged participation in its next conference only for the purpose of unifying the Zimmerwald Left. His resolution had carried. The Bolsheviks refused, of course, to have anything to do with the Stockholm Congress.

As the majority Social Democrats had declared a "class truce" at the beginning of the war and had been supporting their governments ever since, most of the Zimmerwaldists regarded them as representatives of those governments, rather than of the working class. Most of us were opposed to coöperation with them while they were still supporting "civil peace," and the aims of their imperialist governments.

Both Grimm and I represented the Zimmerwald Executive in Russia. While we were opposed to the Stockholm Conference and to its endorsement by the Russian Soviets, Grimm was inclined to favour participation in view of the fact that the Soviets —representing the Russian workers and peasants—had already sponsored it.

A Zimmerwald meeting was called in Petrograd at which all the Russians affiliated with the Zimmerwald group could discuss the Stockholm initiative. At this meeting, besides Grimm and myself, there were delegates from the Mensheviks led by Martov, the Social Revolutionary Internationalists, the Bund, the Polish, Rumanian and Lithuanian Social Democrats, the Bolsheviks and the Intra-fractional Russian Social Democrats. Trotsky, Riazanov and Urizki represented the last-named group; Lenin and Zinoviev the Bolsheviks. There were two main currents of opinion—one for participation, one, the majority, for boycott. Though as an individual I was opposed to participation, I did not consider that the Russian delegates alone had a right to decide this question. An alternative proposal, made by Grimm and myself, called for the convocation of a Third Zimmerwald Conference—in line with our Kienthal decision—to take place before the Stockholm Congress. This proposal finally carried.

During the discussions Trotsky had been particularly hostile and violent towards the conciliatory viewpoint, going much farther in his attacks upon it than did the Bolsheviks, who within the Zimmerwald movement had always comprised the Left Wing, while Trotsky had represented the Centre.

This psychological nuance on Trotsky's part amused me, and as Lenin and I left the meeting where the rest of the delegates were still engaged in personal discussion, I asked him:

"Tell me, Vladimir Ilyitch, what is the difference between the Bolsheviks and Trotsky? Why does he hold apart from your group and create another paper?"

Lenin seemed both astonished and irritated at my naïveté, perhaps because he suspected that I was trying to tease him.

"Now, don't you know?" he answered, curtly. "Ambition, ambition, ambition."

During these weeks since I had returned to Russia I had been meeting Trotsky fairly frequently, for like myself he was not yet a member of either of the dominant Social Democratic factions. Though he had once been affiliated with Mensheviks, he had since organized a new faction of his own. At this time he was quite isolated from both Bolsheviks and Mensheviks who had returned to Russia ahead of him. His journey from the United States, where he had been working on the staff of a Russian paper at the time of the Revolution, had been interrupted by a brief internment in Canada, and after the delays which had prevented him from playing a rôle in the decisive events of those early months, he had arrived in Petrograd in a bad mood. Though he was to join the Bolsheviks in August when a merger occurred between that party and some of the smaller revolutionary groups, at this time he still belonged to an independent group which aimed at uniting all the Marxian internationalists and had recently established a paper in Petrograd. Both Mensheviks and Bolsheviks regarded him with rancour and distrust, possibly in memory of the bitter polemics he had launched against them in the past and partly, no doubt, out of fear of the competition offered by such an effective writer and orator. More than any other figure in the Russian Revolution, Trotsky proved himself capable of arousing the masses by the force of his revolutionary temperament and his brilliant intellectual gifts. But he does not attract personal sympathies, or if he does, he cannot keep them for long—especially in intimate relationships among friends and comrades. His arrogance equals his gifts and capacities and his manner of exercising it in personal relationships creates very often a distance between himself and those about him which excludes both personal warmth and any feeling of equality and reciprocity.

At that time Trotsky was particularly bitter because he assumed that his political adversaries, in order to keep him out of the political arena in Russia as long as possible, had failed to bring sufficient pressure to bear upon the Allied authorities who had imprisoned him. His interpretation seemed to me rather implausible then, but after my own later experiences with the Bolsheviks, I was not so sure of this. In my conversations with them they displayed quite as much hatred of Trotsky as he did of them. Both because of his isolation and the way in which it affected him, and because we both shared the hope of uniting all the Marxian internationalists, we met quite often at this time. A short while after this, when the events which culminated in the October Revolution had absorbed this movement, he was to renounce this hope in language more bitter than that of Lenin. During all the rest of his career Trotsky was to lean over backward to prove himself a good Bolshevik and an orthodox Leninist.

Shortly after our decision to anticipate the Stockholm Congress by a special Zimmerwald convention, an event occurred which played directly into the hands of the Allied War Offices and which tended to discredit the Zimmerwald movement throughout the world.

The newspapers in all of the Allied nations suddenly announced that Robert Grimm, who had been a leader in the Zimmerwald movement since 1915, was a German agent, and on the strength of this statement a tremendous campaign of vituperation was whipped up, not only against Grimm, but against all of us connected with Zimmerwald. The charge was the old familiar one we had heard from the beginning of the war, but this time it was made as a direct accusation based, it was declared, upon concrete proof. We did not need Grimm's categorical denial to assure us of his complete innocence, and while the storm continued to rage about our heads and while both newspaper stories and public opinion became more inflamed, we continued to defend him as best we could. Then suddenly the newspapers printed the text of a telegram which Grimm had sent from Petrograd to the Swiss Foreign Office and which had been identified as authentic. It was then that we understood what had happened. In his zeal to put an end to the war, Grimm had sent a telegram to the Minister of Foreign Affairs in Switzerland requesting him to inquire on what terms Germany would be willing to make peace. Though the establishment of such terms was a necessary first step towards peace, the Allied press had interpreted this act on the part of Grimm as a betrayal of their cause and a conclusive proof that Grimm, and the Zimmerwald leaders in general, were acting in behalf of Germany. It was unfortunate for all of us, and for the Russian masses to whom he was devoted, that Grimm had made this naïve gesture without consulting his most intimate collaborators; it was more unfortunate still that, having done so, he had lacked the courage to admit it and to explain his action when the charges had first been made. He had left Russia before the telegram had been made public and those of us who had collaborated with him and defended him bore the full brunt of the attack, which grew more violent from week to week. Russia was now on the verge of a new offensive and all of those who opposed it, whether Mensheviks, Bolsheviks, or Social Revolutionists, were viciously denounced by all the pro-war elements as German agitators, brought into the country by the German agent, Grimm. Addressing the Left Wing convention of the All-Russian Workers', Peasants', and Soldiers' Soviets, summoned to decide upon the planned offensive, Kerensky shouted:

"I call your attention to the fact that agents of the German government have been agitating in our midst for a separate peace—a separate peace."

This assertion was followed by loud cheers from a majority of the audience and by scowls of hostility in our direction. We were internationalists in the midst of a war. What could be worse?

The whole situation affected me very deeply, and I was torn between discouragement and anger at Grimm. Why had he not consulted us before he sent that stupid and fatal telegram? And why had he not confided in us after the storm broke? After twenty years of exile and work for the Revolution I was now surrounded by a menacing hostility in my own country. More important, however, the puerile behaviour of Grimm had struck an almost fatal blow at the whole peace movement, even though the Zimmerwald leaders and all the Russian groups affiliated with the movement had explained in full our ignorance of Grimm's action and our disapproval of it. The jingoistic and demagogic press merely ignored our statements.

In order to salvage the situation, it was obvious that some one must rush to Stockholm to take over the Zimmerwald activities and to displace Grimm as secretary. It must be some one who had the complete confidence of our members and sympathizers throughout Europe in order that all doubts and suspicions might be allayed. The choice fell upon me and I made arrangements to leave for Stockholm immediately.

In the course of my journey between Petrograd and Stockholm I was to hear the new Russian offensive cheered again and again. Conversation among my fellow passengers seemed to centre on this subject and upon the stories which had appeared in the press. "We must fight to the bitter end," remarked some of the patriots as they left Russia for a neutral country. "All the Germans, all the Internationalists, must be exterminated." "Have you heard the story about the German spy, Grimm, and the whole Zimmerwald crowd?" "What a shame! They should have been shot!"

Fortunately, they did not know who I was.

13

MY UNHAPPINESS AND ANXIETY OVER THE Grimm incident and its possible effect upon the whole internationalist peace movement was enhanced by the fact that after only five weeks I was compelled to leave my native country at the very moment when the progress of the Revolution seemed to be hanging in the balance. I realized by this time that the Revolution in Russia had merely begun, and while no one could foretell how rapidly the revolutionary situation would develop during the next few months, by July, 1917, it was obvious that new internal struggles between the Provisional Government and the more revolutionary workers were at hand. Shortly after I reached Stockholm the Petrograd workers stormed the Tauride Palace with the demand that power be transferred to the Soviets. The government and the press claimed that the Bolsheviks had instigated the uprising, and after its failure hundreds of them were imprisoned, while their papers were suppressed. Among the imprisoned revolutionary leaders were Kamenev, Trotsky, and Alexandra Kollontai. Lenin and Zinoviev escaped and were to remain in hiding for several months. The old charge of "German agents" was revived and spread throughout the press of the entire world. Though most of the Bolshevik leaders were to be released for lack of evidence, the charges themselves were to be revived again and again.

Except for the few days spent in Stockholm in 1917 on the journey back to Russia, I knew nothing of the Scandinavian countries and very little of their people. This was the first time I had come into a foreign country with no knowledge of its language, and I looked forward to my work in Sweden with a certain apprehension. The Scandinavian countries and even the Socialist movement there had always seemed to be something apart from the rest of Europe. It was probably because I had expected to find a phlegmatic, methodical people, a movement dominated by immediate, practical concerns that I was so overwhelmed by the warmth and hospitality of the people, the revolutionary idealism of the Swedish radicals. Several years later, when I was to return to Stockholm from Russia ill and exhausted, the men and women who were my collaborators during this period became my best friends. I understood then what people mean when they say that they have found a second country, a second family.

Though the Scandinavian countries had escaped direct implication in the World War, both their political and social life were dominated by this all-absorbing issue. The neutrality of their country had not saved the Scandinavian radicals from those schisms which had split the movement in the warring countries into patriotic and internationalist camps. In Sweden the controversy was particularly pronounced, due to the fact that Hjalmar Branting, the founder and leader of the Social Democratic Party, had been ardently pro-Ally since 1914. The Left Wing of the Party, together with the Socialist Youth movement, had maintained a revolutionary internationalist position, and in 1916, the Left Wing leader, Höglund, had been imprisoned for advocating a general strike if Sweden should decide to enter the war. A short time before I came to Stockholm the Left Wing and

Youth movement, which had already allied itself with Zimmerwald, had split away from the official Party and had organized the Left Socialist Party of Sweden. Its members were ardent supporters of a Socialist program for Russia and sympathetic to the Bolsheviks. After the organization of the Third International, the Swedish Left Socialists were to join the Comintern and one of the most tragic and typical chapters in the history of Bolshevism was to be its treatment of these generous, honest, and enthusiastic supporters who, like the Italian Socialists, gave the most self-sacrificing and unstinted support to the Russian Revolution at a time when its fate was undecided and when even in the international labour movement the Bolsheviks had few friends. The first victims of the Bolshevik manœuvres were to be its most devoted friends. Their honesty was to prove an embarrassment and a hindrance to the methods of the Comintern leaders, who preferred subordinates whose loyalty had a very different base—self-interest and dependence upon the Bolshevik machine and financial support.

With my arrival in Stockholm the Zimmerwald Executive was definitely established there, three of the Left Socialists serving with me on a committee of four. Among these was Höglund, who had recently been released from prison and who is today the editor of the organ of the Swedish Socialist government and one of the country's ablest members of Parliament. The confidence and sympathy which Höglund inspired in me at our first meeting has grown through all the twenty years I have known him. This is also true of Fred Strom, who with Höglund has played a dominant rôle in the labour and Socialist movement of Sweden. Though seemingly absorbed in political struggles, both these men are poets and writers of merit. Their philosophic idealism is expressed consistently in their personal, as well as in their public, lives. These Swedish leaders, and Kata Dahlstrom, the most beloved Socialist woman agitator in Scandinavia, became my closest friends. (Three years later, in Moscow, I witnessed a demonstration of Kata Dahlstrom's courage when, taking the floor at the Second Comintern Congress, she fought Lenin and Zinoviev for the integrity of her party.) In their homes I had an opportunity to experience the full measure of the simple and spontaneous hospitality of the Scandinavian radicals.

Immediately after my arrival in Stockholm, pressure upon the Zimmerwald Executive to participate in or denounce the Stockholm Congress began again. At a meeting held early in July and attended by Swedish, Russian and German delegates, the committee of three from the Russian Soviets made another attempt to enlist our support for Stockholm. Haase for the German Independents notified us that his party intended to participate in Stockholm. Radek announced that the Bolsheviks would withdraw from Zimmerwald unless we repudiated that Congress. I insisted again, that although I would fight against participation, only a full meeting of the Zimmerwald body had a right to decide this question. My position was upheld and we issued a call for a Zimmerwald Conference to take place five days before the Stockholm meeting assembled. If the latter meeting should fail to take place, our conference should be held anyway.

Through the summer, as both the Stockholm meeting and our own were postponed again and again, due to uncertainties and unavoidable difficulties, the controversy over the Stockholm issue, particularly between the Bolsheviks and the German Independents, became more acute. The Bolsheviks were not unanimous in their attitude on this subject. After the Allied governments had announced their refusal to grant passports to delegates for Stockholm—even to majority Socialists—Kamenev argued for a change of attitude on the subject. Lenin had insisted that there could be no compromise between the "social-chauvinists" and the Bolsheviks. His view, of course, prevailed.

The task of the Zimmerwald Commission was a particularly difficult one at this time. To our propaganda for immediate peace, based upon concerted action of the working class, was now added the additional task of mobilizing the working-class opinion throughout the world to the defence of the Russian Revolution. The determination of Kerensky to continue the war, shown by the July offensive, the suppression of the Bolsheviks after the Petrograd uprising, indicated that a counter-revolutionary wave had set in. In a manifesto issued at this time, we pointed to this situation and ended with the question—"Will the Revolution

[163]

kill the war, or will the war kill the Revolution?" The fact that Zimmerwald was not merely a "peace" movement, but had definite revolutionary implications, made the work of its adherents in the warring countries a highly dangerous one. While we were preparing for an international convention, it was also necessary to guard against spies and *provocateurs*. The movement was illegal even in Germany, where the ruling classes in 1917 would gladly have accepted a "peace without victory," due to military defeats, starvation, and fear of revolt at home. Passports for delegates were out of the question. Not only must they come to Stockholm illegally, but the preparations for the Convention itself must be kept completely secret. This was all the more difficult in view of the fact that Stockholm had become a concentration point for professional spies, journalists, as well as pacifist tourists who had come to Stockholm to report or attend the official Congress. As the latter became more and more uncertain, all of them were searching hungrily for news of some sensational development which they could cable or take home with them. The activity of the underground Zimmerwald movement was known to both journalists and spies.

The date of the Convention was finally set for September 5th. By this time it was obvious that the Social Democratic Congress would never take place. Though delegates to it from the Central Powers and some of the neutral nations had already arrived in Stockholm, the Allied governments, including the United States, refused to issue passports, and the German and neutral delegates were obliged to return home with nothing achieved. The action of the British government in this matter had been encouraged by the chauvinism of the more powerful and conservative trade unions. The seaman's union, led by the violently "patriotic" Havelock Wilson, had issued statements denouncing MacDonald and Henderson, and the Congress in general as "pro-German," and had forbidden its members to man any boats that might carry the English delegates to Stockholm.

A few days before our own Conference convened we issued a statement, pointing to these fruits of Socialist collaboration with capitalist governments and called for "a return to the international class struggle and a break with 'civil peace.'"

It was during the course of these preparations that I finally joined the Bolshevik Party in the summer of 1917. Whatever my personal differences with and opinions of some of the Bolshevik leaders, it seemed to me at this time, as to a number of other Marxists who had never been Bolsheviks, that the salvation of the Russian Revolution lay with the tendency which they represented. The Revolution could not stop with the establishment of a bourgeois republic, and the situation in Russia in the intervening months had strengthened this conviction. Only a program of social revolution, the logical development of the forces set in motion at the time of the March Revolution, could save the country from complete collapse that would bury in its ruins all the hopes and aspirations of the workers and peasants. The development of such a program required a concentration upon Russia's internal problems, and such concentration required an end to Russia's participation in the war—a war which was obviously being waged for aims with which the Russian workers and peasants had no concern. The Menshevik Internationalist group and the Left Wing of the Socialist Revolutionaries were also supporting the demand for peace and for land to the peasants, but the Bolsheviks, with their slogan, "All power to the Soviets," seemed the only group whose program offered an immediate answer to counter-revolution and to the growing demand for "peace, bread, and land." I did not foresee that, having achieved power in the name of this slogan, they would, within a short time, actually liquidate the autonomy of the · Soviets and establish over them a party dictatorship.

The Zimmerwald Conference convened on September 5th, and neither before nor during the meeting did any hint of the gathering leak out. In spite of their eagerness for news, I was not approached by the various journalists in Stockholm, as I had long since accustomed them to my intransigent hostility to interviews and publicity. For years I had published a bulletin in several different languages, which circulated throughout the world, and never once had I signed an article in it or alluded to myself. My discretion was largely a matter of self-discipline, as I am naturally expansive and sociable, and it grew out of my conviction that revolutionary educational work should be anonymous so far as possible, in order to prevent the development of hero-worship and the undue influence of the individual upon the movement. My Swedish comrades were enormously helpful to me in planning and arranging the Conference, and even if they found my discretion exaggerated, they followed my advice. As the delegates from the warring countries arrived secretly in Stockholm, it was obvious that their safety and liberty depended upon our discretion and a strict observance of the arrangements I had made to conceal their presence. Among these were representatives of the Bolsheviks, Mensheviks, both Right and Left, Finland, Poland (Radek), Rumania, Bulgaria, the United States, the German and Austrian Oppositions, besides the Scandinavian and Swiss delegates and those of us who represented the Commission itself.

I was somewhat puzzled by the two American delegates, and one of them at least—who turned out to be no "delegate" at all so far as representing a bona-fide labour group was concerned—proved to be a source of both comedy and embarrassment. Ahsis, a Lett from Boston, represented a small, recently organized group called the Socialist Propaganda League, made up mostly of Slavic sympathizers with the Bolsheviks, which was later to serve as a nucleus for Bolshevik agitation among the Socialists in the United States. The other delegate was purported to be an American millionaire radical and pacifist representing something called the "International Brotherhood," of which none of us had ever heard before. His name was J. Eads Howe and I learned later that he enjoyed a certain celebrity in the United States as an eccentric and "a millionaire hobo."

I do not know yet how he came to be seated as a delegate in that gathering of well-known and serious revolutionaries. After the Conference he was to stay on in Stockholm for awhile, where he hired a small hall and gave Sunday afternoon lectures to the assembled pacifists and English and American tourists. At these meetings he usually distributed very stale cakes and fruits to the audience with all the gestures of a Lord Bountiful. He frequently hinted at this time at the large sums which he intended to bestow upon our peace movement—a fact which induced some of the comrades to treat him more seriously than he de-

served. One day he called at my office and with the air of a con-
spiratorial benefactor subsidizing an international cause, he
slipped five Swedish kronen into my hand. We later discovered
that he received from his family a small income sufficient to
enable him to roam about the world. He was to turn up in
Moscow a year later.

The Conference which began on September 5th lasted for five
days, during which no one outside the groups involved even
knew that it was taking place. Our internal situation was as complicated as was the period in which the meeting was held. There
was enormous tension on all fronts at this time, and in Germany
there was the beginning of breakdown and starvation. The Russian Revolution was in great danger, the Zimmerwaldists in
Russia profoundly split between those who supported the immediate seizure of power by the Bolsheviks and those who believed that such an attempt on the part of a small minority would
be fatal. Our responsibility—and mine in particular—in this
matter was enormous in view of the fact that the most responsible leaders of the Bolsheviks were unable to attend the Conference because of the serious and rapidly developing situation
in Russia. From the very beginning the Convention was divided
between a majority who fully approved the Bolshevik proposal
for seizure of power and a minority which objected to their tactics. The verbal duels which arose over this division between
Axelrod, and other Mensheviks, speaking for the minority, and
those of us who supported Radek, as spokesmen for the Bolsheviks, were made even more tragic to me by the fact that I
recognized fully—even while I supported him in principle—how
completely unscrupulous were Radek's methods, in comparison
with those of the opposition. (After the Convention I was to
have further evidence of this.) But even though we despised
Radek personally and considered him a vulgar politician, we
knew that the Russian Revolution was at stake, and at this moment that Revolution offered the only spark of light on a black
horizon. The majority of the delegates decided that the Zimmerwaldists must support at all cost the struggle of the Russian
vanguard.

We decided that the most effective method of demonstrating

to the capitalist world the workers' solidarity with their Russian comrades, and of igniting anew the spirit of international enthusiasm, would be a general strike. Each of us was aware of the responsibility which such a decision entailed. This weapon had often been threatened but had never been used in war time, and unless it were completely effective it would undoubtedly result in violent persecution and even death for those responsible for it in the countries at war. To be effective, it must take place simultaneously in all the warring countries, for if the workers on either side failed to participate, the strikers on the opposing side would be denounced by their own governments as the agents of the enemy, the general strike itself, a military manœuvre instigated by the enemy's war office. In view of the fact that delegates from England, France, and Italy had been unable to attend the Convention, the decision would have to be kept a secret until their groups were consulted and a general agreement reached. Unless this condition was observed, those who attended the Convention would become victims of the most savage reaction in their own countries and our movement would be practically wiped out.

In order to guard our deliberations and the general-strike resolution in particular, I was given the responsibility of making sure that not a single copy of this appeal would be carried across the border by any of the returning delegates. I was also to find a way by which our appeal could be transmitted to those countries which had not been represented in Stockholm. As secretary of the Zimmerwald Commission, unanimously elected, I was to be solely responsible for this task.

With the conclusion of the Convention I began to consider the possibilities for conveying our appeal into France and England. With the help of my Swedish colleagues on the Commission, I found a reliable young Scandinavian Socialist who agreed to memorize the entire appeal in English and transmit it to the anti-war Socialists in England. In London, the appeal was to be memorized in French by some one who would deliver it in Paris. In this way, no copy of the appeal would fall into the hands of the governments even should our messenger be searched or arrested.

It was understood by the delegates who had attended the Convention that nothing would be said about our decision until our messenger returned from the Allied countries and we had reports from our comrades there. The German Independent Socialists, then accused by their government of inspiring insurrections in the German fleet, were in a particularly dangerous position. If it became known that they had agreed to a general-strike resolution without similar agreements on the part of the English and French, their party would be crushed. For this reason I had pledged myself to them in particular, that under no circumstance would the appeal be made known until we received affirmative replies from the Allied countries.

But the Convention was scarcely over before Radek began demanding that I publish our appeal immediately, in view of the rapidly developing crisis in Russia. The Bolsheviks had already decided to seize power, and the Zimmerwald resolution, calling for an international general strike in support of the Russian workers and the beginning of a general working-class struggle for peace, would increase their prestige enormously, even though the general strike itself never materialized. It would seem to indicate to the more hesitant elements among the workers and peasants in Russia that the program of the Bolsheviks was backed up by international support. It did not matter to Radek and the Bolsheviks whether or not our resolution, endorsed by a handful of Left Wing Socialists at Stockholm, would actually receive the support in the countries represented by these delegates, and they were unwilling to wait until we could find this out. Our mutual and unanimous understanding, our pledges and promises, and my own enormous responsibility meant nothing to Radek, and throughout the month of October he bombarded me with protests and demands. Among his letters—while he had stayed on in Stockholm as a Bolshevik representative, he made his demands in writing—was one in which he threatened to publish the manifesto himself unless I agreed to do so immediately. I understood then that either he or the Finnish delegate who was under his influence must have stolen a copy of the appeal. About the same time, one of the German Independents, Louise Zietz, came over to Stockholm to prevent the premature publication of the mani-

festo, in view of the precarious position of her party. Torn between the threatened extermination of Left Wing Socialism in
Germany and the demands of those who spoke in the name of the
Russian Revolution, I was utterly miserable, but I felt that there
was only one course to pursue—to keep my pledge and obey the
unanimous mandate of the Zimmerwald Convention.

Shortly after I had given Radek my final decision the manifesto was published in the Finnish paper controlled by the Bolsheviks. By this time, however, the November Revolution (October by the Russian calendar) was sweeping aside all other
considerations and put an end to a situation which had grown
intolerable.

14

THOSE OF US IN STOCKHOLM WHOSE EYES WERE
turned toward Russia lived through a period of mounting
excitement and constant anxiety in that first historic week of
November, 1917, when the fate of the Revolution, of Socialism
itself, seemed to be hanging in the balance. We knew that the
outcome was a matter of days, if not of hours, and I felt as one
might who has done all in one's power to assist a beloved patient
and at the end can only await the result of the final life-and-death
struggle.

With the fall of the Provisional Government and the seizure
of power in Petrograd by the Military Revolutionary Committee
expected at any moment, I spent the decisive evening in a café
with a group of Swedish and Russian radicals who, like myself,
were in no mood for sleep. Radek was among them and every
few minutes he would jump to the telephone and bring us back
what news he had been able to gather. Still the word did not

come, and at two o'clock in the morning I went home after Radek had promised he would telephone me at whatever time the news came through. His call came three or four hours later. The Revolutionary Committee had seized power! The Social Revolution had been born!

My first thought—as soon as I was able to think clearly—was my own responsibility and that of the Zimmerwald Executive at this decisive moment. We must rally the workers of the world to the support of the new revolutionary régime and an immediate peace which would permit it to consolidate its power. The war-weary and suffering masses of Europe must be made to realize that their own salvation was bound up with the fate of the Social Revolution in Russia, and the Russian workers must be assured that they were not alone in their fight. The All-Russian Congress of Soviets, at the moment of the Petrograd triumph, had issued a statement to the workers, soldiers, and peasants which contained the following sentence: "The Soviets will at once propose an immediate democratic peace to all nations, and an immediate truce on all fronts." This was the moment for the general publication of our Zimmerwald appeal, and at this moment I was ready to assume the whole responsibility for its publication. The Swedish members of the Zimmerwald Executive agreed with me and put at my disposal their well-equipped printing-shops. A few hours later a special number of their paper appeared with the Zimmerwald Manifesto published in twelve different languages. The Manifesto was subsequently published in leaflet form, and its distribution by the thousands in the trenches and in the navies during the months that followed accelerated the revolutionary movement in Germany and Austria, the strikes and mutinies in behalf of peace. It seemed that at last the Zimmerwald aspiration was being realized—peace was to be imposed by a victorious working class upon the belligerent powers—a lasting peace through Socialism, rather than a mere truce in the old imperialist struggle.

As I was leaving the Zimmerwald headquarters for the printing-shop to give a last glance at the proofs of the various translations, I was interrupted by a call from an American journalist representing a Chicago paper.

"I have come to interview you about the Russian Revolution," he informed me, "and to ask what you have heard from Russia."

"I never give interviews," I replied. "You have probably read the morning papers. You must excuse me, but I must go."

At this moment the telephone rang and my visitor could overhear my conversation with one of the Swedish Zimmerwald leaders in reference to certain decisions of the recent convention.

When I had hung up, he showed no sign of being ready to go. "I understand, from your remarks over the telephone, that you have had a Zimmerwald Convention recently. Could you tell me which countries were represented?"

"The whole world," I answered, shortly.

"What a pity! It would have made a sensational story," he said. "If you had let me know about it in advance, I could have paid you thousands of dollars for such a story."

"Get out, you miserable rascal!" I shouted at him. "Do you think you can corrupt us?" He left hurriedly and never came near me again.

With the triumph of the second Russian Revolution the work of the Zimmerwald movement was not only changed, but enormously augmented. Our office at this time was almost the sole link between the new revolutionary régime and Western Europe and America, and upon my shoulders rested a large share of the responsibility for defending the new government and interpreting its aims to the workers and the revolutionists outside of Russia. I was eager, of course, to return to Russia immediately and participate in the building of the Soviet Republic, but Lenin and the Russian Central Committee insisted that I was of far more value to the movement at this time in Stockholm.

Not only the bourgeois press, but a large section of the labour press of the world was bitterly hostile to the Bolshevik régime, and the most extravagant and calumniatory articles about it were being published daily. The Social Democratic and Anarchist publications which were not directly hostile were hesitant in their attitude, remembering the bitter attacks launched against them in the past by the Bolsheviks and anticipating possibly the events of the coming year. So far as I can remember, only two important daily papers gave unqualified support to the new government at this time—*Avanti,* the organ of the Italian Socialist Party, and *Politiken,* the organ of the newly founded Swedish Left Socialists. The latter, published in a neutral country, had become practically the mouthpiece of Zimmerwald; while *Avanti,* though published in a belligerent country and exposed to the most bitter persecution, heroically defended both the Russian Revolution and the demand for immediate peace.

The influence of these two papers, published in languages not widely known, was small compared with that of the general world press, united in its opposition to the Workers', Soldiers' and Peasants' Republic. Until the November Revolution, Radek and a few other Bolsheviks had published a party bulletin in Sweden dealing with Russian events. But they had now returned to Russia and I was left practically alone to carry on this work in the name of Zimmerwald.

For months, in the bulletin I prepared and published in various languages, and which was sent out to the radical and liberal papers throughout the world, I attempted to counteract the campaign of calumny in the capitalist press by presenting a truthful picture of what was taking place in Russia. To do this effectively it was necessary to have direct and constant contact with Russia, and this was where my greatest difficulty arose. Though Sweden was a neutral country, there was no direct mail or telegraph service with Russia in this period of confusion and breakdown, and our courier service was far from regular. Very often the couriers would arrive with boxes of Russian newspapers, most of which were too old to serve my purpose.

Lenin was following my activity with the utmost anxiety and interest at this time. It was a period in which the fate of the Revolution in Russia seemed to hang upon the revolutionary resistance of the workers in Western Europe to the counter-revolutionary propaganda and intrigues directed against Russia by their own governments. It was necessary that the workers in both the Allied nations and the Central Powers be made to understand Russia's need for immediate peace. Lenin and the Bolsheviks in general were convinced that the Russian Revolution could not survive unless it served as a spark to ignite the fires of revolution in Central Europe, and it was partly as a result of this conviction that the Bolshevik leaders continued to over-estimate the revolutionary sentiment in Western Europe and even America during the next three years, and attempted to create it arbitrarily where it failed to develop.

Once when I had complained about the irregularity of our news service, Lenin wrote me:

"Dear Comrade: The work you are doing is of the utmost importance and I implore you to go on with it. We look to you for our most effective support. Do not consider the cost. Spend millions, tens of millions, if necessary. There is plenty of money at our disposal. I understand from your letters that some of the couriers do not deliver our papers on time. Please send me their names. These saboteurs shall be shot."

Of course I did not send him the names of the couriers, even though I was not sure that they would be shot if I did so and in spite of the handicap to my work. Lenin's reference to the sums he wished me to spend was a surprise and revelation to me, though I knew that one of the first acts of the successful revolutionary régime had been to take over the banks, as well as the industries, and to confiscate the property—including the jewelry and art treasures—of the aristocratic and wealthy classes. My answer to his suggestion that I spend "millions, tens of millions" was probably a revelation to Lenin of my own naïveté. I could not see that our campaign of propaganda, in behalf either of Russia or the World Revolution, required such huge sums. I had always believed, as I still do, that the methods by which the workers emancipate themselves cannot be imposed from above. They must flow from the experience of the workers themselves, as an exploited class, and from their understanding of the goal which they seek to achieve. Thus all my efforts, both before and after the Revolution, were concentrated not upon the artificial "instigation" of revolution by outside agents, but upon the Socialist education of the masses which would enable them to emancipate themselves. Only a revolution achieved upon such a base, I believed, could maintain itself against reaction without or deterioration within.

In spite of my answer to Lenin, large sums of money began to arrive, ostensibly to finance the work of Zimmerwald, but most of which, as I soon discovered, was to be paid out to agents who were creating "Bolshevik" movements and newspapers throughout the world. Though the Soviet régime had no official embassy in Sweden, a commercial delegation had been established in Stockholm to negotiate trade relations. The first office of this delegation was in the Zimmerwald headquarters, and some of the money which I was to spend and distribute was left with me by the couriers of this delegation.

With one of these contributions (I do not remember now whether it was in jewelry or cash) I received, through a Bolshevik delegate, the suggestion that a Communist daily paper be established in Copenhagen. I was amazed at what seemed such a lack of revolutionary common sense. It was a period in which the Bolsheviks were being pictured as fomenters of bloody revolution throughout the world, in which they were trying desperately to achieve or maintain commercial relations with Western Europe and the friendship of the European working class. Everyone knew that there was only a handful of Communists in the entire city of Copenhagen. What would the Danish workers, to say nothing of the government, think if a Communist daily, representing a huge financial investment, should suddenly spring up from nowhere? Certainly there were better ways of stimulating the loyalty of the Danish workers to the Russian Revolution! It was true, as Lenin stated, in a letter addressed to the American workers at this time: "We are in a beleaguered fortress. . . . We are counting upon the inevitability of the international revolution." But the Bolsheviks could not manufacture the international revolution or impose a Communist apparatus from above. This last method, I was convinced, would antagonize rather than win the confidence of the working class.

When the Bolsheviks realized that I did not approve of these methods, the funds for such purposes were distributed through other hands. Though I did not know it at the time, I was witnessing the genesis of that corruption of the international movement which was to become an organized system under the Comintern. My naïve reply—that I did not need so much money for the movement—marked also the genesis of my later dissension with the Russian leaders.

It was during this period that I first met John Reed, while he was on his way back to the United States from Russia. In Russia, immediately after the Revolution, he had been put in charge of the English-speaking section of Karl Radek's Press Bureau and I understood that he was now returning to America to work for the Bolshevik movement there. (During the year that followed he was to play a leading rôle in the splitting of American Socialism and the formation of the Communist Party.) His visit had been preceded by a letter from Chicherin or Lenin, and having heard that his nomination for consul in the United States had been revoked by the Bolsheviks, his proposal for the establishment of a neutral newspaper disapproved, I expected to find some trace of personal resentment in his disappointment. There was none whatever, and I had only to talk with him a few minutes to understand that here was one of the most devoted and genuine revolutionists I had ever met. Very often, Russian radicals or "friends of Soviet Russia," or "naïve" individuals whom Chicherin wanted to get rid of, were sent to me in Stockholm. Reed was none of these. I was amazed to find in an American such a profound understanding of the Russian Revolution and such love for the Russian masses. As a journalist and a poet, as well as a revolutionist, it was probably natural that he should have been stirred by the dramatic boldness of the Revolution itself. But there was something more than an appreciation of the colour and drama of the Revolution, hero-worship of its leaders and sympathy with its aims in Reed's enthusiasm for Russia. He loved the country itself and the great anonymous mass that had made the Revolution possible by its suffering and endurance.

I was surprised and somewhat sceptical when he told me that he had written a book about the Revolution—completed within a few weeks. How, I thought, could a foreigner, with only a rudimentary knowledge of Russia, write an adequate account of such a momentous event? After I had read a few chapters of *Ten Days That Shook the World* I understood to what extent Reed's intuition and creative art, his passionate love for the masses, had contributed to his understanding of the significance

[177]

of the Russian events. This book was published with a preface by Lenin and for a while became a text-book in Russia.

Jack and his wife, Louise Bryant, and I became close friends during the weeks they spent in Scandinavia. Louise was a beautiful and radiant girl at this time. She too had gone to Russia as a correspondent shortly after the first Revolution, and her enthusiasm for the Soviets matched that of Jack. I was to know Louise in three different phases of her life—as Jack's courageous and adventurous comrade, fascinated by the Russian Revolution; as the broken-hearted woman of 1920, after Jack's tragic death, the reasons for which she fully understood; as the sick and shattered woman, without either the will or strength to fight her own weakness, during her last years in Paris. In Stockholm, we had no intimation of the tragedy which our relation to the Russian Revolution would bring to all three of us within the next two or three years.

Reed had to wait for a short time in Christiana, after Louise had left, before he took a boat back to the United States. I, too, was in Norway at this time, on some errand of the Soviet embassies in Scandinavia. We spent our evenings together, reading or talking, and on one occasion Jack induced me to go with him to the cinema to see a Charlie Chaplin picture. It was my first introduction to Chaplin and I enjoyed it immensely. It was also during one of these evenings that Jack tried to persuade me that I must write my memoirs.

Ever since the November Revolution I had been trying to get permission from Lenin or the Party Central Committee to leave Stockholm for a brief visit to Russia, but each time new obstacles had arisen. Before diplomatic relations were established between Russia and Sweden the Tsarist ambassador still claimed to be the official Russian representative. In the two months immediately following the Revolution the Zimmerwald headquarters had to serve in the dual capacity of spiritual and material link between Russia and the rest of Europe, though it was supposed to be quite autonomous and independent of the Soviets.

On returning to my office one day I found a telegram which had been addressed to the Socialist Lord Mayor of Stockholm and which he had forwarded to me because it was written in

Finnish, which he did not understand. It stated that the Soviet government had appointed a Polish-Russian Bolshevik living in Stockholm and employed by a well-known firm, as the Soviet representative in Sweden. This was Vorovsky, who thereafter was to act as *de facto* ambassador for the Soviets.

I had met Vorovsky and his family during the recent Zimmerwald convention. He was a true "intellectual," the most genuinely cultured member of the Russian party I had ever met. As a young man he had been imprisoned by the authorities and his health had never recovered from the rigours of that experience. (In 1922 he was to be assassinated by a Russian monarchist in Switzerland.)

"What shall I do, Angelica?" he asked me when I had shown him the telegram. "The telegram may be false. It may have come from the Whites in Finland. I can't act until I have official confirmation and credentials from Moscow. I can't even rent an office."

We agreed that there was nothing to do but wait for further word and in the meanwhile to use the Zimmerwald office as his headquarters, and so it was that he became a daily visitor to my office. During those visits we probably talked more of literature and art than of politics, and because I had been immersed in political problems for so long, these conversations were a source of delight and release to both of us. Later, after his credentials had arrived, I had to act as his substitute during his trips to Moscow, or to the different peace conferences in which he represented the Russian government. It was a time when Russia was attempting to buy agricultural and other necessary machinery in Sweden, and in the absence of Vorovsky the negotiations between the Swedish firms and the Russian agents who came to Stockholm for this purpose were left in my hands. This was one of the reasons why my trip to Russia was postponed again and again.

In August came the news of the attempt on Lenin's life and the institution of the Red Terror. My alarm at the thought of Lenin's possible death soon gave way to alarm over the sensational reports of continued terror. When I heard that seven hundred political opponents of the Bolsheviks had been shot in reprisal, I was profoundly shocked. Even while I believed that these reports were exaggerated by the enemies of Russia in Sweden and throughout the world, I could not help but recognize how damaging they were at this critical time, even within the labour movement itself. As official reports arrived, confirming the extent of the Terror, I grew more and more disturbed. Revolutions, I knew, were not accomplished without bloodshed, and the suppression of counter-revolutionary activity was both inevitable and fully justified on the part of the revolutionary régime. Russia was compelled to defend itself not only against the assaults of world capitalism but against thousands of conspirators and reactionaries within its own borders. But was wholesale slaughter necessary? Was not the Terror expanding beyond its legitimate bounds? As the secretary of Zimmerwald and the representative of those revolutionary elements in Western Europe supporting the Soviet Republic, I felt it my duty to investigate and to answer these questions at first hand, if only that I might defend the Bolsheviks from their critics and confirm the devotion of their friends. I decided to leave for Russia immediately.

At the Stockholm station, just before I boarded the train, I was handed a letter from Racovsky. In this letter, he spoke, incidentally, of a "terrible tragedy" involving members of my family, which he had described in a previous letter. Never having received this previous letter, I had no way of knowing to what he was referring, but I guessed immediately that something had happened to one of my brothers who had been living in the Ukraine. To my anxiety over the general situation in Russia was now added a more personal apprehension over his fate.

I was to receive no answer for several months. At the Finnish border I was refused permission to cross the country, where bitter warfare was going on between the Reds and the Whites. I was obliged to return to Stockholm.

Months later, in Russia, I learnt the truth in a strange and purely accidental fashion. I was leaving Chicherin's office very late one night, and as the city was in complete darkness at this hour, one of the Red soldiers standing in front of the building offered to accompany me to my hotel. He was a native of the

Ukraine, and as we walked along he described the chaotic conditions there following the Revolution, when bands of marauding and irresponsible soldiers, deserting the front, had indulged in debauches of drunkenness and terror. The murder of one of the wealthiest citizens in Chernigov had been particularly revolting. While his home was being looted the man had been shot and his body cut into pieces. His wife, too, had been wounded by the soldiers. She died a few days later without knowing her husband's fate.

"I remember, comrade," the soldier remarked as I felt myself growing chill with horror, "this man had the same name as yourself—Balabanoff."

Back in Stockholm, I resumed my duties, determined to attempt the trip again at the first opportunity. One day a young woman entered my office while the stenographer was out at lunch.

"I am the widow of a Finnish officer," she explained. "He fell on the Red front fighting the Whites. I have come to ask you to let me work for you as a secretary or typist."

"I am sorry," I said, "but I have a typist and I do my secretarial work myself. Anyway, I am sure you could find much more interesting work than that of a typist. Since your husband died defending the Revolution, perhaps we can arrange to have the Soviet Union give you an allowance until you can find work."

She seemed so downcast, and so eager to work with me, that I was genuinely sorry to refuse her appeal, impossible though it was to admit a strange woman into my office.

She returned several times in the next few weeks and renewed her request—always at the same hour when there was no one present but myself. Finally I decided one day to give her an allowance, though she did not ask me to do so. When Vorovsky returned and I gave him an accounting of the money I had disbursed on behalf of the government, he looked at me with a twinkle in his grey eyes and said: "And now tell me how many orphans and widows and pregnant women you have provided for during my absence."

"Only one," I assured him. "A young girl, a widow of a Red

[181]

officer. I want her to go to the university and become a good militant."

Shortly after this, a sensational "mass murder" took place in Stockholm, followed by an equally sensational trial. A secret anti-Bolshevik League, led by a notorious Cossack officer, had been formed for the purpose of exterminating the Bolsheviks in Sweden. One of the leaders of the group had rented a villa just outside Stockholm and, ostensibly in the capacity of a genial host, had invited the Bolshevik leaders, including myself, and even our commercial contacts, to parties and dinners at his house. The real Bolsheviks had refused to accept these invitations, but seven of their friends were less intransigent. These were never seen again. They were murdered in the villa and their bodies tossed into the sea.

On the night after I finally left for Russia, early in October, and before the trial had revealed the details of this plot, an immense stone was thrown through the window of my room into the alcove in which I slept. The stone landed on the bed which I had occupied only the night before. The trial revealed that one of the conspirators had taken a room in the same house for the purpose of assassinating me. He had not known of my departure. The trial also revealed that the young "widow of a Red officer" had been an agent of this anti-Bolshevik League. She was convicted and sent to prison, along with her fellow conspirators.

In 1922 she was to be released from prison as a concession to the conservative clamour over my own admission to Sweden from the Soviet Union.

15

BECAUSE OF THE TERROR AND RUTHLESSNESS
practised against the masses throughout history by the defenders of economic privilege, particularly in Russia, I was prepared to accept the fact that violence and bloodshed would be unavoidable when the final reckoning occurred. One could not live through the World War without realizing the cheapness of human life in the eyes of the ruling classes and their political representatives. The depreciation of human life and human dignity in a capitalist society had always been contrasted in my mind with its inviolability under the coming Socialist régime, but I knew that, in Russia, Socialism was far from realized. I understood the incredible difficulties and obstacles accompanying the transition in Russia from one system to another.

What I saw and heard, or was told in Russia when I returned there in the autumn of 1918, convinced me that, unfortunate though it might be, the terror and repression which had been inaugurated by the Bolsheviks had been forced upon them by foreign intervention and by Russian reactionaries determined to defend their privileges and reëstablish the old régime. Armed and encouraged by foreign capitalism, reactionary generals like Korniloff, Kaledin, and even Krassnow, to whom the Bolsheviks had granted liberty, were leading White armies against the Revolution, assailing a population ruined by war and Tsarist corruption at a moment when the energies of the entire Russian people should have been concentrated upon the reorganization of Russia's internal life and the consolidation of its revolutionary gains. Peasants and workers who for four years had endured the tortures of war under a corrupt and treacherous leadership, and who had hailed so joyously the proclamations of peace, had had no time to relax, to greet their loved ones, before they were again called upon to defend their revolution on a dozen fronts. How could one expect mildness from such a people? And how could their responsible leaders afford to be indulgent to those who were prolonging their suffering?

One of the interventionist plots which particularly aroused my indignation, and which helped to reconcile me to the Terror at this time, was that in which Bruce Lockhart, the "British agent," was supposed to be involved. The plot had been revealed by a French journalist—René Marchand—as having been hatched by the Allied diplomats in Russia at the American Embassy. Though this man had had no sympathy with the Bolsheviks, he claimed that the callousness of the plot, which involved plans to blow up bridges, wreck the food supply, and kill Lenin and Trotsky, had aroused his indignation. Marchand threw in his lot with the Bolsheviks, but renounced his Communism in 1931. Though the alleged leaders of the plot, including Bruce Lockhart, had been released and returned to their own countries just before I arrived, the trials of the lesser conspirators took place after my return. I attended the trial at the request of Krylenko, who evidently hoped that the revelations would dissipate any doubts I might have about the necessity for terror. His hope proved correct. I was not only convinced of the guilt of the accused, who were for the most part humble subordinates who went through their confessions in a mechanical

monotone, but I was indignant at the Bolsheviks for having released the higher-ups, including Lockhart, whom the government had exchanged for Litvinoff, then in gaol in England. I
realize now that I was somewhat naïve in accepting the entire
story at face value. I do not doubt that the Allied diplomats in
Russia were plotting against the Bolsheviks and that hundreds
of such plots were fomented by the various interventionists and
their spies, but I believe now that the details of this particular
scheme might have been embroidered by the Cheka for propaganda purposes.

I knew, of course, that the Terror was not confined exclusively
to spies and active counter-revolutionists, and I suspected that
many who were innocent suffered with the guilty. Though hundreds had been executed in reprisal after the shooting of Lenin
at the end of August and after the revelation of the "Lockhart
plot," suppression on a large scale was not yet directed against
the non-Bolshevik revolutionists. Even at its worst, I knew that
there was no comparison between cruelty and extent of the Red
Terror and that of the White. The Red Terror had been intensified by Allied encouragement to the counter-revolutionists. I
accepted it as a revolutionary necessity, even while it depressed
and tormented me.

The tragedy of Russia and, indirectly, of the revolutionary
movement in general, began when terror became a habit rather
than an act of self-defence. Even before I left Russia I had come
to the conclusion that its leaders had become accustomed too
soon to follow the path of least resistance—the extermination
of opposition in any form. (When I expressed this opinion once
or twice to some of the Russian Bolsheviks, they looked at me as
though I had dropped from another planet.) The path of least
resistance can very easily become a trap and the price one pays
for taking it may ultimately come too high. This has certainly
been the case with Russia. The trials and executions of the past
two years which have dishonoured not only Russia but the entire
revolutionary movement, may cancel in the memory of mankind
the gigantic social and technical achievements of the Revolution. These crimes did not begin with Stalin. They are links in
a chain that had been forged by 1920. They were implicit in the

development of the Bolshevik method—a method which Stalin has merely amplified to incredible proportions and used for his own non-revolutionary ends. As long as I was in Russia I intervened whenever and wherever I could to save the innocent victims of these methods—whether among the "bourgeoisie" or the working class. Even in 1918 I was convinced that if the sacrifice of human life is sometimes a tragic necessity—in order to save a much larger number of lives—then each drop of blood, each tear that might have been spared is a dishonour to those responsible for it. I am not the first to have said this, but I am writing it out of my own experience and with the blood of my heart.

When I returned to Moscow from Stockholm, Lenin was still recuperating at a house in the country known only to his most intimate associates. When I stepped off the train at the station I was told that he wished to see me immediately. I did not need to be told why. He wanted to hear the latest news from the west. Though the Bolshevik armies had succeeded in stemming the advances of the interventionists—the Czechs in Siberia, the English at Archangel, and the Allied-financed White Generals in the east and south—Lenin was fully aware that the defence and consolidation of the Soviet system depended to a large extent upon resistance to intervention and development of revolutionary sentiment among the workers in the rest of the world. The experience of the next twenty years was to prove how right he was. Many of the abuses and deviations of the Soviet régime in this early period were due to the fact that the social revolution had begun in an economically backward country and then failed to receive the support of its class allies in the more progressive nations of the world. The Russian masses were compelled to dedicate all their resources to defence instead of reconstruction because the workers of other nations were not sufficiently class conscious and well organized to defeat their own interventionists and prevent the subsequent blockade which completed the tragic isolation of the Revolution in its most critical years. The ruthlessness of the Bolshevik methods developed in this period, which in turn demoralized and alienated the revolutionary movement throughout the world, later intensified that isolation, and led finally to a new cycle of abuses and repressions, the triumph of Russian nationalism, and the dependence upon military and diplomatic alliances for protection and support. The irony of history was to be expressed in this vicious circle.

The car which rushed me through Moscow and out into the country was driven by the former chauffeur of the Tsar. He had been instructed, evidently, to outdistance any car that might try to follow us and we travelled at breakneck speed. When we arrived at our destination, Lenin was sitting on a balcony in the sun. At the sight of him and the thought of how close he had been to death, I was overcome with emotion and embraced him silently. Krupskaya was present and I thought how much older and more haggard she looked since I had last seen her. The strain of the past few months had told more heavily upon her than upon her husband.

Lenin's questions began almost before I sat down. It was obvious that in spite of all his revolutionary realism he shared the illusions of the other Bolshevik leaders regarding the revolutionary developments abroad. The war was drawing to a close with the inevitable defeat of the Central Powers. It was almost incredible that the German masses as well as the army had been able to hold out so long. I believed, as did Lenin, that defeat would be followed by revolution in Germany and Austria, but of its success I was less assured. I was certainly far more realistic in my appraisal of the situation in the Allied and neutral countries, and was surprised at Lenin's somewhat exaggerated estimate of Communist influence in the labour movements abroad. Only in Italy was there whole-hearted support of the Bolsheviks among the organized workers and in the other western nations even the anti-interventionist sentiment did not rest necessarily upon working class sympathy with the Bolshevik aims. It was possible, of course, that a revolution in Central Europe would galvanize and solidify the international labour movement as the isolated revolution in Russia had so far failed to do.

We discussed the work of Zimmerwald and the European situation throughout the afternoon. Only when the time came for me to leave did we refer to what had happened to him and indirectly to the Terror that followed. When we spoke of Dora

Kaplan, the young woman who had shot him and who had been executed, Krupskaya became very upset. I could see that she was deeply affected at the thought of revolutionaries condemned to death by a revolutionary power. Later, when we were alone, she wept bitterly when she spoke of this. Lenin himself did not care to enlarge upon the episode. I had the impression that he had been particularly affected by the execution of Dora Kaplan because of its relation to himself; that the decision would have been easier had the victim of her bullet been one of the other Soviet Commissars. On a later occasion when I expressed my feelings about the execution of a group of Mensheviks accused of counter-revolutionary propaganda, Lenin replied: "Don't you understand that if we do not shoot these few leaders we may be placed in a position where we would need to shoot ten thousand workers?" His tone was neither cruel nor indifferent; it was an expression of tragic necessity which impressed me deeply at this time.

When the car came to take me back to Moscow, Lenin sent it away and insisted that I remain over until the evening. The dinner was eloquent of the scarcity of that time, but Lenin insisted that I share some of those extra rations which had been provided for his convalescence.

"Look," he said. "This bread has been sent to me from Jaraslow, this sugar from comrades in the Ukraine. Also the meat. They want me to eat meat during my convalescence." He spoke almost as though this were an unreasonable demand upon him.

I had brought with me some of the cheese and condensed milk—even one beloved bar of chocolate—which I had brought from Sweden, and when I wanted to leave these with him, he insisted that I take most of it back to Moscow and give it to the comrades there.

During the course of the evening I broached the subject that I had been thinking about for several weeks—a brief trip to Switzerland for the purpose of reëstablishing contacts with my Italian friends and of becoming better acquainted with the general European situation, particularly that of Italy. I had spent so much time in the Scandinavian countries that I had begun to feel isolated from the movement I knew best.

Lenin opposed my proposal.

"Don't do it. There is every chance that you will not be able to return to your Zimmerwald work and you know how important that is to us at this time. No one can substitute for you."

"But I will be gone only a short time," I assured him, "and I give you my word I won't participate in any activities or speak at any public meetings. If I indulge in no political work, the authorities can have no pretext to take action. In two weeks I shall be back."

He shook his head. "Think it over. I am sure you will run into difficulties. You are secretary of Zimmerwald; you are known all over the world. There will be trouble."

I assured him again and he let the matter drop. Picking up a copy of Barbusse's *Under Fire,* he asked: "Have you read this? In the end he anticipates the abolition of private ownership."

I had read it and had been impressed most by its psychological approach to the war problem. It seemed to me characteristic of Lenin that he should have been most impressed by this propagandistic ending with its scene of fraternization between the French and German soldiers.

I had not heard directly from any member of my family since the Bolshevik Revolution and after my arrival in Petrograd, I learned that my brother and sister who had lived there had escaped to Odessa with their families.

A few days after my return, I received a telephone call from a woman who had been a schoolmate of mine at Kharkoff, a spoiled and selfish aristocrat whom I suspected of having written an article against me that had appeared in the Russian papers at the time of the Grimm episode. There had been personal references in the article which only a schoolmate could have known. She asked for an appointment and implored me to see her immediately.

"Why do you speak so formally?" she asked over the telephone. "Don't you remember, we were the best of friends at school?"

I suspected that she or her husband was in trouble with the Cheka, but I consented to see her.

When my former schoolmate arrived, she informed me that her husband, a provincial governor, had been arrested as a counter-revolutionary.

"He is completely innocent, Angelica. You have only to meet him to know it. He is the most innocuous and stupid man. You can imagine it—he lived with me eighteen years without ever suspecting that I had any lovers ———"

"To live with you eighteen years and still believe in your faithfulness, Marousia, must mean that he is very stupid," I replied. "However, if I am going to help you, I must know the truth. I am not interested in what he thinks, but are you sure that he does not *act* against the Revolution? I will have to investigate and find out if he is guilty of illegal activity. Then I will let you know."

She thanked me profusely and affectionately as though I had been her best friend. The investigation, made at my request, established the fact that her husband was indeed too innocuous and cowardly to have been guilty of the charges against him, and a few days later he was released. When she telephoned to thank me, I asked her if she had written the article about me, and though she denied it, she was obviously embarrassed. Years later I heard of her in Paris, where she kept an antique shop and where her son acted as co-editor of a monarchist paper.

There were many technicalities to be overcome before I could leave for Switzerland, but finally the Swiss authorities agreed to let me enter if a group of Swiss citizens who had been caught in Russia by the Revolution were allowed to return to their homeland. This was arranged and I received a diplomatic pass which allowed me to travel as a member of the Red Cross administration. I wanted to be independent of the Russian government and of our Embassy in Switzerland, so that if Lenin's apprehensions should prove justified, I alone would bear the responsibility.

I arranged for a short stop-over in Berlin on my way to Switzerland, and when I arrived there the Russian ambassador Joffe sent his car to meet my train. I was whisked to the Embassy on Unter-den-Linden, that beautiful tree-lined street which offered an artificial oasis of quiet and luxury in Berlin to those who could afford it.

The task of Joffe was a complicated one. Since the shooting of the German ambassador Mirbach in Russia by the Left Socialist Revolutionaries as a protest against the peace terms of Brest-Litovsk, and particularly with the growth of Bolshevik sentiment in Germany, the Germans had regarded the Russian Embassy with increasing mistrust. It was Joffe's duty, as a diplomat, to abstain from any connexion or interference with the political situation in Germany. But as a representative of the Bolshevik Party he was forced to advise and subsidize the German Bolsheviks—carrying out to the letter the secret instructions he received from Moscow, even when he disagreed with them or believed them inapplicable to German conditions. He worried continuously over the conflict between his diplomatic duties and the revolutionary traditions of the generation to which he belonged. He was particularly concerned about the manner in which he was forced to live. The Russian government insisted then—as it does now with its representatives—that he live as all the other diplomats did, with a great show of luxury. His staff, however, had to live quite differently, on a more proletarian standard. This inequality was a source of bad feeling and gossip within the Embassy and of embarrassment to Joffe. When I came to visit him, I asked myself: Should I take my meals with Joffe, in his private apartments, or downstairs with the staff? Joffe himself settled this by insisting that I eat with him. As we sat at breakfast that sunny morning, we had no hint of the tragedy that was to overtake both Joffe and his wife. After the expulsion of his friend Trotsky, Joffe was to commit suicide. Later, his wife killed herself while an exile in Siberia.

The day after my arrival I got in touch with several of the German Zimmerwaldists, members of the Independent Socialist Party. We met in one of the halls of the Reichstag building for an informal exchange of views. The terrible tension in the political atmosphere which I had noticed as soon as I entered Germany was reflected in the attitude of the German militants at this time. The war was ending in the defeat of the German government; peace or conquest was a matter of days or weeks.

[191]

But life in Germany would never be what it had been before. Gone was the proverbial punctuality, the scrupulous honesty and loyalty of the average citizen. In its place there was merely confusion and desperation. I realized that the war itself, and particularly the starvation and suffering of the past year, had altered everything and everybody. The monarchy, the Junkers, would go, but what then—in the face of probable Allied occupation? Had the German people the spirit and vitality left for civil war? The Socialist militants were tempted by the example of Russia, but the seeming indifference of the workers in victorious France and England worried them. Would the workers who had left Russia to its fate come to their defence? The split in the German labour movement, the dissension even in the anti-war Left, was another handicap.

I left them with a feeling of profound depression.

On the train as we were approaching Switzerland my attention was attracted to a dispatch in a Swiss newspaper. It read: "Angelica Balabanoff, the well-known revolutionist, is on her way to Switzerland from Russia with many millions for the purpose of provoking a revolution here and in Italy."

The report was so ridiculous that it merely amused me, even when I saw that it was repeated in the headlines of the other Swiss papers. When some of my Italian comrades met me at the station in Zürich, they too joked about my "many millions."

The following day I was approached on the street by a man I had never seen before.

"Would you do me the honour, signora, to have dinner with me?" he asked.

"Why should I?" I replied. "I don't know you."

The stranger, who was very well dressed, continued to walk along beside me.

"I have heard of how generous you are, signora. And I am in great need. If you could loan me a small sum, you will never regret it. Just 60,000 francs, a mere trifle to you now."

During the week that followed I was flooded with letters from people who had houses, furniture, estates to sell. Spies and *provocateurs* came to my hotel with various stories, posing as journalists interested in the Zimmerwald program, or as revolutionists wanting money to start an insurrection. It was all so stupid and naïve that I found it hard to believe that it was instigated by the police, or that the government placed any credence in the newspaper story. The Swiss authorities knew me and they also knew that if the Bolsheviks had wanted to provoke a revolution in Switzerland they did not need to send the money by me. The Soviet government had a regular embassy at Bern and the funds could have been transported more easily by diplomatic or commercial couriers. As a matter of fact, the police did not even bother to investigate the story. But I learnt soon afterwards the source of these reports and the subsequent pressure for my expulsion.

On my arrival in Zürich I heard from some of the Italian Socialists a story that had already gained wide circulation among the radicals. A young French intellectual, named Guilbeaux, a voluntary exile in Switzerland, was editing an anti-militarist paper in Geneva. This paper, *Demain,* had been looked upon as an unofficial organ of the Zimmerwald movement ever since the Bolsheviks had introduced Guilbeaux into the Kienthal Conference in 1916. I had been dubious about him at that time, and had said so, as the war itself had already taught us the unreliability of free-lance anti-militarists and pacifists with no responsibility to any working-class organization. Now, I was told, some of the radicals suspected that Guilbeaux's paper had received a contribution from a pro-German "journalist." In view of all the suspicion and attacks directed against us as "German agents," I determined to go to Geneva and have the matter out with Guilbeaux. He neither denied nor affirmed the charge itself, but answered cynically:

"What of it? Why shouldn't we use capitalist money in our propaganda? Didn't Lenin take advantage of German strategy to get to Russia?"

"But what effect do you think this sort of thing has upon the confidence of the workers in our motives? Can't you see how it plays into the hands of the Allied governments?"

He merely laughed.

After my return to Russia, I discussed the Guilbeaux incident with Lenin. He, too, seemed unconcerned. Guilbeaux, for a few years at least, was to be a reliable Bolshevik supporter.

One day, in Zürich, I received a telegram from the Russian Embassy in Bern asking me to come there at once. The member of the diplomatic staff who met me at the station told me that the Swiss Foreign Office wished me to leave the country. The reason given was that I was a prominent "revolutionist" and that my "influence upon the masses was enormous." The Russian ambassador had asked if that was any reason for my expulsion, and then the truth had come out.

"We are a small country," the Swiss diplomat had replied. "We can't afford to get into trouble with the larger nations. We have had trouble enough. The Allies, and especially Italy, have requested the expulsion of Dr. Balabanoff."

I told the Russian ambassador, Berzine, an Old Bolshevik whom I had known for many years, that I would refuse to leave the country under such conditions unless the leaders of the Swiss labour unions decided that it was better for their movement that I should do so. When I took the matter up with them, a special meeting of the trade union and Socialist executives was called immediately. The members agreed unanimously that I should not go.

"What would become of our movement," one of the veterans asked, "if we could be intimidated whenever the government wishes to render a service to the great powers? If the government can prove any specific charges against Comrade Balabanoff let them do so."

A few days later, the first anniversary of the October Revolution was to be celebrated in Bern and I again made the trip from Zürich to attend it. On the train, I read in one of the Swiss newspapers a renewal of the attacks and charges against me made at the time of my arrival. The articles were obvious attempts to arouse public opinion and create a demand for my expulsion. The situation was now far more serious than it had been even a week or two before. All of Europe was on the eve of cataclysmic events. The rout of the German army was accompanied by revolutionary disturbances in Germany and Austria, and with the signing of the Armistice it seemed probable the social unrest in

Italy and possibly in France might take an insurrectionary turn. Even in neutral Switzerland, the bourgeoisie was in a panic. During the war it had taken full economic advantage of the country's neutral position and had reaped tremendous profits both at the expense of the warring nations and its own working class. The Swiss unions and the Socialists had been threatening a general strike and to the final ultimatum which they had just published they had added a protest against the move for my expulsion and a demand that I be permitted to remain in Switzerland. The newspapers were now claiming that as an agent for the Bolsheviks I had fomented the general strike, and were demanding not only my own expulsion, but that of the Russian Embassy as well.

When I arrived at the hotel in the People's House in Bern I was advised not to leave the building, as I was certain to be arrested. The next day the general strike began and with it all telephone and telegraph communication was cut off. Though the newspapers were forced to cease publication, secretly printed sensational supplements appeared on the streets. From these we learned that all the "Bolshevik agents," including those attached to the Russian Embassy, were to be expelled immediately. As it was impossible to get in touch with the Swiss labour men by telephone, and as I had been warned not to leave the hotel, there was nothing for me to do but wait, and I did so in complete bewilderment. Finally, at six o'clock in the morning, I received a message from the Russian Embassy asking me to get ready and to come there immediately. We were all to be expelled—no one knew just how or where in view of the fact that no trains were running.

As I drove to the Embassy with the messenger, I saw that the streets were filled with soldiers and that trucks mounted with machine-guns were patrolling the city. The civilian population was not permitted to loiter or to gather even in groups of two or three. I discovered later that in order to avoid a counter-demonstration the whole expulsion move was being carried out so swiftly and secretly that even the Socialists and labour leaders did not know that it was taking place.

At the Russian Embassy all was confusion. Among the thirty

or forty Russians who had been summoned, there were a number of women and children, quite bewildered by the sudden turn of events. The French propaganda mission was housed in a neighbouring building and it was obvious that the large group of French officers supposedly recuperating in Bern, were fully aware of what was going on. Many of them, with their wives or other members of their families, were gathered outside the Embassy to watch the expulsion and stage a demonstration against the "Bolsheviks." No attempt was made to disperse them, though passing Swiss citizens were forced to "move on."

Government trucks, flanked by soldiers on horseback, were sent to fetch our luggage, but we were ordered to walk to the station. As we started the French surged forward and began to shout insults and to spit at me, while some of the women tried to strike me with their fists and umbrellas. Fearing for the children in our group, I detached myself from the other Russians and faced them.

"Oui, c'est moi, Angelica Balabanoff," I announced. *"Que voulez-vous?"*

I do not know what happened then. In a pandemonium of shouting and horses' hoofs I lost consciousness.

When I opened my eyes I found myself in one of the railway stations to which I had been dragged in the midst of the riot by four cavalry soldiers. A wound on my arm was bleeding badly, but when I asked one of the soldiers to get me a bandage from a near-by pharmacy, the officer in charge refused to let him go.

Coming over to where I was half-sitting, half-lying on a bench, the officer informed me that I was to be taken to where the other Bolsheviks were already waiting inside the station house.

"If you dare to move until you are summoned," he remarked, "the soldiers will shoot."

Shortly after this I found myself being loaded into one of the automobiles—each containing a heavily armed soldier in addition to the military chauffeur—in which the Russians were to be transported. We were warned not to speak with the soldiers, all of whom were French Swiss and therefore more likely to be pro-Ally. The officer in charge treated us like a band of vulgar adventurers. He refused to tell us where we were going or when we would stop. Only once during the journey were we permitted to leave the cars, under guard, and get some food at a confectionery shop.

When we arrived at the German frontier, where we were to take the train across Germany, we were handed over to the authorities, who received us with the utmost suspicion, informing us that we should probably have to remain in the town several days, during which we would be under formal arrest. Several members of the Embassy staff and myself were told that we might go to a hotel, under guard, but I preferred to stay with the majority who were compelled to sleep on bundles of hay on the floor of the local school. We received no papers and were permitted to write no messages.

Our expulsion from Bern had taken place on the day of the Armistice. The revolution in Germany had already reached the stage of the Russian Revolution at the beginning of the Kerensky régime. Workers' and Soldiers' Councils had been formed, but except where these were dominated by the Left Wing elements they had no revolutionary character. Only the day before the Armistice—as I was to learn later—Frederich Ebert, the most conservative of the trade-union leaders among the Right Wing Social Democrats, had been appointed president of the People's Commissioners at a meeting of the Workmen's and Soldiers' Councils in Berlin. That same meeting had refused to listen to Liebknecht and other Left Wing leaders or to include them among their nominees. The monarchy and all that it stood for had been overthrown, the country was in a state of confusion and chaos, the population worn and hopeless. Power had passed into the hands of the German working-class leaders who did not know what to do with it. Trained in a tradition of gradualism, they sought only to restore the continuity of Germany's political evolution at a time when the industrial and military breakdown of German capitalism called for a complete break with the past. To accomplish this feat, Ebert, Noske, and the other labour bureaucrats whose influence, even in the Social Democracy, had gradually displaced that of an older generation of Marxists while it stifled that of the new, were to use the remnants of

[197]

Prussian militarism to suppress the German revolutionists within the next few months.

Cut off from all news of what was happening in the world outside during those four or five days in Germany, we knew nothing of all this. We did discover, however, that the chairman of the local Workers' Soviet was an old Social Democrat and I asked for an interview with him. I found him embarrassed and suspicious of us (had we not been expelled from Switzerland as dangerous Bolsheviks?), torn between the impulse to accept us as comrades and the need to treat us as adventurers. When he found that I was a friend of Hugo Haase and Clara Zetkin—I had asked permission to send them telegrams—his suspicion was somewhat relaxed. We were to be sent on the following day, he informed me, but he could not tell us by what route. Our train was to be guarded by German soldiers as far as the Polish frontier.

As we left Germany I experienced again the depression with which I had left Berlin a few weeks before. The old oppressive military bureaucracy had been destroyed and to this extent the suffering of Germany had not been in vain. But this destruction had brought with it no sense of liberation, none of the enthusiasm needed to build something new in its place. The German workers and their leaders felt themselves defeated in the defeat of their own oppressors.

I remembered at this time the brilliant critical analysis of the German Social Democracy which Rosa Luxemburg had written in gaol in 1914, after her arrest for anti-militarist activity. The pamphlet had been signed by the pseudonym "Junius" and it was a confirmation of prophecies I had heard her make at a German Congress in Hanover many years before when she had engaged in a brilliant polemical duel with the German Revisionist, Edward Bernstein. Even then she had foreseen the development of that pernicious opportunism which was to result in the tragedies of the post-war years. In January, 1919, during the revolutionary disturbances in Berlin, she and Karl Liebknecht were to be the most famous victims of these tragedies. Rosa Luxemburg, then a frail and elderly woman, was beaten to death by drunken officers, her mutilated body thrown into a river. To render their victory more symbolic, these forerunners of Hitlerism who had assassinated her and Liebknecht, drank beer out of her shoe in the orgy that followed.

At the Russian frontier, where we were transferred to a Soviet train which had been sent to meet us, we learned that Joffe and his staff had just arrived. The Russian Embassy with its ten "expert propagandists" had been expelled from Germany for a violation of the "non-interference" clause in the treaty of Brest-Litovsk. The Germans had, of course, suspected the Russians of financing the German revolutionists from the beginning. They had finally arranged to have one of the boxes of the Russian couriers, who enjoyed diplomatic immunity, "accidentally" broken open by a porter. It was filled with revolutionary appeals to the German workers.

16

KNOWING HOW DESPERATE WAS THE HOUSING situation in Moscow, I had anticipated difficulties in finding a place to live. I was surprised, therefore, when, just outside of Moscow, a member of the Foreign Office entered my compartment in the train and asked me if I would prefer to stay in a private apartment or in a hotel.

"Please don't make any special arrangements for me," I told him. "I shall live like any one else."

He told me that Joffe and his staff, and the delegation from Switzerland were to be taken to two private houses and suggested that I go with the latter.

The house to which we were driven upon our arrival in Moscow was one of the luxurious private homes expropriated by the government. The moment I entered it I was struck with a vague sense of familiarity and distaste. Everything about it seemed as cold and cheerless as the marble stairway and the cheap Michelangelo statue that stood in the entry. The following morning at breakfast, when I asked the waiter to whom the house had belonged, his answer confirmed my vague impression. It had been the home of a very wealthy family into which one of my brothers had married. I decided to leave this house at once. A few days later I moved to a room at the Hotel National, which was reserved at this time for members of the government and those devoting their entire time to Soviet activity. I had returned to Moscow prepared to live like the average Russian citizen or at least the humblest of party members, considering it logical that those who had led or instigated the Revolution and who were therefore responsible, in part, for the suffering and disorganization which the transition necessarily entailed, should not only share the physical discomforts of the masses, but should expect to make even greater sacrifices than those who followed them. We had intellectual and spiritual compensations denied to the average citizen—the joy of working for the realization of our ideals, the assurance that these sufferings were only transitory and that they would be compensated for by the achievement of peace and plenty for all. I realized that the privations which might seem irrelevant to me—in view of our hopes—were almost unbearable to those who had no such faith. I felt a sense of shame, therefore, even in my comfortable room at the National when I knew that others—both workers and intellectuals—had to wait for months, to beg, insist, and scheme to get any shelter at all.

And yet what could I do? If I refused to accept these privileges, it would seem like political coquetry or self-righteousness, an implied criticism of those other devoted revolutionists who, though they might share my feelings on this subject, had already accepted these conditions. Most of them were working day and night for the Revolution, sacrificing their health, carrying the burden of terrific responsibility. Certainly they needed the best that could be obtained under the circumstances—clean, hygienic rooms, heated whenever possible, adequate food, motor-cars for transportation. . . . These comforts, elementary though they might be, constituted an immeasurable advantage over the living conditions of the working class and even more immeasurable advantage over the non-Bolshevik professional class, and I was never able to forget this fact. When I thought of the women who worked all day in cold factories, returning to unheated rooms and a piece of black bread, it was difficult for me to enjoy my own food. And when, seated in the automobile of the ex-Tsar, I watched these women walk from work at the end of the day because the street cars were so overcrowded and ran so irregularly, it seemed to me that so far as physical comfort was concerned there was a greater distance between them and myself than between the pre-revolutionary Russian citizen and the Tsar.

So far as food was concerned, I could refuse to accept the first categories of rations, and in this respect I lived in Russia as did the average citizen. I got a sort of secret satisfaction, when I was addressing large meetings, from the knowledge that, though many in my audience were actually starving, the greater portion of it was fed as well as, if not better than, myself. Nor was I alone in this. I once read in a German Social Democratic paper that Lenin, Chicherin, Bukharin, and Balabanoff were the only Russian leaders who lived like ordinary Russian citizens. I could add other names to the list. I know that Trotsky's family (and he himself when he was not at the front) shared many of the general privations. There were numerous other revolutionaries who heroically endured the sacrifices which they imposed voluntarily upon themselves. The very few privileges they enjoyed reflected also the wishes of the masses. I resented this at first, as a manifestation of that humility which centuries of slavery have impressed upon a subjugated class. It seemed to me that they exaggerated in particular the merits and capacities of those leaders who had once belonged to the ruling class. I came to understand, however, that there was an instinctive gratitude among the masses to those intellectuals who had not deserted the workers when the Revolution had assumed a proletarian character; and among the class-conscious vanguard of the revolutionary movement, the preservation of its leadership was an act of self-defence.

Even when I had misgivings that the continuation of this attitude would lead in time to the toleration of even greater inequalities, I noted the striking faculty of discrimination among the Russian workers, between those "responsible Communists"— the men and women who had given their lives to the Revolution and who were now burdened with its work and responsibility— and those who had joined the Party in its moment of triumph for political and material reasons. Towards the privileges and airs assumed by the latter they were frequently resentful and even rude. At this time there was little of that fetishism of leadership which developed later and there were obvious gradations of loyalty to and enthusiasm over the various commissars. Lenin and Trotsky, whom the workers considered largely responsible for their victory and indispensable to its continued success, were greeted quite differently from such leaders as Zinoviev and Kamenev. The same gradations could be noted in the greetings to different members of the various foreign delegations when these began to visit Russia in 1920.

A number of incidents impressed upon me the subtle judgments quietly passed upon various leaders by the rank and file. I remember an occasion during the winter when the material situation was at its worst and when I received a telephone call from a secretary in the Foreign Office.

"Comrade Balabanoff, please help us," he asked. "The car in which Comrade Lansbury was driving has been stopped in the snow. It is impossible to repair it and we don't know how to get another one. If you could use your influence ——"

I called the Kremlin garage and asked for a car.

"The car will be at your door in five minutes," I was told by the chauffeur in charge.

I thanked him and then asked: "Will you please explain to me why Comrade Balabanoff can get a car immediately, when other comrades who have asked find it impossible to get one at all?"

"May I ask you a question?" he answered. "Who is the comrade whom we fetch to work in the morning earlier than any one else, and who returns later at night? And who is it who has never once asked to have a car for a drive?"

I had been prevented from taking my luggage from Switzerland, and I had come to Moscow in a light coat. As the weather grew bitterly cold, Lenin and other comrades insisted that I provide myself with a fur coat. As there was no money and no legal commerce at this time, I was presented with the necessary documents to present at the fur warehouse. The "salesman" in charge, a man I had never seen before, became almost angry at my reluctance to choose one of the more expensive and elegant furs.

"Who, if not you, deserves to wear a good fur?" he demanded. He had read of my anti-war activity, and more recently of my expulsion from Switzerland, and he was determined that I must have the best. He was quite upset when I chose a cheaper coat.

If I had not become a philosophic materialist through study and observation in my youth, my experience in Russia during this period of "War Communism" would have made me one. Day by day I could see how material need transformed and deformed human beings and clipped the wings of the young social revolution itself. Here I saw men and women who had lived all their lives for ideas, who had voluntarily renounced material advantages, liberty, happiness, and family affection for the realization of their ideals—completely absorbed by the problem of hunger and cold. Hunger makes slaves of human beings and interferes with every manifestation of human life. It deprives one of will power, weakens one's resistance, and makes one impatient, irascible, and unjust. How can men and women, exhausted by privation, knowing that their own children, their old parents, are suffering for food, find the will and energy to concern themselves with monumental social problems confronting them on every hand? I saw individuals who had devoted their entire lives to the struggle against private property, running home with a parcel of flour or a herring, eager to conceal it beneath their coats from the envious eyes of a hungry comrade. The women who owed to the Revolution all their new rights and dignities became suddenly old and worn, physically deformed by their own suffering and incessant worry for their children. Little by little, it became their sole concern to get a "ticket" which might enable them, sometime in the near or distant future, to get a dress, a coat, or a pair of shoes for their children.

The greatest heroes of the Russian Revolution are to be looked for not among its leaders, perhaps not even among those who died defending it on the numerous fronts. They were to be found among the workers who, resisting cold and hunger, went on working in factories and offices throughout this terrible period of blockade, civil war, and disorganization; perhaps, too, among those anonymous, secondary commissars who had to quiet these people, to appeal to their patience, to promise them for tomorrow what they could not get today. Sometimes when the discontent became too menacing and the commissars had promised too often to be believed, some of the better-known leaders who had more influence or greater authority would be asked to speak at certain factories, to arouse the enthusiasm of the workers by speeches about the success of the Revolution, the victories at the front, promise of revolutionary assistance from abroad.

On several occasions I received the message: "Please, comrade, come to Factory X today. There is no bread today, after we had promised it. The workers are exasperated. We must quiet them."

I confess I would refuse to go. I understood too well what was going on in the minds of these workers, to speak to them of anything but bread. I hated to think that they would listen to an agitational speech from me on any other subject without howling and interrupting.

Once, in Moscow, when the food shortage was at a climax, I was invited by a military institution of Red officers to deliver a speech at a meeting in celebration of a revolutionary anniversary. The first category of rations was supplied to the soldiers defending the Revolution and for the dinner which was to precede my speech some extra food had been supplied. When I arrived at the hall, before the dinner was over, I was invited to share it. I had not eaten a regular meal for so long that I was afraid to eat before I spoke, lest I should become ill, and replied that I preferred to eat later. More than three thousand young men received me with loud and prolonged cheers, and then followed my address with the closest attention. When I described the suffering and humiliation of the masses under capitalism, the hopes and achievement of the Revolution, the enthusiasm it had aroused among the workers throughout the world, they

[205]

listened breathlessly to my anticipation of the day when the Russian people would not be alone in their attempt to construct a new society. Though I was completely exhausted when I finished, I knew by their applause and their shining faces that my words had reached their minds and hearts. As we returned to the room where my dinner had been left for me, I hoped that my physical strength would be restored by the food. That hope sank as I saw that a coating of ice had formed over the food on my plate. The kitchen had been heated just long enough to cook the dinner, and with the return to the normal temperature of a Moscow winter day, the meal had frozen. Afraid to swallow the frozen food in my exhausted condition and afraid also of hurting the feelings of my hosts, I asked them to excuse me.

"I feel too happy, too excited, by the meeting to eat, comrades," I told them.

As we were driving back to my hotel, the young officer who accompanied me turned to me suddenly and said:

"You spoke so persuasively of the coming world revolution. We believe that it is coming. But will our leaders be here to welcome it when it comes? Some are already old. Others are exhausted by work and starvation." I knew that this last alluded to me.

"Why are you so pessimistic?" I asked him. "It will not take so much time for the revolution to come and new leaders will arise."

After my expulsion from Switzerland and the Allied propaganda that had accompanied it, I realized that it would be impossible to carry on even the post-war work of the Zimmerwald group—which at this time was practically embodied in my own person—in Western Europe. That work consisted largely of holding together and keeping in contact with those Left Wing, anti-war forces which had broken with or were opposed to the dominant Social Democratic policies. It had been the aspiration of the Zimmerwald movement to unite all these forces into a single international alliance at the close of the war—an alliance not dominated by any single party, such as the Bolsheviks were to impose when they organized the Third International.

In Moscow, these activities were seriously handicapped because of the Allied blockade. No regular mail, no newspapers, no books were being received from Western Europe, and for news of what was going on in the rest of the world we were obliged to depend largely upon a few couriers and illegal visitors. In view of these limitations, I was all the more eager to devote myself to some useful work—outside of addressing meetings—in one of the Soviet departments, and I asked the Commissar of Justice to let me work for a while, incognito, at some subordinate position in the Cult department. My incognito lasted only a few weeks, unfortunately, and when my fellow workers discovered who I was, so much curiosity and comment was aroused that I was obliged to leave. During this time, however, I learned much about the cunningness, the deep common sense and sense of humour of the Russian peasants.

During the war, in those provinces menaced by the Germans, the numerous church bells in the towns and villages had been moved to the capital to prevent them from falling into the hands of the enemy. The Germans, so badly in need of metals, would melt them down and reforge them into armaments. Now that the war was over, delegations of peasants were coming to Moscow from remote villages to get back their church bells. Because of the lack of fuel and the general disorganization of transportation, these journeys sometimes lasted for weeks. The peasants travelled in unheated freight-cars, sometimes even on the roof of a train. After reaching Moscow, they could expect only continued cold and hunger, and they were faced with the same torturous journey back to their homes.

In dealing with these delegations I found that not one of the men would admit that he, himself, was concerned either with the church or religion, and when I asked why they had not waited until the bells could be returned by the government, they would usually reply to the effect that "we have so many backward old women in the village who still care about such things." Some of them would anticipate my questions in advance and would hasten to assure me, "If all were like myself and family, the bells could remain where they are"; or, "We could wait, of course, but how would it be in case of fire or some other need for an alarm?"

In their shrewd and humble way they were adapting themselves to the new régime. They spoke now as though they had always been Bolsheviks, were perfectly at home in the new régime, and already understood all the new laws—and how to evade them.

During this period of work in the Commissariat my attention was attracted by the complaints of two such pilgrims who had travelled for three weeks in cold and hunger to reach Moscow. It had then taken them three days to find out where to apply.

"Is this the way we are received in our Republic?" they grumbled. "We have had to sleep on the streets because the 'Peasant House' of which we have heard so much, is overcrowded. And now we hear nothing but 'Come back tomorrow.' Our village has been very loyal to the Soviet government and we did not come here just because of the church bells. We want also to see Lenin or Kalinin, so that we can describe to them the conditions in our *gubernja*."

"But," one of them added, sighing, "it is the same old story. It is as difficult to see Lenin or Kalinin as Nicholas II."

"But can't you imagine how busy our comrades are here?" I asked them. "If you will call the day after tomorrow, at the first Soviet House, Room 103, I shall try to arrange an appointment with Kalinin. Lenin is not here just now."

"Are you not Comrade Balabanoff?" the younger peasant asked me. "I was a war prisoner in Germany and I heard of your Zimmerwald work there."

I offered them tea and apologized for the lack of bread, as there was neither bread nor sugar in Moscow at this time.

"What a pity we did not know you had no bread! We could have brought you some *suchari* (dry black bread) from our village."

Two days later, I took them to the Kremlin and was surprised at their interest in the art treasures there. There was not a shade of humility in their approach to these works of art which were now a part of their own heritage. After their brief visit with Kalinin, they came to thank me.

"Our journey has not been in vain," they assured me. "If only all the visitors were treated as we have been!"

Late in the year we had received word in Moscow that the English Labour Party had issued a call for an international Socialist and Labour Congress to be held in Paris or Bern. To Lenin and the other Bolsheviks the call was the signal for the post-war revival of the hated Second International. It was also the signal for the immediate launching of that new Third International for which Lenin had fought at Zimmerwald and Kienthal and which now, in his moment of triumph and world acclaim, he was in a position to push through. The revival of the Second International, or at least the reaffiliation with it of the Left Wing elements, must be prevented and the leadership of the Russian movement over these elements must be asserted at all costs. Even though a genuinely representative International Congress could not possibly be held in Russia at this time, it was necessary that some sort of preliminary gathering be announced to offset the effect of the Social Democratic call.

On January 24th Chicherin sent out, by radio, an invitation to an international Left Wing gathering to be held in Moscow early in March. It denounced the convention proposed by the English party as a "gathering of the enemies of working class," and asked all "friends of the Third Revolutionary International" to refuse to participate. The manifesto which had been written by Trotsky, ended with the call: "Under the banner of Workers' Councils, of the revolutionary fight for power and the dictatorship of the proletariat, under the banner of the Third International, workers of all countries, unite!"

The organization of a new International had been implicit in the victory of the October Revolution. The proposal of an obscure *émigré* group in Switzerland had become by 1919 the order of the day. The period was one of revolutionary disturbances in Germany, Austria, Hungary, and Finland, and of profound industrial unrest even in the Allied nations. Half of Europe, at least, seemed ripe for social revolution under determined leadership. In the rest of the world the revolutionary vanguard was inspired by the Russian success. If I was more realistic in my appraisal of the labour movement in Western Europe than the Bolshevik leaders, I was no less convinced than they that the time for a new international alignment was at hand. It did not occur to me—nor to other Left Wing Socialists at this time—that my concept of this new alignment had little relation to what Lenin, Trotsky, Zinoviev and the other Bolshevik leaders had in mind. This fact was not to be completely clarified until the second Congress of the Comintern in 1920.

Looking back upon this period—1918 to 1920—I came to realize later to what extent the mechanics of Bolshevik strategy were obscured by the enthusiasm and solidarity of that time. We lived in a world besieged by blockade and counter-revolution, in which the conquests of October were threatened on a dozen fronts. Confidence in our own solidarity and in the wisdom, integrity, and courage of our leadership was as much a psychological necessity as confidence in the Revolution itself. It was no time to anticipate or to worry over difficulties and details or to heckle over small deceits.

It was shortly after this, however, that I made my first protest over what I then considered an isolated "mistake."

I heard that Radek was organizing foreign sections of the "Communist Party," with headquarters in the Commissariat of Foreign Affairs. When I went there to investigate, I found that this widely heralded achievement was a fake. The members of these sections were practically all war prisoners in Russia: most of them had joined the Party recently because of the favour and privileges which membership involved. Practically none of them had had any contact with the revolutionary or labour movement in their own countries, and knew nothing of Socialist principles. Radek was grooming them to return to their native countries, where they were to "work for the Soviet Union." Two of these prisoners—Italians from Trieste—were about to return to Italy with special credentials from Lenin and a large sum of money. I had only to talk with them for a few moments in Italian to understand that they knew nothing of the Italian movement, or even of the elementary terminology of Socialism. I decided to go direct to Lenin with my protest.

"Vladimir Ilyitch," I said, after I had described the situation,

"I advise you to get back your money and credentials. These men are merely profiteers of the Revolution. They will damage us seriously in Italy."

His reply fell like a stone upon my spirit.

"For the destruction of Turati's party," he answered, "they are quite good enough."

This was my first intimation that Lenin's attitude towards the non-Bolshevik sections of the movement was that of a military strategist to whom the demoralization of the "enemy" is a commonplace of war. It is taken for granted that the instruments of such demoralization must be men devoid of scruples and more important—professional calumniators. (The new International was to breed these last like flies.) Yesterday, the enemy had been an impersonal system of exploitation; it had now become the right wing of the labour movement itself. Tomorrow it was to be the dissident Left Wing Socialists who questioned in any detail the Moscow formula; in time, after Lenin's death, it would be the Old Bolsheviks themselves. By 1937 the October Revolution would be liquidated in the name of "Leninism" and the cycle would be complete.

A few weeks after this conversation with Lenin, complaints arrived from our Italian comrades that the two emissaries had spent the money entrusted to them in the cafés and brothels of Milan.

Early in February, 1919, Lenin sent for me and asked me to go to Kiev to assist Racovsky who was then acting as the president of the People's Commissars for Ukraine—a position analogous to that of Lenin in Russia proper. In theory, the Bolsheviks had set up an independent republic in the Ukraine. In actuality that section of it in which Soviet rule had been established was completely dominated by the Moscow régime. I was to take over from Racovsky the work of Commissar of Foreign Affairs, and in this capacity as well as in that of Zimmerwald secretary I was to function again as a link with the outside world. In the Ukraine it would be easier to maintain contact with Central Europe, even though the internal and military situation was so unsettled.

Shortly before I left Moscow, word came of the brutal murder of Liebknecht and Luxemburg by the German army officers.

17

THE LAUNCHING OF THE NEW INTERNATIONAL which was to become an object of terror throughout the world in the next few years took place in one of the rooms of the Kremlin early in March, just a month after the close of the Bern conference. At Bern, serious differences had arisen between the Right and Centre delegates, particularly on the subject of Russia and the Bolsheviks and the reconstitution of the Second International. Several of the Socialist parties—the Italian, Swiss, Serbian, Rumanian, and American had not been represented at all. But the Right Wing had predominated and the methods of "dictatorship," as employed in Russia, had been decisively condemned.

I was barely settled in Kiev when Racovsky and I were summoned back to Moscow for the Communist Conference—Racovsky to act as representative of the Revolutionary Social Democratic Federation of the Balkans and I as the secretary of

Zimmerwald. The meeting had already begun when we arrived, and as I sat through the second day's session it seemed to me that not even the long and impressive speeches of Lenin, Trotsky, and Zinoviev were able to lift the occasion to the level of an historic event; as I looked about the room at the delegates and guests, I had an intimation of what was amiss. There was something artificial about the gathering which defeated the spirit in which it had been called. (Arthur Ransome, the English journalist who was present on this occasion, later remarked on this "make believe side to the whole affair.") Most of the thirty-five delegates and fifteen guests had been hand-picked by the Russian Central Committee from so-called "Communist parties" in those smaller "nations" which had formerly comprised the Russian Empire, such as Esthonia, Latvia, Lithuania, Ukraine, and Finland; or they were war prisoners or foreign radicals who happened to be in Russia at this time. This situation was due in part to the blockade, transportation difficulties, and the haste with which the meeting had been prepared. Holland, the Socialist Propaganda League of America (made up mostly of Slavic immigrants) and the Japanese Communists, were represented by a Dutch-American engineer named Rutgers who had once spent a few months in Japan; England by a Russian *émigré* named Feinberg on Chicherin's staff; Hungary by a war prisoner who later escaped with a large sum of money. Jacques Sadoul, who had come to Russia in 1918 as an attaché of the French military mission and who had stayed to throw in his lot with the Bolsheviks, had been suggested as a French representative, but possibly because the Bolsheviks were not sure of his vote, another delegate was produced. Word had come that Guilbeaux, the "anti-militarist" editor, was on his way to Russia in an unofficial capacity, and I learnt on my arrival in Moscow that a special train had been sent to the border to meet him and to rush him to the Congress in time to vote. He was to act as representative of the French "Left Wing," and in that capacity he was granted five votes. I was astonished and disgusted at this news, but after my previous conversation with Lenin on the subject of Guilbeaux, I knew it would be useless to protest. (Guilbeaux has since become a violent nationalist in France.) The Swiss delegate was

Platten who had arranged with the German government for Lenin's return to Russia, who had accompanied him on the so-called "sealed train," and who had been in Russia ever since. Boris Reinstein, of the American Socialist Labour Party who had also come to Russia in 1917, declined to act, except in a fraternal capacity, on the grounds that he had no credentials from his party. In fact, the only duly elected delegate from Western Europe was a young German named Eberlein, who represented the Spartacus Union, which had been led by Liebknecht and Luxemburg.

The Præsidium, with Lenin in the centre, flanked by Eberlein and Platten on either side, sat on a raised dais at one end of the room. On the wall behind them was a huge red banner inscribed with the slogan, "Long live the Third International!" The gathering had been called presumably as a preliminary conference, and on the first day, when it became obvious that the meeting represented little more than the Slavic parties, opposition had developed to the immediate formation of the International. It was Eberlein, the German delegate, who had protested most vigorously when it was proposed by the Russians that the gathering constitute itself the first Congress of the Third International. He declared that he would not commit himself to any formula that had not been first approved by the membership of his organization. In view of this opposition from a German Sparticist, representing the only real Communist Party in Western Europe at this time, the proposal was decisively defeated.

I knew that the Bolsheviks were eager to establish the continuity of the new International with the war-time Zimmerwald movement and then to liquidate what was left of the latter. When this matter came up, after the lengthy reports of the various delegates on conditions in their own countries—conditions on which most of them had no first-hand information—a proposal was made that as Zimmerwald secretary, I formally transfer the functions and documents of Zimmerwald to the new International. This proposal was contained in a declaration signed by Lenin, Trotsky, Racovsky, Zinoviev, and Platten, as representatives of the "Zimmerwald Left." After denouncing the

"Centrist" elements of Zimmerwald as "pacifists and wavering elements," it declared:

The Zimmerwald Union has outlived its purpose. All that was really revolutionary in it goes over to the Communist International.

The subjoined signatories—declare that they consider the Zimmerwald organization as liquidated and they beg the Bureau of the Zimmerwald Conference to hand over all its documents to the Executive Committee of the Third International.

In refusing to comply with this request, I explained to the delegates that I had no authority to transfer the Zimmerwald documents without consulting its affiliates. I realized fully that Zimmerwald was liquidated in fact. It had been created by the World War for a specific purpose, and now that the war was ended, that purpose no longer existed. New conditions had arisen which demanded a new instrument of struggle. While I believed that most of the groups and individuals associated with Zimmerwald were in complete sympathy with Soviet Russia, the conditions under which this preliminary conference had been called—the transportation difficulties, the failure to obtain passports—had precluded their representation. Until they had an opportunity to consider and act upon its program, I had no right as the secretary of Zimmerwald to act in their name.

Though some of the Bolsheviks were annoyed by this display of "legalistic" squeamishness on my part, they merely passed a resolution to the effect that "the First Congress of the Communist International resolves that the Zimmerwald agreement be liquidated."

Though the proposal that the meeting inaugurate the new International had been defeated the day before, a fortuitous circumstance had in the meanwhile changed the entire tone and complexion of the gathering. In the very midst of one of the sessions an Austrian ex-war prisoner who had spent several months in Russia before returning to his native land, arrived on the scene. Breathless, full of emotion and bearing all the marks of an adventurous journey, he asked for and was given the floor. He had just returned from Western Europe, he reported, and in every country he had visited since he left Russia, capitalism was disintegrating, the masses on the verge of revolt. In Austria and Germany, particularly, the revolution was at hand. Everywhere, the masses were fascinated and inspired by the Russian Revolution, and in the approaching upheaval they were looking to Moscow to lead the way.

The convention was immediately electrified by this over-optimistic—though probably sincere—report. Four delegates took the floor and proposed a resolution for the immediate launching of the Third International and the drafting of its program. Eberlein continued to protest in the name of his party, but he was overruled. The resolution was passed. The Third International was born! Immediately after this, Lenin, Trotsky, Zinoviev, Racovsky, and Platten were chosen as the members of its first Bureau. I had refused to vote on the ground that I had no mandate from Zimmerwald to do so.

The following sessions were marked by a far more optimistic and combative spirit. The Bolsheviks were jubilant now that their long-cherished dream had been fulfilled. The new Communist Manifesto, drafted and presented by members of the Bureau, denounced both the Right and the Centre of World Socialism, declared that the imperialist war was passing into civil war, and called upon the workers of the world to "flock to the banner of workmen's councils and fight the revolutionary fight for the power and dictatorship of the proletariat."

Though I had discounted much of the report of the Austrian visitor, I too was caught up in the general enthusiasm in which the International was finally launched. In the midst of the speeches and felicitations, Lenin passed me a note which read:

"Please take the floor and announce the affiliation of the Italian Socialist Party to the Third International."

I replied on the same scrap of paper:

"I can't do it. I am not in touch with them. There is no question of their loyalty, but they must speak for themselves."

Another note came back immediately.

"You have to. You are their official representative for Zimmerwald. You read *Avanti* and you know what is going on in Italy."

This time I merely looked at him and shook my head.

I did have credentials—though not as a delegate to the Congress—from the Italian Party. I knew the sentiment of its majority and probably its Executive would be willing that I should speak in its name. But—this was a technical, a political right, not a moral one. What did I know of the immediate problems confronting the Party members in Italy or what effect such an announcement on my part, in Moscow, would have upon the Party situation in Rome and Milan, where the post-war reaction, following upon the war-time persecution of the Party, was at its height? No, they had the right to make their own decisions and to publicize them when and how they saw fit. Here in Russia, where the Revolution was victorious, where we were protected by the might of the Red army, what right had we to commit our comrades in capitalist countries to the resolutions we were passing, or to demand that they should apply them without an opportunity to see or discuss them?

When the Congress formally adjourned at the end of the third day's session, I decided to return to the Ukraine immediately. Meeting Trotsky as I was leaving the hall, I bade him good-bye.

"Good-bye? What do you mean?" he asked. "Don't you know that you are to be the secretary of the International? It has been discussed and Lenin is of the opinion that no one but you should have this position."

As we spoke, he led me into the small Kremlin hall where Lenin was sitting. I was both amazed and overwhelmed by this unwelcome suggestion. I realized immediately why I had been chosen, in spite of the evidence I had given in Stockholm and even at the Congress itself of what the Bolsheviks probably considered political "naïveté." Among the anti-war, Left Wing forces whom the new International was courting, my name was synonymous with Zimmerwald and with the prestige of Italian Socialism. As an active leader in the European Socialist and Labour movement for nearly twenty years, I had the confidence of working-class groups which still looked upon the Bolsheviks, and upon a new International with a certain distrust. I do not mean that I was fully aware, or even suspected, that I was to be used as a "front" for the Comintern Executive. I did understand, however, that my appointment as secretary had a definite political significance. There were other reasons why the appointment was unwelcome. As long as the international movement was operating under the difficult and tragic circumstances created by the war, it had never occurred to me to refuse my share of its work and responsibility. Now that it could function freely and legally in a country where Socialism had triumphed, I preferred to realize the aspiration of many years—to work with and for the Russian masses, as I had just begun to do in the Ukraine. There were plenty of Bolsheviks in Moscow who could function as secretary of the Third International.

I was prepared to explain all this to Lenin and Trotsky, but I hardly had time to voice my first objection to Lenin when he interrupted me. Closing one of his eyes as usual, when he wished to speak categorically, he replied:

"Party discipline exists for you too, dear comrade. The Central Committee has decided." (When Lenin had decided something before the Central Committee had ratified his decision, he usually anticipated their action in this fashion so as to avoid superfluous discussion.)

I knew it would be useless to argue.

When I returned to my hotel a few minutes after this conversation with Lenin I received the confirmation of my appointment by telephone.

"Comrade Balabanoff, this is a message from the Executive Committee. You have been nominated general secretary of the Third International. Comrade Racovsky has been informed by Vladimir Ilyitch that the supreme interest of the movement requires your presence here and that you can't return to the Ukraine."

That same evening the inauguration of the new International was celebrated in the largest hall in Moscow, and amid the general enthusiasm, all my doubts and hesitations of the past three days were swept away. I was particularly fêted at the gathering and for a few moments I felt profoundly happy. The optimistic speeches of the foreign representatives (or those who were supposed to be representatives), the overwhelming enthusiasm of the workers who listened to my translation of their words, the revolutionary songs of defiance and victory, as well as those which recalled the heroes and martyrs of the past—how could one resist the infection of the occasion? We were all carried away by our emotions. It was one of the few moments in my life when it seemed to me that I had not lived in vain. Here was the result of the tenacity of the Zimmerwald movement—the ties of international brotherhood had been renewed. I was almost grateful to Lenin and Trotsky for having induced me to accept the nomination and for having given me the opportunity thus to serve the international working class again.

If I had been a little less enthusiastic on this occasion, or if I had understood more fully the tactical and psychological approach of the Party I had joined, I would have realized even then that the latter would make my collaboration with the Bolsheviks impossible.

The following day, Borodine, whom I had known in both Sweden and Moscow, presented me with a list of the equipment I was to ask for in connexion with my new position—a separate building, assistants, a staff of secretaries, furniture, various office machinery, private cars. I felt frightened and oppressed by these exterior accompaniments of privilege and officeholding. I had already been shocked by the display and theatricality of public life in revolutionary Russia (the Bolsheviks seemed to be masters of stage direction) which seemed to me unsuited to the Revolution's proletarian character.

I spoke to Lenin on the subject, hoping that he would help to protect me from these material complications.

"Vladimir Ilyitch," I told him, "I should like my office to remain as it is—in my own two rooms. I do not need a separate building. Please promise me that there will be no bureaucratic trappings about our office."

"Don't worry," he replied. "No one will interfere with you." Then he added, "We have appointed a counsellor to help you in your complicated relations with other countries—Comrade Vorovsky."

"Vorovsky!" I exclaimed. "You could not have made a better choice." I was delighted to hear that I was to work with Vorovsky again.

Just before I left, Lenin remarked, "I hope you will not

[219]

create any difficulties for us in regard to those with whom you must collaborate."

I did not know at this time to whom he was referring. A few days later, when Vorovsky came to the first meeting of the Comintern Bureau, which took place in my room, he remarked:

"You know Angelica, you have one bad—or good—quality. You know too much about the members of the international movement, and if you disapprove of them morally, or object to them personally, you don't wish to work with them."

"You are perfectly right," I answered. "But knowing that, why did they nominate me for secretary?"

"Because of your international prestige," he replied.

Shortly after this I was told that Zinoviev had been appointed chairman of the International. I understood then the meaning of Lenin's remarks.

It is difficult to write frankly of a man who has died the most disgraceful of deaths—execution by a revolutionary power on charges of treachery and counter-revolution. Now that those who trembled before him and flattered him have joined his calumniators, it is not so easy to express my opinion of him as it was when, for doing so, these very same people—and Zinoviev himself—branded me a "counter-revolutionary."

After Mussolini, whom I knew still better and over a longer period, I consider Zinoviev the most despicable individual I have ever met. But not even this fact, the cowardly charges of his enemies or his own "confession" can convince me that he and his co-defendants were guilty of the crimes of which they were accused. The background of such frame-ups and confessions was developed under Zinoviev himself and they were implicit in the development of the Bolshevik method, the Leninist strategy, since the Revolution. No one who watched that development as I did in its early period can be surprised at its inevitable fruits. Within the confines of the revolutionary movement itself, the Bolshevik leaders were *capable of anything* to achieve their own political and factional ends, but *none of them was capable of counter-revolutionary conspiracy with the class enemy*. If a tribunal existed for the judgment and punishment of those who have damaged and dishonoured the labour movement, who have killed its spirit, who have been responsible for the moral and sometimes the physical extinction of its best militants, both Zinoviev and Stalin would head the list of those condemned. But the tribunal which sentenced Zinoviev for betrayal, for so-called Trotskyism, knew that they were condemning a man who was merely the victim of manœuvres as unscrupulous as his own.

I had first observed Zinoviev in action at Zimmerwald. I had noted then that whenever there was an unfair factional manœuvre to be carried out, a revolutionary reputation to be undermined, Lenin would charge Zinoviev with the task. I don't remember having exchanged a single word of personal conversation with him during the intervening years, but when I came to Russia he had begun to flatter me, to use me for the *mise en scène* he was attempting to create and which I hated so profoundly. "This is the comrade," he would say, when introducing me to a large crowd in Petrograd or Moscow, "to whom we owe so much. It was she and Comrade Serrati who contributed most to the internationalist position of the Italian Party during the war and to its support of our Revolution." He wished to use me to work up the enthusiasm of the audience, which would, of course, applaud frantically.

Now Lenin had put this master of intrigue and calumny, to whom the end justified any means, in charge of the organization that was to cleanse and solidify the revolutionary forces of the world!

I have often been asked how it was possible for Lenin, who knew Zinoviev so thoroughly, to protect and reward him as long as he lived. I can only answer that in his collaboration with Zinoviev, as in his general strategy, Lenin was guided by what he believed to be the supreme interest of the Revolution. He knew that he had in Zinoviev a reliable and docile tool and he never doubted for a moment his own ability to control that tool to the advantage of the Revolution. Zinoviev was an interpreter and executor of the will of others, and his personal shrewdness, ambiguity, and dishonesty made it possible for him to discharge these duties more effectively than could a more scrupulous man. Lenin was more concerned that his decisions be made effective than with the manner in which they were carried out. It was his fundamental psychological error that he did not foresee what would happen to the Revolution when these means became the end; that he failed to understand that his own famous *raison d'état*—"The Proletarian State is justified in any compromise it makes, provided that power is maintained"—would serve as a shield for the failure or corruption of those who spoke in the name of the Proletarian State. I have a feeling that Lenin had some intimation of all this before the end of his life and it may have been because of certain misgivings on this score that he wrote the letter or "Testament" which has been so widely quoted by Trotskyists and denied by Stalinists in the past few years. (Trotsky, by the way, refused to admit its authenticity while he was still a member of the Communist Party.)

After Zinoviev assumed office we came into conflict almost immediately. The man was so accustomed to lying and cheating that he could not understand why I should attempt to establish some factual basis for our work. At first, the meetings of the Executive continued to take place in my room. Then Zinoviev's demand for a "headquarters" became insistent and his choice fell upon the former German Embassy, one of the few large houses where the furnishings had been kept intact and in perfect order. Knowing my friendliness with many of the German and Austrian Socialists, I was urged by the Executive to write and ask them to have their Soviets authorize the use of this building as the headquarters of the Third International.

I considered it presumptuous to ask the German comrades for the building which the Soviets had given to them and I was reluctant to write. I did so, however, at the insistence of the Executive, and the building was ours.

I was surprised to find that the topics of discussion at our Executive meetings had so little relation to the work we had been elected to do. (Later, when I discovered that our meetings were mere formalities and that real authority rested with a secret Party Committee, I was to understand the reason for this.) I had decided to dedicate all my energy to the building up of the new International and I had conceived of our work as that of strengthening and solidifying the Left Wing forces throughout the world—not by artificial stimulation or by the wrecking of existing movements, but by propaganda and comradely aid. I knew that their respect could only be won by the quality of our program and the superiority of our leadership. But it soon became obvious that Zinoviev and the rest of the Bolsheviks had other methods in mind—methods which I considered as dangerous to Russia as to the labour movement abroad—the effects of which were to become obvious within the next two years. Why bother to win the loyalty of a party or a union movement when it was so much easier for the Bolshevists to wreck it and create from its ruins a docile sect, dependent for its very existence upon the Comintern? Why discuss methods, confront honest differences of opinion, when with the resources of the nation behind them, it was so much easier to discredit their more formidable opponents, to buy off the less scrupulous and weaker? I was not fully aware of all this during these early months as secretary of the Comintern. The worst of its abuses developed gradually within the coming year.

I was most disturbed at this time and during the coming year to find how many of our agents and representatives were individuals long discredited in the labour movement abroad. They were chosen because they had nothing in common with the labour movement and could, therefore, obey the most contradictory and outrageous orders quite mechanically and with no sense of responsibility. Adventurers, opportunists, even former Red-baiters, all were grist to Zinoviev's mill. They departed on secret missions, supplied with enormous sums—and as emissaries of Moscow to the revolutionary workers abroad, they moved in the reflected glory of the October Revolution. If the prestige of their mission impressed thousands of the faithful, the power and money which emanated from them attracted new opportunists on every hand. The arbitrary creation of new parties, and new labour movements during 1919 and 1920 (especially after the Red Trade Union International was formed), had behind it the facilities and resources which only the control of a governmental apparatus can provide. Expensive agencies with numerous personnel were established overnight. The International became a bureaucratic apparatus before a real Communist movement was born.

I think that Zinoviev determined to get rid of me somehow, soon after my first protest. I learned that my name was being used on documents and appeals which I had never seen. These documents emanated from Zinoviev and were, of course, approved by Lenin. When I complained about this, Zinoviev's replies were evasive. The Executive had made the decision informally, they had intended to consult me, of course; as a disciplined Party member, I would accept these decisions; and so on. It was the secret Party Committee, not the Comintern Executive, that had met "informally" and issued statements in my name. But I was still far from suspecting all that was going on. My name was still necessary to the Comintern, but my participation in its deliberations was an embarrassment.

In the middle of the summer, Zinoviev made a glowing report of expansion at one of the Executive meetings.

"Since our movement is spreading so rapidly," he reported, "we should create another office of the International in the Ukraine. Comrade Balabanoff should be in charge of it and Racovsky and Sadoul can help her."

Though not yet suspecting the motive for this suggestion, I was surprised and annoyed.

"Why should I leave Moscow again?" I asked. "I am secretary of the International and this is our headquarters."

Zinoviev continued to insist, and the other members backed him up. I decided to talk the matter over with Lenin. He too advised me to go.

"The Ukraine is the most important issue in our fight just now," he said. "Why should we keep all our best speakers in Moscow?"

As I was leaving for the Ukraine, I met Bela Kun, returning from Hungary where the short-lived Soviet Republic had been overthrown with the help of the Rumanian army. I had heard so much of Kun's devious personal and political record, that I had been surprised, on returning to Moscow, to hear that he had been sent to Hungary to "make a revolution." The mere fact that the man was said to be a drug addict seemed to me sufficient reason for not trusting him with revolutionary responsibilities. This first meeting with him confirmed my most disagreeable impressions. His very appearance was repulsive. Yet the Bolsheviks, including Stalin, were to make use of him until 1937.

18

MOSCOW IN 1919 AND 1920 WAS A PEACEFUL haven compared with the Ukraine. This rich and fertile country had become a volcano, constantly erupting with civil and international wars, accompanied by White and Red terror, pogroms, typhus epidemics, and the complete disorganization of its industrial and agricultural life. Some parts of the Ukraine had changed governments fourteen times since 1917. Conquests and evacuations followed in rapid succession as nationalists, Germans, Poles, Bolsheviks, White generals, guerrilla rebels moved back and forth. The Ukrainian nationalists had struggled against both Kerensky and the Bolsheviks. After Brest-Litovsk, the Germans had dissolved the Ukrainian Rada and put Hetman Skoropadsky in command. After the German defeat, Petlura had triumphed, only to be driven back by the combined forces of the rebels, the peasants and the Red Army. The struggle with Denikin followed and after his defeat, the Bolsheviks again gained an insecure control. The organization and disci-

[225]

pline of the Red Army in the Ukraine were very inferior to that of Central Russia; but it was given effective assistance by the guerrilla bands of Ukrainian peasants and soldiers not under Bolshevik control, and by a sort of "international brigade" made up partly of Bolshevik sympathizers and partly of self-seeking adventurers from various countries.

This was the situation in which Racovsky had been functioning as president of the Commissars since he was chosen for that office by Lenin early in the year. In the Ukraine this office required even more personal courage, energy, and diplomacy than in Russia. Racovsky was not a Russian, he knew little of the traditions and conditions of the Russian population, and before the war he had never been a Bolshevik; yet Lenin's choice of Racovsky for this particular position indicated that Lenin knew how to choose the right man for the right place.

Born in a wealthy Rumanian family, Racovsky had early been attracted by western culture and had gone to Switzerland, where he had studied medicine and had come into contact with Plekhanoff, Axelrod, and other Russian Marxists. Returning to Rumania and Bulgaria, where he worked among the peasants, he soon gave up the medical profession and devoted himself entirely to the revolutionary movement. His exceptional brilliance and wide culture had made him one of the most distinguished figures on the Executive of the Second International.

It was probably the fact that he was far more versatile and adaptable than the typical Russian Bolshevik that influenced Lenin's appointment of Racovsky to the highest office in the Ukraine. Lenin's choice of such former Mensheviks as Trotsky and Racovsky as his collaborators, after his rise to power, proves that where the interest of the Revolution was concerned he was not a fanatical and inflexible factionalist. Once these brilliant men had demonstrated their devotion to the Revolution and the Bolshevik Party, Lenin acted as though he had forgotten their Menshevik approach of the past. The fate of these two men who rendered such matchless service to the Soviet Republic is a symbol of the history of Bolshevism itself. Several years later, Racovsky was forced to write or sign a shameful repudiation of

[226]

his friend and comrade, Trotsky, in order to save his own life. This capitulation, like that of the other Bolshevik leaders—in both the Left and the Right Oppositions to Stalin—merely postponed his fate. In the purges of early 1938, he was sentenced to twenty-five years imprisonment—a sentence which means death.

Racovsky and I had become friends as members of the Executive of the Second International. We remained friends until I began openly to criticize and oppose the Bolshevik tactics. Then, guided by that military solidarity which dominated the Bolshevik leaders, he would try to convince me that I was wrong, even when he knew that I was right. Like many other honest revolutionaries, he probably believed that after the civil war a change would take place and the abuses of the "War Communism" period would be overcome.

The work with Racovsky was a welcome change from Moscow. Here our work was as real as it was physically and emotionally exhausting. There were fewer experienced and reliable people in the Party, and less time for display and theatrical demonstrations. In Moscow, I had been treated like a prima donna, permitted to appear or to speak only on the more important occasions. In my office I had been made a figurehead. Once when I had asked Lunarcharsky to let me help him in the educational activities of his Commissariat, he had replied: "But you can't expect us to give you a subordinate job!"

Because of the intensity of the military situation, the general disorganization, Racovsky was overwhelmed by his various responsibilities. Besides acting as secretary of the Comintern, I was obliged to substitute for him as Ukrainian Commissar of Foreign Affairs. As propagandist for the government among a people so confused and divided in their political loyalties and yet so eager to learn, I addressed meetings every day and night.

Because of the unsettled political and military situation, espionage and repression practised by the Cheka were far worse than in Central Russia. Thousands of the intellectuals and former bourgeois had fled to the Ukraine from Moscow and Petrograd to escape political persecution. Mensheviks, Socialist Revolutionists, and Anarchists in the Ukraine were caught

[227]

between the Red Terror and the White. In addition, the country was a hot-bed of plotting White officers and interventionist agents. Many of the peasants of the countryside who had united with the workers against Denikin and Petlura were as opposed to the methods of the Bolsheviks as to those of the Whites, the Germans, and the Poles. Many of them were imbued with Social Revolutionist and even Anarchist traditions and were consequently hostile to political dictatorships. They had flocked to the standards of local leaders, like the Ukrainian Anarchist, Nestor Makhno, whenever they were threatened from the Right or the Left.

The condition of the general population was little better than that of the prisoners in the concentration camps. The suffering and tragedies of these people will remain with me to the end of my life. The rooms in the house in which I lived with the staff of the International were crowded day and night with despairing and desperate people of many nationalities—people who were hungry and ill, people mistreated or menaced by the Cheka, others who had friends or relatives in prison or in the work camps. The sufferings they had undergone at the hands of the various invaders were incredible. I suffered as much from the misery and injustice at which I guessed as from that of which I was told. I did what I could to alleviate this misery and to remedy specific injustices, but I realized how inadequate were my efforts.

Because of them, however, legends arose and survived about my activity in the Ukraine. Racovsky was unwittingly responsible for some of these stories, as, in order to tease me, he would tell exaggerated and witty tales of how I attempted to open all the jails in the Ukraine and how I was capable of ruining the state's finances in an effort to feed all who applied for help. Later, years after I had been expelled from the Party, people who did not accept the official statement of the Russian Central Committee *did* accept the explanation that I had been "too soft-hearted" to understand the necessities of the Revolution and Terror. I feel that this judgment is almost as false as the official one. I had never tried to help any one out of "soft-heartedness" alone. My sensitiveness to human suffering has probably been

[228]

the dominant factor in my emotional and intellectual development—my childhood rebeliion, my break with my family, my devotion to the revolutionary movement. But in this there has never been any conflict between my heart and my brain. Since I left Russia I have met a number of people who have reminded me that I once saved them, or the lives of those near to them. In doing this I had never subordinated to my individual feelings the interests of the Revolution.

After I left Petrograd for Stockholm in 1917, I had had no contact with my own family. This was not merely because I had so little in common with them, but also because I feared at that time that my political activities would get them into trouble. After the October Revolution I thought of them more frequently; they were no longer members of a privileged class, they were defeated people. I guessed also that they were in need, because I knew that they were neither shrewd nor bold enough to survive by illegal means. Not having the courage to face human suffering unless I am able to help alleviate it, I had avoided any opportunity to get in touch with them. The situation was more complicated than otherwise in the case of my relatives, because as an influential member of the party in power I did have the political power to alter their lot. Morally, I felt that it was impossible to do so. When I thought of them after the Revolution, I remembered that they were not the only ones to expiate the injustices of which the Revolution was the result. Though I had used my influence more than once for people who were strangers to me, I felt that to use it in behalf of my own people would damage the prestige of the Revolution in the eyes of those who would hear about it. These people would say: "See, the difference is not so great. Before the Revolution, the Romanoffs could interfere in behalf of their relatives and friends, now the Balabanoffs can do the same." It seemed to me that it was just such similarities between the old and the new régime that would discourage enthusiasm during the terrible period of transition.

The fact that my relatives in Petrograd, like so many of the bourgeois refugees, had gone to Odessa in order to be nearer Turkey in case the Bolsheviks triumphed in the Ukraine, had spared me the necessity for such decisions.

Then suddenly one morning in Kiev, I received a long-distance telephone call from Lenin in Moscow.

"Comrade Balabanoff," he said, "I beg you to leave at once for Odessa. The situation at the front is precarious. We must have a new campaign for the mobilization of the youth. The population must be encouraged and inspired with enthusiasm for this new sacrifice. Our best speakers must be rushed there. Comrade Joffe will accompany you and join you in the campaign."

The mention of Odessa made me shudder; it reminded me of my relatives. I felt somehow that a terrible experience awaited me there. I knew that if I told Lenin or Racovsky why I did not wish to go, they might understand and release me. Yet, it was impossible for me to make such a plea. A day or two later Joffe, former ambassador to Germany, arrived from Moscow and we left in a special train for Odessa.

Of all the cities and towns I had visited since the October Revolution, Odessa made the most painful impression. Disorganization and starvation were even more evident than in Kiev. Far from the centre of the Revolution and lacking the industrial population which impresses its discipline and vigour upon the social atmosphere, even under such conditions, it seemed like a wraith of that beautiful seashore city which in normal times had been so animated. Though in the midst of the most fertile zone in Russia, it was suffering as acutely from the shortage of food as the rest of the Ukraine. A part of the population, mostly the young Jewish artisans, was loyal to the Bolsheviks and full of enthusiasm. But the new government was not yet sufficiently well established to organize the ration system of food distribution that prevailed in Moscow and other Russian cities or to prevent speculation. In order to get food, one had to enjoy the special privileges of a party member or functionary, or one had to buy it illegally. Being as much opposed to one method as the other, I would have starved had not some of the Soviet officials insisted on bringing me some canned food. There was no bread to be had, no tea, nor any kind of fat. The physical strain of working under such conditions was as great as the emotional and nervous strain to which I was subjected daily by dozens of personal interviews, pleas, and complaints.

Early each morning the waiting-rooms of my office would be crowded with visitors who wished to see me in my capacity as Commissar of Foreign Affairs. With these interviews over, I had to take up my duties as secretary of the Third International. These would be interrupted by the necessity to rush off to four or five meetings. When I returned late at night, I was too exhausted to eat, even if there had been food.

One day, on my arrival at a meeting in an overcrowded hall, one of the enthusiastic young Communists who was awaiting my arrival announced:

"Comrade Balabanoff, there is a woman waiting to see you. She refused to go to your office."

My heart almost stopped beating as I guessed who it was. And yet, when I walked into the small waiting-room behind the stage, I did not recognize my sister. The old, trembling woman who stood there was dressed like a beggar, with a shawl covering her head. Until she spoke, I could scarcely believe that this was Anna. After we had stared at each other for a moment, and I had motioned to the young Communist to leave us alone, she began to speak rapidly, in a low, broken voice. She had learnt several days before that I was in Odessa, but she would never have come to me for help if it were not for the mobilization order. They had suffered hunger, privations of every sort, and she could stand everything but this—that her son should be mobilized to fight for the Bolsheviks! She would not complain or ask for anything, except that I should save him. Certainly I could do this much for a member of my family.

Inside the hall, I could hear the impatient calls of the audience: "We want Comrade Balabanoff! Long live Comrade Balabanoff!" I had come to this meeting to emphasize the need for mobilization, to arouse the enthusiasm of the youth to save Socialism in Russia in order that it might pave the way for freedom in the rest of the world. And here I was, myself immobilized by the living tragedy of this mother—my sister—who was so obsessed by the fear that her own son would be drafted that she could not think or complain of anything else.

I told her that I must go into the meeting and asked her to come to my rooms the following morning.

Her visit—at six o'clock the next morning—inaugurated one of the most painful weeks of my life. In retrospect, I ask myself how I could have resisted her pleas. She would come to my room each morning, trembling and weeping, and it was only incidentally that she told me how she and her husband and family were living. They all lived in one room in which there was no lighting—even candles were too difficult to obtain. In the morning she would wash the family linen (she was now over sixty) in cold water and would then attempt to dry it by the window when there was sun. They had had no heat during the winter and very little food. Her son had been obliged to give up his scientific writings, because their room was too dark for either reading or writing—he who had had one of the finest and most expensive of scientific libraries, who had never gone to a second-class hotel or worn ready-made clothes. All of this, however, was incidental to her terror that he would be mobilized into the Red army which he hated. This was all that she asked—that I should save him.

I think that from the beginning she realized that I would refuse to take advantage of my political position to grant her request. (How could I, who was urging working-class and peasant mothers to send their sons into the Red army, ask for the exemption of my own nephew?) In spite of this, however, she continued to come, and when she saw how little I had to eat, she sometimes brought me small bits of dried bread. Her monologue would last for hours—I could neither interrupt her nor make her understand that I had other work to do. Every few minutes we would be interrupted by some of my co-workers, or by people who were waiting to see me and who did not know who she was. She always came dressed like a beggar, as she was afraid that counter-revolutionary spies, or individuals who would join the counter-revolution as soon as it triumphed, would denounce her for having been in touch with me. Once I went with her and met the rest of the family. My brother-in-law was a broken and ageing man, but I was most deeply touched by the attitude of my nephew. He was only five years younger than I, we had grown up together, and though we differed so widely in temperament and interests, we had always respected each other's opinions. He was interested only in science and had been given every opportunity to develop his aptitudes. It was only during the war that he had begun, reluctantly, to work in the diplomatic field, and had become secretary to the Finance Minister, Count Witte. When I met him in Odessa it was only externals, his clothing and general appearance, that gave any evidence of what he had been through. I knew that he was agitated by our meeting, but he failed to show it; there was not a word of recrimination, of hostility or lament. His objections to Socialism—by this time to Bolshevism—were intellectual rather than emotional. He believed that the Bolsheviks had ruined Russia—his own ruin was incidental to that.

While we were talking I learned for the first time of an incident that occurred in Petrograd immediately after the October Revolution. My nephew had been arrested with the other members of the government, and when he was brought before the Bolshevik Commissar he had been asked whether or not he was related to Angelica Balabanoff. (My sister had married a cousin of ours and so our names were the same.) My nephew, who was too proud to accept any consideration because of his Communist aunt, even though his own life might be at stake, had denied any relationship to me. Soon after that the family had escaped to the Ukraine.

His sister's attitude toward the new régime was not so impersonal. Her hatred towards it was coloured by her bitterness over the loss of her own privileges. During her childhood and adolescence her mother had protected her from any contact with life—with the result that in spite of a keen and serious mind, she had developed into an unhappy and hysterical girl.

A year later, when I returned to the Ukraine with the Italian delegation, I heard that the family had escaped to Turkey. Several years after that, on meeting my nephew in Paris, I learned that my sister and her husband had died of starvation in Constantinople.

Shortly after my return to Kiev from Odessa I became involved in a situation which was to provide one of the most serious shocks to my Bolshevik illusions—the Pirro incident which

[233]

Alexander Berkman later described at some length in his book, *The Bolshevik Myth*.

During the summer a Count Pirro had come to Kiev as "Brazilian ambassador" to the Ukraine and had set up his headquarters in one of the more elaborate houses in the city. He made no secret of his antagonism to Bolshevism or his friendliness to those who were oppressed by the régime. In organizing his staff of secretaries and office workers, he made it clear that he would accept no Bolsheviks—a fact which attracted to the Embassy a large number of desperate people who could secure no employment under the government. A number of these were placed, and others were put on the waiting list. It was rumoured that Pirro had also agreed to give Brazilian passports to individuals who were trying to escape from the country.

During this period the Cheka, under Latsis, Extraordinary Commissioner at Kiev, was conducting a vigorous drive against money-hoarders and "speculators." Hundreds of people were rounded up and put into concentration camps, among them many poor Jews accused of speculation or of trying to leave the Ukraine. Foreigners were also obliged to pay a certain sum before they were permitted to leave, and as Commissar of Foreign Affairs I was attempting to have the workers among them—musicians, governesses, teachers, etc.—exempted from this tax. Again my offices were besieged by friends and relatives of the accused, seeking my intervention.

It was in my attempt to alleviate this situation and to save a few of the innocent, that I first learned of the activities of Pirro. The prisoners included a number of people who were accused of contact with Pirro, among them his own secretary. I learnt later that many of these prisoners were executed.

When I heard of Pirro's activities I went to Latsis.

"If any one is to be arrested because of contact with Pirro, why shouldn't you arrest Pirro himself? The man is obviously acting as a foreign agent; at least he should be expelled."

"We will take care of him," Latsis answered. But though Peters himself came down from the Moscow Cheka to supervise the work in Kiev, and though "conspirators" with Pirro continued to fall into the hands of the Cheka, nothing had happened

[234]

to Pirro himself when the advance of the Poles compelled our evacuation.

When I returned to Moscow I went to see Djersinsky, supreme chief of the Cheka. Djersinsky, like Peters, his assistant, has been called a fanatic and a sadist; his appearance and manner were those of a Polish aristocrat or an intellectual priest. I do not think that in the beginning he was either cruel or indifferent to human suffering. He was merely convinced that no revolution could be consolidated without terror and persecution. Lenin had entrusted him with the most difficult task of the Revolution— and here, too, he had chosen the "right" man for the right place—one who never forgot his own long tortures in Siberia before the Revolution had liberated him. As he became absorbed in his special functions, he became more determined not to be influenced or diverted by appeals to his humanity, lest in doing so he should violate his revolutionary duty. After my return to Moscow I observed how much more formal and single-tracked he had become. He seemed irritated at my attempt at intervention, and when I spoke about the Pirro matter he looked at me in astonishment. Didn't I understand that Pirro was a Cheka agent who had been sent to the Ukraine to act as a *provocateur?*

I was too shocked to answer him. I decided to go to Lenin, to explain what I had witnessed in the Ukraine, to protest against the senseless cruelty of the Cheka and the methods they were using.

After I had finished speaking, particularly of the Pirro affair, Lenin looked at me with an expression which was more sad than sardonic.

"Comrade Angelica," he said, "what use can life make of you?"

There was no implied superiority or reproach in his tone. He spoke as a father might to a child who lacks certain attributes of success, an understanding that life imposes compromises and adaptations—in this case conditions and methods inherited from the old régime. He knew better than to try to convince me that I was wrong, and I left him in a mood of deep depression. I was opposed to these methods, not only because I considered them unworthy of a Socialist régime, but because I knew that they would, in time, corrupt those who used them.

[235]

19

WHEN WE WERE FORCED BY THE POLISH AD-
vance to evacuate Kiev and return to Moscow early in
1920, I was surprised to find how the attitude toward Racovsky,
in official circles, had changed. Though he had remained in Kiev
as long as it was possible to defend an inch of Soviet soil, instead
of being welcomed and cheered for his courage and resourceful-
ness, he was put in a position of having to defend himself. I felt
indignant that a Socialist government should blame one of its
officials for a military defeat which he had been unable to prevent and I expressed myself to Lenin on this subject at the first
opportunity.

I found many other things changed, too. In my former office,
the ex-embassador to Switzerland, Berzine—a sick, irascible Old
Bolshevik whose vanity had been flattered by his diplomatic
post—had been installed as my substitute. I saw that he was so
happy to occupy my office and "rank" in Moscow that I decided

to leave him in peace, and to depart from Moscow again on a propaganda trip. The Central Committee eagerly agreed, but the military situation suddenly became so acute that I abandoned the plan. One of the White armies led by Yudenitch was advancing on Petrograd, and even Moscow was threatened. Every member of the Party was mobilized for military service or for propaganda work.

During those weeks of danger I made an average of five speeches a day, and though I was physically exhausted through lack of food and constant strain (my temperature was constantly below normal), I should have been glad to work even harder. The Revolution seemed in a more serious danger of military defeat than at any time since 1917. In the vast meetings I addressed, I found the Russians, men and women, ready to sacrifice their lives and those of their children in an effort to defend their hard-won conquests from these military representatives of the old régime. The name of Trotsky, who had organized and galvanized the Red army into an effective fighting force, was even more enthusiastically acclaimed at this moment than that of Lenin. He seemed to personify victory and courage, and when he left Moscow to head the defence of Petrograd, the hopes of the Revolution seemed to rest upon his shoulders. Notwithstanding the danger, however, Moscow was quiet and comparatively serene.

Shortly after the defeat of the reactionary army at the gates of Petrograd, I was amazed to receive an official order from the Central Committee to leave Moscow for a sanatorium. I thought at first that the order must be the result of an error. In the Soviet Union, women and children were especially privileged in such matters, but other women in the Party, to say nothing of thousands of ordinary citizens, were suffering as seriously from overwork and under-nourishment as I. No special concern had been shown about the state of my health before this. When I made further inquiries I discovered that there was no error—the Central Committee wished me to "take a rest in a sanatorium."

A sojourn in a sanatorium was one of the most cherished—and difficult to obtain—privileges at this time, a privilege for which applications must be made months in advance, because only here was it possible to obtain special food for the sick or invalided. Even among the active Party members envy and resentment always arose when it seemed that permission to enter a sanatorium was granted to some one who was not seriously ill or who was not otherwise entitled to it. The knowledge of this fact made me even more indignant.

"I am neither sick nor old enough to retire," I told the General Secretary of the Party, Krestinski (later ambassador to Germany). "I am strong enough to work and I want to keep on working."

"Look here, Comrade Balabanoff," he replied when he saw that I would refuse to accept the order, "we have a piece of work which will certainly satisfy you and which is extremely important to us. We would like you to take charge of a propaganda train which we are preparing to send to Turkestan."

If I had been surprised by the order to go to a sanatorium, I was even more amazed at this suggestion. A trip to Turkestan meant months of weary travel into a primitive and typhus-ridden district at a time when I was supposed to be ill enough to go to a sanatorium! While I recognized the extreme importance of such a trip, I wondered why I happened to be chosen at such a time. These propaganda trains were the method of establishing contact between the central government and the rest of the country. The publication of newspapers was hindered by the shortage of paper, ink, and printing machinery; other means of communication were poor and irregular. But propaganda was so essential to the consolidation and defence of the revolutionary régime that almost every other activity must be subordinated to it. At a time when travelling had become almost impossible or unbearable, due to lack of fuel and equipment (very often the trains would be compelled to stop while the passengers went into the surrounding country to cut wood for fuel) and when Trotsky had declared that there were one thousand "sick" locomotives in Central Russia, new, modern trains were built to carry the government propaganda and assistance into the more remote districts and to bring back first-hand information. Such miracles are possible only in periods of tremendous faith and enthusiasm, of a will-to-sacrifice inspired by a common goal.

Since such a large section of the population was illiterate, the trains were decorated with elementary but attractive slogans and pictures. They carried hundreds of poster illustrations relating to hygienic, agricultural, industrial, and educational problems, and stopping at each station, they offered the population moving pictures, musical and other programs. Each train carried two representatives of every commissariat whose duty it was to enlighten and instruct the local administrative bodies as to their functions. It also carried an official of the Cheka, and all those who had any complaints or protests to make were invited to bring them to this representative of the central power. Wherever the train stopped, an introductory and a concluding speech were made. This was to be my function.

"Why do you think that I am the person to go to Turkestan?" I asked Krestinski. "I can't even speak the language. A backward population, with a warrior's psychology—a man would make a better impression."

"We need a very popular name—a prima donna," he replied. He did not realize how much this remark displeased me and he continued: "The preliminary work will begin immediately. The representatives of the Commissariats will submit for your approval the reports they will make during the trip; then a general discussion will follow. The arrangements will take some time, and in the meanwhile the delegates will come to see you at your convenience."

"I shall have time, then, to decide whether or not I will go," I answered.

Krestinski did not reply.

During the next few weeks the plans for the trip went forward as though all had been decided; the delegates from the Commissariats arrived with their reports and we spent hours in discussing them. I was surprised, and somewhat amused, to see how quickly some of these ardent revolutionaries had become not only good officials, but good bureaucrats. Occasionally, some of my friends would ask me: "Are you really going to Turkestan?" and one of them warned me: "This is a manoeuvre of Zinoviev. He is trying to get rid of you."

In spite of what I knew about Zinoviev, I paid no attention

to this warning. I was still sufficiently naïve to believe that there was some legitimate reason behind the decision to send me to Turkestan. Then suddenly I heard an announcement which added to my hesitation—the news that a commission from the British Labour Party and Trade Union Congress was coming to Russia in May to investigate the Russian situation. Not only was this a highly important historical event, but I looked forward to the opportunity of renewing contact with the western labour movement. Two of the members of the delegation were men I had known and worked with in international trade-union conventions—Tom Shaw of the Textile Workers and Ben Turner.

My hesitation regarding the Turkestan trip became a decision when, soon after this, came another announcement that the visit of the English commission would be followed by one from Italy, consisting of Socialist, trade-union, and coöperative leaders, specialists and technicians from the municipality of Milan. Among those named was Serrati—and others of my comrades with whom I had worked and suffered during the early years of the war and who had been among the first to understand, to defend and aid the Soviet Union! I would be able to see them again, to receive and honour them in a Socialist country which, being the cradle of the Social Revolution, was as much their country as mine! Who should greet them upon their arrival, if not their friend and the secretary of the Third International, with which the Italian Socialists had already voted to affiliate? Who else was there to explain everything to them in their own language? I decided that I must make every effort to remain in Moscow.

I telephoned Zinoviev my objections to leaving Moscow at this time and the reasons for them. To my surprise, he declared that the Central Committee of the Russian Party had decided that I must leave for Turkestan. I still did not believe that the Central Committee had made this decision. It was Zinoviev's idea, which he had transmitted originally through Krestinski.

"Aren't you convinced yet that Zinoviev wants to get rid of you?" one of my friends asked. "Don't you realize what six months of life on a train in Turkestan will mean to your health?"

I decided to clear up the situation once and for all. As secretary of the International my work was under the jurisdiction of the Comintern Executive, not the Party Central Committee. Theoretically, at least, the latter was merely one of the affiliates of the Comintern. I knew, of course, that the Bolshevik leaders controlled the International Executive, but it was the latter which I would force to go on record in this matter.

The next meeting of the International Executive was to take place in Petrograd in Zinoviev's magnificent offices, and I went there to attend the session. After the preliminary business was out of the way, I brought up the issue abruptly.

"I should like Comrade Zinoviev to tell me why I have to leave Moscow at the very time that the delegations from Western Europe are arriving. I was elected secretary, presumably, because of my contacts with the labour movement abroad—especially Italy. Then why must I be separated from my Italian comrades on their arrival in Russia? And what can I do in Turkestan that any other Party propagandist can't do?"

An icy silence followed my words. Irritated by this direct and undiplomatic offensive, Zinoviev had begun nervously to write notes to members of the Executive while I was speaking. It was obvious that they were well aware of Zinoviev's plot. Several of them began to emphasize the urgency of the Turkestan trip, repeating the same weak arguments I had already heard. Zinoviev finally said:

"I am sorry the Party Central Committee did not inform you of the reasons for sending you to Turkestan. It was their decision."

"Even if it were," I replied, "the decision also came from you. You are the president of the International. I should like you to tell me what those reasons are."

Most of the other members looked horrified. How could I speak like this to Zinoviev the almighty?

As usual, when he became angry or excited, Zinoviev's voice was shrill and petulant:

"Well, if you don't wish to obey the Party Central Commit-

[241]

tee, we shall take up the matter tomorrow. We have urgent problems to deal with now."

While the session was still going on, I received a long-distance call from the Kronstadt Soviet, asking me to speak at a meeting that had been arranged for the following morning. I interrupted my answer to inquire of Zinoviev if the next day's session of the Executive was definitely set for three o'clock and if the matter of my trip would be taken up at that time.

He replied in the affirmative, adding, "You will have plenty of time to go and get back for the afternoon meeting."

I explained the situation to the Kronstadt chairman. "We will see that you get back to Petrograd in plenty of time," he answered. "So please come."

The next morning I observed that the weather was very threatening. The only communication between Petrograd and Kronstadt being by small boats, I wondered if I was not taking too great a chance in leaving Petrograd at this moment. I phoned the Kronstadt chairman again, and when he agreed that, due to the weather, they might not be able to get me back for the Executive meeting, I asked him to release me from the engagement.

When I came to Smolny that afternoon, a half-hour before the meeting was supposed to convene, some of the members of the Executive were already leaving.

"What is the matter?" I asked them. "Why are you leaving?"

"We have just finished," one of them replied. "The schedule was changed; we began at ten this morning."

At this moment I saw Zinoviev hurrying towards the door. Stepping in front of him, I asked: "Didn't you repeat to me yesterday that this meeting would begin at three? What do you mean by discussing a question which concerns me in my absence?"

He neither looked at me nor answered my question directly. Shifting the responsibility, as usual, he replied:

"The Executive has decided that you must obey the Central Committee's request that you go to Turkestan."

"I will not go," I answered.

[242]

"Party discipline—" he began, in his softest, most effeminate tones.

"I know what party discipline is and I don't transgress it. But you, Comrade Zinoviev, will regret what you have done today."

With these words I expressed my half-formed decision that I could no longer collaborate with Zinoviev and his institution. I was not naïve enough to think that I could fight these methods without resorting myself to identical means—intrigue, lies, co-operation with heterogeneous elements, opposing a certain current or personality for very different reasons. I knew that I was quite incapable of functioning on such a level, that the victories obtained by such means were victories of personal ambition or rivalries, not the victory of principles or ideals. Those who began to use such methods in the interest of the cause would in time become the slaves of their own means. To coöperate with Zinoviev meant that one must become his accomplice. Only Lenin or Trotsky could control him and I had no illusions that they would do so. Like the other Bolshevik leaders, including Kamenev, Bukharin and Radek, they would consider my scruples *petit-bourgeois*.

After my return to Moscow from Petrograd, it was John Reed who put into words that which I had already begun to suspect. We had been meeting frequently since his return to Russia from the United States, drawn together by our common, though as yet unacknowledged, disillusionment and growing despair. Reed had been travelling about the country with Party credentials under the most dangerous and difficult conditions, getting in touch with the peasants and the miners, sharing the cold, hunger, and filth of the average Russian life. Clothed in a long fur coat and a fur *shapka*, he looked like a typical Russian from the Caucasus. I do not think that any foreigner who came to Russia in those early years ever saw or came to know as much about the conditions of the people as did Reed in the spring and summer of 1920. He was becoming more and more depressed by the suffering, disorganization, and inefficiency to be found everywhere, but like the rest of us who saw these things, he understood the difficulties of the situation—enhanced

[243]

by the blockade, sabotage, the shortage of materials—and his irritation and discouragement were directed not at the government itself, but at the growing indifference and cynicism of the bureaucracy of all gradations. He was particularly discouraged when he saw his own efforts and those of the other friends of the Revolution defeated by indifference and inefficiency. Sensitive to any kind of inequality and injustice, he would return from each of his trips with stories that were heartbreaking to both of us. The fact that he talked only with me of such matters was not due to caution or diplomacy, but to the fact that he knew that I, too, was in the same mood. He was merely thinking out loud.

I remember meeting Reed at one of the huge entertainments which the trade unions arranged in the sumptuous building they had inherited from the former aristocracy. It was during a period of the greatest scarcity of food and fuel, and the government leaders were trying to take the workers' minds off the material situation with musical and dramatic performances. Though some of the artists who performed on this occasion were among the best in Russia, there was something about the quality and manner of their performance that irritated me. They were obviously giving inferior performances, playing down to a working-class audience which was not supposed to know any better. I was all the more irritated when I saw that the officials who organized the affair were so radiant and proud of their accomplishment.

"*Parvenus, petit-bourgeois,*" I thought to myself. "They don't see how the artists are insulting these workers."

I rose and started to leave the hall, and as I did so, Jack Reed came over and joined me. "Let's go," he said. I have never heard a voice so full of humiliation and sadness.

It was strange that Jack, a foreigner, should have understood both my own and the general situation before a Russian like myself.

"They want to get rid of you," he told me after my return from Petrograd, "before the foreign delegations arrive. You know too much."

"But surely," I replied, "they don't doubt my loyalty."

[244]

"Of course not, but neither do they doubt your honesty. It is that they are afraid of."

I knew that my refusal to go to Turkestan, under orders from the Comintern Executive, would probably result in my removal, but I had already indicated that I was willing to pay this price. (In the 1930's, a similar breach of discipline would probably have resulted in my imprisonment or worse. In 1920, the Soviet leaders were still responsive to working-class opinion abroad.)

About a fortnight after the Petrograd meeting of the Executive, Reed ran into my room.

"Tell me, Angelica, are you still the secretary of the International or not?"

"Of course I am, at least nominally," I replied.

"If that is so, why aren't you attending the Executive meeting?"

"I knew nothing about it. Where is it held?"

"Well, I know," he answered. "Those cowards are meeting in Litvinov's commissariat, so that you won't know where they are."

Though I was feeling ill, I dressed and went to the meeting. As I entered the room, Zinoviev grew quite pale and the other members were extremely embarrassed. I waited for the meeting to close without saying a word. Then I asked Zinoviev to explain why I had not been notified and what had taken place.

"Oh," he replied, without looking up, "we thought that Trotsky had told you. The Executive Committee has already decided to remove you—because of your refusal to go to Turkestan."

The news of my removal, the realization that I was no longer even nominally responsible for methods and activities I despised, gave me a sense of liberation I had not felt for years. But what impressed me most at this moment was the cowardice of this man who, pretending to be a revolutionary leader, had not even the courage to face an individual or to assume responsibility in an unpleasant situation.

In spite of the sense of liberation following my removal from office, my realization of the means by which this had been accomplished, the motives behind it, and the suspicion of how widespread and pervasive these methods had become—together with my weakened physical condition—resulted in a sort of physical and nervous breakdown in which my whole organism was shaken. I was touched at this time to receive from John Reed a picture of himself. In the corner of it he had written: "To the best revolutionist I have known in Russia." I knew when I read these words what John Reed must have suffered—he who had known and worshipped the leaders of the Revolution.

During these days of illness I also had a visit from Radek. He had just come from Berlin, where he had been sent by Zinoviev and where he had been jailed for his Communist activity. He brought news and letters from Italian comrades, and from old friends in Germany. He seemed very bitter about my removal. "Are they crazy?" he exclaimed, referring to the action of the Executive. "You are the one person in Russia well known throughout the western labour movement. I have had proof enough of it. These people, and the Italians in particular, will resent your removal. That rascal Zinoviev! You will have to come back!"

I realized that his attitude in this matter was dictated more by his competition with Zinoviev than by any other consideration.

Radek was to me a strange psychological phenomenon, but never a puzzle. Even during the war I had observed how easily he could jump from one prediction to another. Today he would prove that the events on the various fronts had to be so and so; tomorrow, when just the contrary had happened, he would then attempt to prove that it could not have happened otherwise. These objective judgments did not matter so much, but when Radek's own factional or personal position was at stake, he employed the same intellectual trickery with more serious results. He was—and is—a strange mixture of amorality, cynicism, and spontaneous appreciation for ideas, books, music, human beings. Just as there are people who have no perception of colours, so Radek had no perception of moral values. In politics, he would change his viewpoint overnight, appropriate for himself the most contradictory slogans. This quality, with his quick mind,

[246]

his sardonic humour, his versatility and his vast reading, was probably the key to his journalistic success. His adaptability had made him very useful to Lenin, who never, however, took him seriously or considered him reliable. As the outstanding journalist of the Soviets, Radek was instructed to write certain things, which did not ostensibly emanate from the government or from Lenin, Trotsky, or Chicherin, just to see what the diplomatic and public reaction in Europe would be. If the reaction was unfavourable, the articles would be officially disavowed. More than that, Radek himself would disavow them. Having no sensibility and much mental elasticity, he could express the opinions of others and actually believe they were his own, support an argument which he had fought against with zeal.

Because of this insensibility, he had no resentment about the way he was treated by other people. I have seen him attempt to go with people who refused to sit at the same table with him, or even put their signatures next to his on a document, or to shake hands with him. He would be delighted if he could merely divert these people with one of his innumerable anecdotes. Though a Jew himself, his anecdotes were almost exclusively those which dealt with Jews and which put them in a ridiculous or degrading light.

Radek was looked upon as an outsider—a foreigner—in Russia, so far as the traditions of the revolutionary movement were concerned. But he appropriated so thoroughly the political mentality—as well as the language—of the Russian Bolsheviks that he felt completely at home there. His attitude was that of a revolutionary parvenu who does not hesitate to take full material advantage of the position into which the Revolution has thrown him and who feels more important because of these advantages. None of the Russian revolutionaries of the Old Guard, except Zinoviev, shared this point of view.

For all of these characteristics I feel about Radek, as I do about Zinoviev—that though he was capable of anything within the confines of the revolutionary movement, he would never sell himself to the enemies of the Revolution. These would be his enemies, too. Another reason for believing in his innocence is this—that in no other state and under no other circumstances would Radek occupy such a position of prestige and power—and even of income—as he had in Soviet Russia, and he was even more at home in the Russia of Stalin, with its greater rewards and inequalities, than in the Russia of Lenin and the early revolutionary days.

I remember an incident which impressed upon me the parvenu snobbery of this "Soviet Puck," as the American journalists have called him. Once as the Comintern Executive was leaving Petrograd for Moscow, we did not find at the station the special train in which we had come. The one placed at our disposal was far less pleasant, although the average Russian citizen would have been delighted at the opportunity to travel under such conditions. We were just about to take our seats when an ugly altercation arose between Radek and the conductor. Radek declared he would not allow the train to leave Petrograd unless a better coach was found for us. His ultimatum was accompanied by the most vulgar insults—made more provocative by his insufficient knowledge of Russian. How did the conductor dare to ask for his name? Didn't he know Karl Radek when he saw him? We tried to stop the disgraceful outburst, but it was impossible to appease Radek's dignity. The altercation aroused the attention of other travellers and the railway staff. Finally a young man in officer's uniform came into the coach and said, after offering Radek a military salute:

"I am a military commissar travelling with some colleagues in a special coach. We will be glad to give it up to you and travel in yours."

We all expected Radek to be decent enough to refuse. Instead, he accepted the offer as homage due to his rank. Later, when I indicated to him how humiliated and ashamed I had felt at this incident and that I thought the conductor should have rebuked him for his insults, he lost his temper and shouted: "It is *you* who dishonour the Soviet Union, if as a member of the government you are willing to travel under such conditions. They may be good enough for other people, but not for us."

A few days after my meeting with Radek, while I was still

[248]

sick in bed, my telephone rang and I heard Zinoviev in his most mellifluous tones, inquiring about my health.

"I have heard you don't feel well, Comrade Balabanoff. I should like to call with my wife. I should also like you to know that the Russian Central Committee has decided that you may again take up your work in the Comintern. Perhaps Comrade Trotsky has told you of our decision."

"Take up my work!" I exclaimed. "The Executive has to explain to me why I ever had to give it up." I hung up the receiver without waiting for his reply.

How typical this was of Zinoviev! As long as he was surrounded by the creatures whom he manipulated, he had been courageous enough to get rid of me. But as soon as the Party Central Committee had sensed the reaction to my dismissal in other countries and no longer backed him up, he was ready to be humble and even flattering.

When I met Trotsky, soon after this, I learnt a little more about the reversal of the decision. Trotsky explained that he had been very much opposed to my exclusion from the Executive and had urged some kind of compromise. He still urged it, now that I told him of my refusal to accept office again.

"If you don't want to be secretary of the International," he said, "why not be the Italian representative or correspondent on the Executive—just as Marx was the correspondent for Germany in the First International, Engels for Russia?"

I refused because I knew what this meant. As a member of the Russian Party, I would be bound by the decisions of the Russian Central Committee. Therefore the Italian Party would be acquiescing in the decisions of the Russian, without either discussion or vote. I explained this to Trotsky and declined his offer.

Trotsky's own tragic fate was to illustrate all that I felt and thought about my own inability either to work with or compete with the Comintern leaders on their own ground. If, after the Soviet Republic was consolidated and the factional struggle first began against him, after the Central Committee decided that the time had come to lessen the popularity and self-confidence of the former Menshevik, Trotsky had shown his own superiority to the Jesuitry of his rivals, by refusing to use their methods, how different his fate might have been! It is far more likely that when the moment of disillusion with the bureaucracy came, he would have become the leader of a revolutionary labour movement throughout the world, and that the authority and the number of his disciples would be many times greater than they are now. If from the *beginning*, he had defended party democracy, fought the repression of honest dissent, the calumny of political opponents by the Party machine, how much more sympathy and solidarity he would have found in Russia from the first day of his persecution to the last shameful campaign against him!

But to have denounced those methods consistently, Trotsky should have fought them from the very beginning when he was most powerful, when he was a part of the bureaucracy, and when the Russians themselves were still convinced that the country could not be saved without him. He could not have eradicated the disease, perhaps—this was too inherent in Bolshevism itself—but he could have avoided some of its most monstrous applications and he could have protested far more successfully—and aroused others to protest—when he himself became the victim. But not only was Trotsky himself, after 1917, a good Bolshevist, a hundred-per-cent "Leninist," he was also too weak and too self-conscious to have made such a fight while still part of the ruling group.

"Too weak?" How can I use that word to describe a man whom I consider one of the most powerful intellects of our time—a man who has done for Russia what no other modern statesman has done for his country (because none has had to work, to destroy and reconstruct under such complicated and unprecedented conditions); who has faced danger and death without hesitation, endured heroically persecution on an unprecedented scale?

Yet, there are different ways of being courageous, or rather of being indifferent to what may come. One may defy death but be unable to face reproach or a threat to one's popularity. This was, and still is, the case with Trotsky. He was daring enough, with Lenin, to face the hostile opinion of the whole world. But he was not sufficiently independent to fight those tendencies exemplified in Lenin's puppet, Zinoviev, nor to refuse an alliance with Zinoviev even after the latter had first capitulated to and become the puppet of Stalin. He was afraid of being thought less "revolutionary" than those who attacked him and in the field of demagogy and political shrewdness he was no match for Zinoviev, Stalin, and the whole party apparatus.

This fear of being suspected of not having wholly abnegated his original sin—Menshevism—and his immeasurable self-confidence, have continuously projected themselves like a shadow between this brilliant man and the situations in which he is personally involved, so that he has failed to apply to his own movement the criteria he applies to others. It is as though history and logic and the laws of causality which he understands and knows how to handle so well, stopped short before his own personality. It is an attitude which was encouraged, of course, by his matchless success in the early years of the Revolution, the overwhelming popularity he enjoyed. He was so sure in those days that, whatever might be the fate of others, whatever the dangers of popularity and success, for him—Leon Trotsky—life would make an exception. Instead, he has become the foremost victim of the perversion of the Revolution!

Within the Russian Party itself, the first organized opposition to the policies of both Lenin and Trotsky was led by a woman—Alexandra Kollontai. Alexandra was not an Old Bolshevik, but she had joined the Bolshevik Party even before Trotsky had done so and much earlier than I. During these first few years of the Revolution she was a frequent source of both personal and political annoyance to the Party leaders. On more than one occasion the Central Committee had wanted me to substitute for her in the leadership of the women's movement, thus facilitating the campaign against her and isolating her from the women of the masses. Fortunately, I understood this intrigue and refused these offers, emphasizing that no one could do this work so well as she, and trying to augment her prestige and create sympathy for her whenever possible.

By the Ninth Congress of the Russian Party, the last vestiges of trade-union autonomy and workers' control in industry was

[251]

swept away to be replaced by the control of the political commissars over the trade unions and the workers' soviets. Kollantai had become the leader of the "Workers' Opposition," a protest movement against the bureaucratic suffocation of the labour unions and the democratic rights of the workers. As there was no possibility, even at that time, of publicly criticizing the Central Committee or of placing an unofficial opinion before the Party rank and file, she was courageous enough to have a pamphlet secretly printed for distribution to the delegates at the Party Convention. I have never seen Lenin so angry as when one of these pamphlets was handed to him at the Convention—in spite of the fact that "opposition" within the Party itself was still supposed to be legitimate. Taking the platform, he denounced Kollontai as the Party's worst enemy, a menace to its unity. He went so far in his attack as to make allusions to certain episodes in Kollontai's intimate life that had nothing whatever to do with the issue. It was the kind of polemic which did no credit to Lenin, and it was on this occasion that I realized the lengths to which Lenin would go in the pursuit of his strategic aims, his opposition to a party opponent. I admired Kollontai for the calm and self-control with which she answered Lenin's attack. Among the examples she quoted of the methods which were used by the Central Committee against Party "rebels" was the attempt of the "Central Committee to send Angelica Balabanoff to Turkestan to eat peaches."

Like many other rebellious members of the Party, she was sent away soon after on a diplomatic mission. For old revolutionists like Kollontai it was a punishment to be separated from the field of revolutionary activity, but after years in Norway, Mexico, and Sweden as Soviet ambassador, she seemed to become reconciled to her position and to fall completely into line.

20

WHEN JOHN REED FIRST TOLD ME, EARLY IN February, that the famous American Anarchists, Emma Goldman and Alexander Berkman were in Petrograd and that they wished to get in touch with me, my first reaction was one of irritation. Most of the Anarchists I had known during my activity in Western Europe had always seemed to me either hypercritical or utopian in their attitude, without appreciation or consideration for objective conditions and circumstances. Such an attitude applied to Russia in this period, when there were so many obstacles in the path of the Revolution, when superhuman efforts were necessary to overcome them, could lead only to superficial and unjust conclusions. As a member of the Party, it is also possible that I accepted too readily some of the official charges made against so-called "Anarchist" dissenters in Russia at this time.

Reed dissipated my apprehensions about the two Americans

by giving me a pamphlet containing the speeches they had made during their trials for anti-war activity. After I had read it and after hearing Jack's praise of their courage and devotion, I felt a little ashamed of my prejudice. Nothing that I saw and heard of them in Russia after their arrival changed the impression I had received from their pamphlet or from Jack's description, and I followed their activities closely enough to speak with some authority. I feel it is my duty to bear witness to this fact because of the bitter attacks launched against both of them among European and American radicals, after they had left Russia and had criticized the Bolshevik régime.

When Emma came to see me at the National, just after she arrived in Moscow from Petrograd, much of the initial enthusiasm with which she had entered the Workers' Republic had already been chilled. In Petrograd she had learnt of the repression of the Russian Anarchists and other political dissidents, the activities of the Cheka, the pervasiveness of the Party bureaucracy. Though she was shocked and indignant, she had not yet lost faith in those whom she considered the *real* leaders of the Revolution. She was still eager to work with and for the Revolution, even while she protested against what she considered its abuses. She had already visited Lunarcharsky and Kollontai when she came to see me, and was convinced that both of them recognized these abuses, but felt it impolitic to protest. When she called I was still ill, as a result of my own recent experiences, and when we began to speak, she suddenly broke down and wept. It was in this fit of weeping that she poured forth all her shock and disillusionment, her bitterness at the injustices she had witnessed, the others of which she had heard. Five hundred executed at one time by a revolutionary government! A secret police that matched the old Okhrana! Suppression, persecution of honest revolutionists, all the unnecessary suffering and cruelty —was it for this the Revolution had been fought?

I tried to speak of the tragic necessities of the Revolution in a backward country, to explain away her own doubts as I had tried to banish my own. External conditions, life itself, rather than theory, had dictated the course of the Revolution. I realized how inadequate my explanation must seem to her. She was eager to talk with Lenin and I promised to arrange an interview with him for her and "Sasha" Berkman.

Ordinarily, I hated to be asked to introduce anyone to Lenin, but this time I was sincerely glad to do so. I wrote him a note enclosing the pamphlet Reed had given me, and in a short time I received a reply.

"Dear Comrade," he wrote, "I read the pamphlet with immense interest" (he underlined the "immense" three times). "Will you make an appointment with E. G. and A. B. for next week and bring them to me? I shall send a car for you."

After we had arrived at the Kremlin and had passed through the many guarded doors into Lenin's office, Lenin, as usual, began firing a volley of questions at his visitors as soon as he had greeted them. It was as though he was trying to extract from them the last possible grain of information about conditions in the United States. He was eager, as always, to get an estimate of revolutionary sentiment in the labour movement abroad and he expressed his concern that two such valuable workers should have been torn from their labour in America at this critical time.

Emma and Sasha listened and answered his questions with warm deference, expressing their eagerness to collaborate in the work of revolutionary Russia. They hoped that Lenin would suggest some work they would be fitted to perform. Among other activities, they had thought of the possibility of founding in Russia a movement, and a magazine to be called the Friends of American Freedom, just as for more than two decades there had been in the United States a society of the Friends of Russian Freedom. Would he approve of such an effort? From the almost imperceptible change in Lenin's expression, I knew what the answer would be. But as usual, he did not give it directly.

Before we left, however, Sasha Berkman could not forbear to speak in behalf of the Anarchists in Soviet prisons.

Lenin denied that any Anarchists had been imprisoned for their beliefs, insisting that the Soviets were suppressing only those who were "bandits" or followers of Makhno. He advised his visitors to find some useful work to do in order to keep their balance under the revolutionary régime. He would submit their

[255]

suggestion to the Central Committee and send an answer through me.

When I told Emma and Sasha that the decision on their plan was a negative one, they showed no resentment or discouragement. This would have been only one of the fields of their activity—there were so many other things that they could do. I realized that their final assignment could not possibly satisfy them: they were to supervise the renovation of some of the expropriated mansions in Petrograd into workers' rest-homes. Though this type of activity was so different from that which they had planned or hoped for, they undertook it with the utmost good-will. They were happy to make any contribution to the "Workers' Fatherland."

Both of them possessing very active temperaments and coming from a country of such comparatively high standards of efficiency as the United States, they probably suffered more than Russians or average Europeans because of the horrible conditions in Russia at that time—when everything but time itself was wanting. To the shortage of material and the general confusion was added the indescribable waste of time and energy generated by an oppressive bureaucracy. Hours and days might be spent getting an order for the transference of a mattress, though no one seemed to know just why. It was a situation calculated to exhaust the patience of any one who had not spent his life in Russia or who had not already accommodated himself to bureaucratic red tape. When, after this exhausting experience, they were given more satisfactory work—the organization of a revolutionary museum—they had to deal with the same type of difficulties and delays. Yet, though they were becoming more and more disillusioned with the régime, and found themselves in increasing disagreement with its leaders, they cheerfully went on working without complaints or recriminations.

I would like to mention here two indications of their courage and generosity which augmented their prestige in my eyes.

When they came to Moscow I asked them to be my guests, both because it was so difficult to find a place in which to sleep and because with me they would be immune from the espionage of the Cheka; but they refused to do so. Generally they came to

Moscow to see their friends who were not Bolsheviks, to bring relief to, or to plead the cause of, their Anarchist comrades who were being persecuted and arrested by the authorities. Some of these had gone on hunger strikes in prison and their situation was desperate. I could see how depressed both Emma and Sasha were becoming as they saw these persecutions taking place in a Workers' Republic. And yet, after that first interview with Emma in Moscow, they never complained to me—because they sensed what a torture it was to me to listen to these stories without being able to disavow such activities dictated by the Party to which I belonged. Only on one or two occasions, in which I was the only one who could possibly help, did they come to me for aid.

Years later I met Alexander Berkman frequently during his sojourn in France, and his last letter reached me when he was no longer alive. To those of his friends who never saw him after he left the United States, I should like to convey the impression which he made on me, both in Russia and in his later exile. Neither his experiences in Russia nor the bitterness of his *émigré* life ever shook his great courage or his boundless devotion to his ideal. Perhaps it was the impossibility of serving as he had wished to, and was fitted to serve, the country which had symbolized his hopes that was the indirect cause of his voluntary and untimely end. His death was as brave as his life had been.

Shortly before the long-heralded arrival of the English delegation I received a message from Chicherin, telling me that I had been appointed to prepare for and receive the British delegation in Petrograd. I was asked to come to his office to discuss the matter with him. When I arrived I found Radek already on hand. The food question was being discussed and Radek had just proved the "absolute necessity" of placing our guests under extraordinarily privileged conditions and of providing them as well with the wines and liquors which were forbidden in Russia at this time. I protested vehemently against this.

"Why should we make exceptions for our English comrades? Can't they live a few weeks as our people have lived for years? What have we to conceal? Why should they not see what it means in Russia to fight for freedom? Radek's proposal about wines and liquor is humiliating. We do not need to bribe these people; they are not coming here for a good time. We should offer them a clean and comfortable place to live and the opportunity to see and hear all they wish."

I left for Petrograd immediately, and with the help of some women comrades prepared an apartment in the Narishkin Palace, formerly owned by a Russian princess.

Among the members of the Commission, Clifford Allen was the only one who was definitely sympathetic to the Soviets. However, the labour leaders, who were themselves of proletarian origin, men like Tom Shaw, Ben Turner, and Ben Tillett, were quite ready to be impressed by Russia's positive achievements. In Petrograd I felt that Mrs. Snowden was most concerned with the negative aspects of the new régime, that she was more distressed over the fate of the upper classes than over the sufferings of the masses. After reading her book, I realized that this judgment was not altogether correct. Bertrand Russell, who accompanied the delegation unofficially, and about whom no one among the Soviet officials seemed to know anything, probably had more opportunity than any of the English delegates to get an unofficial view of things. After the delegation had gone to Moscow, no one paid any attention to him.

With me, personally, Mrs. Snowden was more than polite and gentle, but I felt that she deeply distrusted as "official" any statements about Russia and the Soviets. The same feeling, of course, pervaded most of the other delegates—certainly with much justification so far as Petrovsky, Lozowsky, and others who came up from Moscow to welcome them were concerned. It was this attitude which finally induced me to say to the delegation:

"Don't think that we Russians feel that we have to act like salesmen, to praise our merchandise or cheat you. Here is the reality. This is the Revolution. It is up to you to judge whether in your country liberty and Socialism can be obtained at a lesser price." They probably guessed that my attitude was unique.

The receptions, parades, demonstrations, theatrical performances, etc., staged for the English delegation as long as they were in Russia, were as much intended to impress the Russian workers with the significance of this visitation "from representatives of the British Workers" as they were to impress the delegation itself. Every effort was made to use the English delegation for propaganda purposes, to make the Russians feel that the Commission represented the sympathy, approval, and solidarity with Bolshevism of the English working class. Such an impression would, of course, inspire the hopes of the Russian masses that the blockade would soon be lifted by revolutionary protest abroad and that the workers of England would come to their aid.

Though one or two of the English delegates were flattered and impressed by all these demonstrations, I saw that the others were fully aware of the manner in which they were being used and that they resented the constant official surveillance, disguised as attention, under which they were forced to make their investigation.

As long as the Commission remained in Petrograd I fought vigorously against this policy, but without much effect. It was so stupid not to let these foreigners see what the British blockade was doing to Russia, the misery and starvation it had produced, so that they could arouse the consciences of their own people when they returned home.

One Sunday Mrs. Snowden asked me apologetically whether or not the churches were still functioning and whether she could attend a religious service. I told her that she could go wherever she chose, and put a car and chauffeur at her disposal. Afraid that the chauffeur might have been instructed to take her to some "show place," she pretended that she preferred to walk, as she "hadn't had enough exercise in Russia."

When we arrived in Moscow I found that an entire hotel had been renovated for our English guests and that their visit in Moscow was to be initiated by an impressive banquet. Sasha Berkman had come down from Petrograd with us to assist as an interpreter, and as we sat down to this elaborate dinner I noticed that he looked at me sympathetically, as though he guessed what was going on in my mind.

After that neither of us took part in the public exhibitions, demonstrations, visits to factories, schools, etc., which crowded the days of the English delegates, and in which they were always accompanied by numerous officials and interpreters. Their guidance was now out of my hands—and besides, the Italian delegation was on its way and I was to act as its hostess.

From the viewpoint of the Bolsheviks, one serious incident marred the visit of the English delegation just before they left Moscow. In the fight against the recent destruction of trade-union autonomy, several of the unions, including the bakers', had gone on strike. In reprisal their executive committees had been dissolved and some of their leaders imprisoned. The printers' union had organized a closed mass meeting to protest against this action and had invited several members of the British delegation to attend. In the midst of this meeting, during which a small Bolshevik group in the large audience continued to howl and heckle, a strange man in dark glasses appeared on the platform. After a brief and impassioned attack upon the Party bureaucracy, he had removed the dark glasses and revealed himself. It was Chernov, the Socialist Revolutionary leader for whom the Cheka had been looking. Before the Bolsheviks present could take action the doors of the building were locked by the printers, so that no one could leave or enter while Chernov was being spirited away. The whole affair, Chernov's appearance and speech in particular, made a tremendous impression upon the English delegates who were present. After their departure from Moscow the officials of the printers' union were imprisoned as a result of this affair.

Though I had prepared weeks in advance for the reception of the Italian delegation in the house in which the English delegates had lived in Petrograd, I was fearful that at the last moment something would go wrong. When I received a telegram announcing that they were approaching Finland, I phoned immediately for an extra train for their journey to Petrograd, and then left for Petrograd myself.

The Italian delegation comprised a mixed Commission, made up of representatives from the Socialist Party, the Federation of Labour, and the coöperative movement. The Commission had been sent to Russia to investigate the possibility of material and technical assistance to Russia by the Italian coöperatives and labour movement.

[260]

I knew that the welcome of the masses to the Italian delegation and Serrati in particular would be far more spontaneous
and enthusiastic than that accorded the English commission.
The attitude of the whole Italian Party during the war, the immediate and enthusiastic support of the Bolshevik Revolution—
facts which the Bolsheviks themselves had so frequently emphasized in public meetings—gave them a special standing in the
hearts of the Russian workers. Ever since that historical meeting
of the Italian Executive in 1914, when we were confronted with
the treachery of Mussolini, the greatest responsibility of the
Party had rested upon the shoulders of Serrati, and during the
war period he had been the one most bitterly attacked by the
ignorant and reactionary.

By the summer of 1920 the population of Petrograd had
known almost four years of cold and starvation, of national and
civil war. The city was like a ghost of its former self, its ranks
thinned by revolution and counter-revolution, its immediate
future uncertain. How was it possible that these suffering people
(stronger and more combative members were at the front) could
display the interest and enthusiasm, the patience and tenacity
with which they awaited the arrival of the train carrying the
Italian commission? One can explain it only on the basis that
the Russian masses believed profoundly in the Revolution and
its leaders, and that they were proud to receive their foreign
comrades in the capital which they had so recently defended
against counter-revolution. They also hoped and expected that
the visit of the Italians meant help and relief in their long fight
against hunger and misery, their struggle to reconstruct their
world. Among the huge crowd there were also groups and individuals who had no sympathy with the revolutionary movement, but they, too, hoped for relief from "civilized" Europe.
They, too, were flattered that this miserable, starving country had
attracted visitors from abroad. Some, of course, were attracted
merely by curiosity. For such a long time they had seen and
heard only people who were suffering and who could speak only
of their immediate needs. How did these foreigners look? How
would they speak—these people who were not tortured by hunger, to whom a coat, a pair of shoes, was not a long-cherished

but never-obtained ambition? The nervous tension, the spirit of fraternity arose as the train arrived. The singing of the "Internationale," the shouts of greeting, were only a feeble expression of the intimate feelings of these people.

I have seen many huge gatherings and mass manifestations in Russia, with beautiful banners, parades of the youth and military forces, manifestations both of joy and of mourning, but none has been so spontaneous and unanimous as those which followed the arrival of the Italian delegation in Petrograd. These demonstrations took place every evening until we left for Moscow. The masses, sensitive as are all collective groups, understood the response to their greeting; knew that this delegation had come not to criticize, but to study, to learn and to help. On the evening of its departure from Milan, Mussolini, not yet at the climax of his power and with the vulgarity characteristic of him, had written that the delegation was going to a country of "vermin" and pauperism. Serrati replied that they had come to a Holy Land.

Even in material details, the Italian delegation proved its comprehension and solidarity. They had brought with them about a hundred enormous cases filled with food—canned goods, rice, oil, sugar, etc.—medicines and soap, needles for the tailors' coöperatives, and other much-needed supplies. One needed to have witnessed the sufferings of the Russian people to judge how welcome these contributions were. Of the many delegations which came to Russia in this and subsequent periods, the Italians and the Swedes were the only ones who proved their fraternal solidarity in this manner.

A few days after the arrival of the delegation in Petrograd I received a message from Zinoviev asking me to come to his office and to bring with me some of the Italian Socialists whom I considered "the most radical." At the moment this request aroused in me no particular suspicion, but as soon as I repeated the invitation to Serrati, he seemed to understand what it meant.

"Look here, comrade," he warned me, "Zinoviev must understand that we have come here to learn the truth about Russia, so that we can answer the attacks of her enemies and arouse the support of her friends. For Russia's sake, as well as for that of the Italian workers, don't encourage any attempt to split our delegation. To be useful our report must be unanimous. We must not give to the outside world the impression that there is any difference among us, or that secret, factional meetings are being held. The Party members in our delegation have been sent here not as representatives of factions, but of the Party as a whole. We must be loyal to that mandate."

I was convinced that he was right and as time went on and I had further opportunity to observe what was taking place, I realized more and more how wise Serrati had been and how thoroughly devoted to Soviet Russia he was. Before we left for Petrograd, Zinoviev informed us that he would travel to Moscow in the same train and that he had called a meeting in his coach to which the Italian Socialist and trade-union leaders were invited. Oh, fallacy of human power! Zinoviev received us in that particular carriage which the Tsar had used for audiences with his representatives and staff members when he had travelled about the country. Now Zinoviev had taken on all the airs and manners of a Tsar. His whole attitude differed from that with which he dealt with these same people before his elevation to power in the Soviets.

He began by announcing that the Second Congress of the Third International had been called for a date within the next few weeks and that he wanted the Italian delegation to be prepared for participation and for voting on that occasion. We were amazed at this sudden announcement, because there had been no word of the Congress before the delegation left Italy. Serrati again proved his perspicacity when he objected that the delegation had not been sent to Russia for a political purpose, that no one in Italy had known that an international convention was to take place, and that there had been no discussion of such an event and no mandates for voting given to the Socialists who happened to be members of the commission.

When I heard Serrati make this honest statement I knew that he had signed his political death warrant. He had shown that he was too honest, too aware of his own responsibilities, to act as Zinoviev's accomplice. As the other Socialists present agreed with Serrati's position, Zinoviev had little to say, but I knew that war

[263]

would be declared against him by the almighty president of the International. When I translated Zinoviev's remarks to the trade-union members of the delegation, D'Aragona, then secretary of the Italian Federation of Labour, Bianchi, an official and the intellectual leader of the I.F.L., and Colombino, the general-secretary of the metal workers, I realized that it was his purpose to split the Italian trade-union movement, too, though he met with the same opposition from these delegates as he had from Serrati. This was the recondite plan of Zinoviev and the other Bolsheviks—to abuse the devotion of the Italian Socialists to the Russian Revolution and its leaders in order to make them tools of division in their own and other countries. Serrati was the greatest obstacle to this criminal aim, and he had to be eliminated.

It had been decided that the Italian delegation would be given every opportunity to travel about and to visit the towns and country outside Petrograd and Moscow. Knowing how tiring were the delays and demonstrations in the capital, and how soon many of the delegates needed to return to Italy, I tried to arrange for their departure as soon as possible. The majority of the delegates chose a trip down the Volga and into the Ukraine. After I had spoken to Lenin about the matter, boats and trains, all spotlessly clean and well equipped and stocked with the best of food were placed at our disposal with a speed very unusual for Russia at that time.

While we were still in Petrograd and Moscow, I had been surprised to find that the Russian engineer who had been an informal representative of the Soviets in Italy and who had been chosen to accompany the delegation to Russia, had been replaced at the last moment by a Russian student who knew nothing about the movement but who even followed the delegation into their most confidential interviews with Lenin, meetings at which only the Italian Socialists and myself were supposed to participate. When I drew Lenin's attention to the undesirability of this young man's presence, he quieted me with the remark, "He is one of ours."

I understood then that the student was a Bolshevik spy, the aid of another spy—"the eye of Moscow." These men had not only to report everything that concerned the Italian Socialists to Zinoviev, but they had also to spy upon each other, each concerned with proving that he was the man whom Zinoviev, the Soviet mouthpiece, the dispenser of money and power, could trust. Each report sent in by the Italian Socialists to Moscow would be read by one of these spies, who would send with it his own report—the results of his own espionage, provocations, and lies. Zinoviev in turn would answer the delegates in one way, his agents in another. In this way he induced the Italians to believe that he approved their activities and recommendations, while at the same time he gave orders for their undoing—a situation intended to arouse distrust of them among the rank and file.

As we were leaving Moscow we learned, to our surprise, that two of the Italian delegates were not going with us. Why? Because they had "important work" in Moscow—interviews with prominent Bolsheviks, etc. This answer augmented our surprise. Why had these two been chosen for this "important work"? One of them, Bombacci, was a sentimental and naïve man whose cheap vanity had been stimulated by his reception. Whenever Zinoviev wished him to speak at a meeting, he would write in a note to the chairman: "Let Bombacci take the floor now. His long hair and flowing beard are an attraction. What he says is not worth translating." The other, Professor Graziadei, had been a life-long critic of Marxism and one of the most Right Wing members of the Italian movement. Why this choice? To divide the Italian Socialist delegation so that Serrati would have to fight, not only against the Bolsheviks, but against some of his own people as well—and in this way to produce the impression that the Italian movement was split within itself and that Serrati did not represent the majority. These two individuals had been chosen, rather than others, because of their weakness and vanity, their inability to resist flattery and applause. They had been received and flattered in the Kremlin, the ex-residence of the Tsar, in a setting which spoke of power and money!

Whereas Lenin looked upon these two men as tools whom he could use and then get rid of, the two pilgrims themselves imagined that they were chosen for their positive qualities to be the leaders of the Italian movement, under the Bolshevik wing.

While we were absent they were shown to Russian audiences as authentic representatives of the Revolution—in opposition to Serrati, who had "betrayed" it. Their speeches were translated into whatever Zinoviev wished them to say. They became completely inebriated with the ovations of the crowds and the flattery of Zinoviev's satraps.

Shortly after the arrival of the Italian mission, Emma Goldman and Sasha Berkman had left Moscow on their new assignment to collect material throughout the country for a Museum of the revolutionary period. An American friend of theirs, Henry Alsberg, then a newspaper correspondent, accompanied them on this trip. I ran into them again in Kiev, and invited them to a banquet given for the Italian delegates and some French trade unionists who had recently arrived to attend a Red Trade Union Congress. I presided at the banquet, where the best of foods were supplied for the visitors, and as on previous occasions I knew that Sasha and Emma shared my feelings about this display.

When we returned to Moscow, we found a changed atmosphere. Serrati and the delegates who had supported him were met with hostility and suspicion. Rumours of Serrati's "treachery" were being whispered about. An ever-growing current of mutual suspicion pervaded the delegation. The two Italians who had stayed in Moscow had become complete tools of the Bolsheviks. Counting upon the impunity which their prestige, money, and success had granted them, the Bolsheviks had already made use of their agents residing in Italy to complete the details of their plot.

Inside the Italian party there had always been a minority current hostile to parliamentarianism. Its leader was at that time a brilliant young lawyer of Naples, named Bordiga. The Bolsheviks had always scorned and disapproved of this movement and of its leader. They considered it petty-bourgeois and harmful to the labour movement. But for the purpose of splitting the Italian party, this, too, was "good enough." They had invited Bordiga to come to Russia to attack Serrati.

Serrati's only weapons in such a conflict were the truth, his devotion and experience, and his own independence of character. How could these prevail against the leaders of a successful social revolution, against the prestige of a Lenin and a Trotsky? I knew that, however unequal the battle, he would not hesitate to fight for the integrity of his Party; and I think he foresaw the consequences even then. Zinoviev had cabled the Executive of the Italian Party to name three of the Socialist commissioners in Russia as delegates to the Second Comintern Congress. Knowing nothing of the situation that had developed in Moscow, they cabled back credentials for Serrati, Bombacci and Graziadei.

21

TO THOSE WHO WERE IN CLOSE TOUCH WITH the labour movement during this period or who have watched since then the fatal effect of Bolshevik influence upon the movement in other countries, what I have to say about the development of the Italian tragedy, both during and after the Second Comintern Congress, will come as no surprise. On the contrary, it will recall their own experiences in other countries, with other details and personalities, but with identical methods involved. The realization that their own experience was not exceptional may help them to understand the enormity of the tragedy.

Of all the Socialist movements, the Italian had been the most appreciated by the Russians. The Italian Socialists, and Serrati in particular, had saved the Bolsheviks from virtual isolation from Western Europe. But in 1920, when the political and economic situation in Italy was so acute, Zinoviev had decided that

both the Party and Serrati were to be destroyed. That very revolutionary integrity and independence of the Italian movement
that had distinguished it during and after the World War made
it a thorn in the side of the Comintern leadership and compelled
the bureaucracy to employ against this powerful movement
every dubious weapon at its command.

To understand that fight, it is necessary to understand the
ramifications of the Comintern itself, as they had developed by
the end of 1920. Very few organizations in the world—except
perhaps the Catholic Church—can be compared with the Comintern in the number of its publications, agencies, and representatives throughout the entire world, stimulated by the ambition to
penetrate and proselytize the masses everywhere. It had behind
it the unlimited resources of the Soviet government at a time
when this government was less concerned with the immediate
condition of the Russian masses than with the control of the
revolutionary labour movement of the world. No revolutionary
group in any country, dependent upon the resources of its own
members and the support of poverty-stricken workers, could
compete with such machinery or with its unscrupulous and well-
financed agents—many of whom, as I have pointed out previ-
ously, were men with no background in the labour movement or
who had been discredited in it long before.

Ostensibly, it was the purpose of these numerous agencies,
newspapers and representatives, to translate the Moscow gospel
to the workers of the world. Actually, however, it was almost impossible to find in any of their documents an explanation of
what the Bolsheviks really required of their followers—why they
split some parties, excommunicated others, declared still others
(even farther to the Right) infallible; why certain leaders were
denounced as spies, traitors, social fascists, etc., while others who
had actually betrayed the movement, before and during the war,
were accepted into the fold and made Communist officials in
their own countries. The only criterion actually employed—in
spite of these lengthy "political" theses—was complete verbal
acceptance of Moscow's direction.

The theses and demands sent out to the various movements
and parties for their unqualified acceptance and for the guid-

ance of the faithful were written in the artificial political jargon invented for the use of the Russian Bolsheviks. In translation, they were still less intelligible. A word with a Latin root would be Russified; it was then translated, by people who had no idea of its origin, into a word which had quite another significance, or none at all. Or the deformed Latin-Russian word would be introduced bodily into the text of another language. But these long theses and artificial slogans were intended, not to be understood and discussed, but merely to be followed. Hundreds of newspapers copied them, thousands of agents would introduce them in various ways in every country.

Though occasionally brilliant from the theoretical viewpoint, most of these endless theses were merely continuations of the monotonous factional polemics carried on between the Social Democrats and the Bolsheviks before the war and the Revolution, or rather they were the accentuation of older Bolshevik polemics. In the beginning they had certain new and useful theoretical formulations, even though these were expressed in a way that made them accessible only to the intellectuals. Theoretical enlightenment is a necessary weapon for any mass movement. But the demagogy of the Comintern began when it pretended that these theses—and their application—were the expression of the attitude and the will of the masses themselves.

A leader or agent would be summoned to Moscow and ordered to have certain resolutions passed in his own party or labour organization. Surrounded by the prestige thus given to him as a "mouthpiece of Moscow," he would return and introduce this thesis to an audience incapable of following it, but impressed by the authority of Moscow. The conclusion was clear. If Moscow called some one a "traitor," it must be so. Had not the Russians been victorious in their Revolution—and therefore, must not their formula be correct? "Down with the traitors, the Social Democrats, the Centrists! Long live Soviet Russia and the Comintern!"

These very theses and pilgrimages themselves soon became a source of intrigue. Certain members, envying the prestige of the "envoys" and "spokesmen," would begin to denounce them for not being sufficiently devoted in advocating or applying the party line. The spokesmen would be accused of "deviations." Zinoviev would then immediately charge these complainants with spying upon his envoys. An underground competition for Moscow's favour, developing into a net of intrigue, became the very essence of Bolshevik propaganda in every country in the world. Members would vote a certain way, not because of conviction, but because they were partisans of one leader or another. (In the United States, as elsewhere, this situation developed constant and brutal struggles for power among Communist leaders from 1920 on.) Soon, all formalities of "democracy" were abandoned. Moscow named all the leaders and disposed of votes and Party decisions as it saw fit. The most contradictory tactics and slogans would succeed each other with amazing rapidity; the hero of yesterday would become the "renegade" of today, and vice versa. There was no reason, in principle or tactics, for the excommunication of certain leaders or parties. For the most part, these acts represented attempts on the part of the Bolshevik leaders to conceal their own mistakes and blunders, their cowardice or lack of responsibility.

The tactics of the Comintern leaders—who were also the Russian leaders—which have resulted in the widespread defeat, or rather suicide, of the European labour movement, flow logically from the psychological approach of the Bolsheviks, with its lack of any ethical concept. In the international field, as in Russia's internal politics, this approach led them to follow the path of least resistance in that sphere in which it is most dangerous to do so—the sphere of human relationships between the powerful and the powerless, those who command and those who obey. Here, too, they used the method of natural selection in reverse—choosing their collaborators not for their good or positive qualities, but for their bad or negative ones—because these could be more easily manipulated. It is an historical tragi-comedy that these brilliant dialecticians did not foresee that the dialectic process also applied to them—that they failed to realize that once you begin to manœuvre with human beings you set into motion certain forces which will go their own way, which cannot be stopped, and which may eventually destroy their initiators.

It is the tragedy of the international labour movement that

[271]

the first social revolution occurred, not only in a backward country, but in a country which was compelled, because of the circumstances of the time, to create a new militarism. Because of the prestige of this first victory, the revolutionary movement thereafter was to bear the imprint of Russia's specific experience and the methods which grew out of it. This situation has enabled the Bolsheviks to introduce into the world movement that system of military caste, ruthless suppression, espionage, and bureaucratic corruption which are the fruits of capitalism and war, and which have nothing in common with Socialism.

In the few days preceding the beginning of the Second Congress, I became more and more distressed as I suspected that the intrigues of the past year were about to bear fruit in the splitting and disorganization of the Left Wing forces of the world. I was most concerned, naturally, with the Italian situation. It was obvious, from Zinoviev's choice of conspirators, that he was preparing to attack Serrati from both the Left and the Right. As the Bolsheviks knew that I agreed with Serrati, I had been deprived of the opportunity to speak or vote at the Congress. Though for years I had represented the Italian Party at all international conventions—and Lenin had insisted on my representing that Party at the first Comintern convention—I was now considered a member of the Russian Party whose delegates were elected by the Russian Central Committee. A larger number of delegates had come from the parties of Western Europe and America, which had not been represented the year before—including the Swedish and Norwegian Left Socialists, the Independent Labour Party of England, the Dutch Communists, the German Independents, the two American Communist parties. (American Communism had split into two sections at its birth; the Communist Labour Party was represented by John Reed and two other Americans; the Communist Party by Louis Fraina and a man named Stocklitzky).

Even among the "delegates" who were entitled to vote—as opposed to the fraternal delegates who were not—there were a number who belonged to parties which had not yet affiliated with the Third International. This was the case with the French Socialists, supposedly represented by Guilbeaux. The split in the

French Socialist Party, which resulted in the organization of French Communism, did not take place until several months later—as a result of the mandates of the Comintern. We were amazed to discover that among the fraternal delegates from France was Marcel Cachin, who had been most violently patriotic of the French Right Wing Socialists. It was Cachin who had acted as a French agent in the wooing of Mussolini in 1914 and it was Cachin who had come to Russia in 1918, as an agent of his government to persuade the Russian workers to continue the war. Now he was to be received into the Comintern Executive and made a leader of the French Communist Party, a rôle he has occupied ever since.

It was announced that the American Socialist Party had withdrawn from the Second International, but had not yet endorsed the Third. Like a number of other anti-war Socialist groups, it was awaiting the answer to certain questions on matters of organization and tactics which it had put to the Comintern Executive. The answers to these questions, given by the Second Congress, not only wrecked any hope of Left Wing unity among those forces whose faces were already turned towards Moscow, but resulted in the withdrawal of a number of parties—including the Italian and later the Scandinavian—which had already voted to affiliate. The same thing occurred in relation to the Red Trade Union Congress in 1920, from which the American I.W.W. and the more radical sections of the European labour movement withdrew at this time. Those sections dominated by Syndicalist tendencies, in particular, were bitterly opposed to control of their unions by a political party—Communist or otherwise. These labour movements, like the radical political parties, were also to be split wide open during the coming year or two.

When the Congress finally convened in Petrograd (to be moved next day to Moscow) in the former throne-room of the Tsar, the Russian Bolsheviks were at the very crest of a wave of power and confidence that had been rising since 1917. They had successfully routed the White armies and interventionists and had established themselves as rulers of all Russia. Throughout the world the rift between the Left forces and the Social

[273]

Democracy had deepened and practically all of the former groups were ready to enter the Comintern. Revolutionists from every section of the world were making pilgrimages to Moscow and were hailing the Bolsheviks. It was a moment when the Bolsheviks could have built a powerful and united movement on the basis of mutual agreement on revolutionary fundamentals, internal equality and self-respect. Whatever politically vacillating elements remained in such an alignment would have dropped away or could have been disposed of by democratic means. But in this moment of supreme self-confidence it became obvious that the Bolsheviks wanted nothing of the kind; that they were concerned only with the organization in each country of a militarized and miniature Bolshevik Party completely dominated by and dependent upon Moscow itself. Any elements—and these included many of the best in the international movement—which pleaded for any degree of autonomy, for the right to adjust their tactics to objective situations in their own countries, which objected to the automatic expulsion of any individual on orders from Moscow, or which questioned the Russian "thesis" on world affairs, were to be denounced as "centrists" or even "counter-revolutionists," unfit for membership in the Comintern.

The mandate round which most of the conflict in the Congress centred, was embodied in the famous "Twenty-One Points." Zinoviev could scarcely conceal his satisfaction and malice when he flung these "Conditions of Affiliation with the Third International" into the faces of the assembled delegates and at the revolutionary movement throughout the world. These Conditions were based upon the "thesis" that the class struggle was "now passing into civil war."

As I was the only translator available for the Congress, I was able to judge more clearly than most of the delegates the character and trend of that event. Through the interminable discussions (the Congress lasted for three weeks) I was forced to repeat lengthy polemics in Russian, German, French, Italian, to translate hundreds of questions and answers. I had a feeling that I was participating not merely in a political, but also in a personal, tragedy, involving some of my dearest friends. It was obvious that John Reed, as he watched the proceedings, shared my feeling. For Reed, waging his own particular battle with Radek and Zinoviev, that tragedy lay not so much in his inability to defend himself effectively against these men, as in the realization that he was struggling against a *system* which had already begun to devour its own children. His resignation from the Comintern was a symbol of his despair.

In the general fight against the Comintern Conditions, Serrati was supported by delegates from other countries—Sylvia Pankhurst from the British Independent Labour Party, the Swedish and Norwegian Left Socialists and others. He discussed each of the Bolshevik assertions. The Italian Socialists had agreed in the past that it might be necessary to part with certain Right Wing leaders; but this was a matter which the rank and file must discuss and decide. Men like Turati, Treves, Modigliani, and others, while not Left-wingers, had supported the Party position in a disciplined manner during the war—in meetings, in articles, and in Parliament. Their fate could not be handed down from above. He pointed out that in Italy the rigid centralized control of the Party press which the Bolsheviks demanded would merely wreck the Party. The *leit-motif* of his remarks was: "We shall remain at our posts and fulfil our duty, which means to express our opinions openly to all and to you too—as has always been the case in our international Party. We ask that the Comintern let us judge the situation as it is developing in Italy and to let us choose the measures to be taken to defend Italian Socialism."

As most of the delegates present had no understanding of what was happening in Italy in this period, but relied for their information upon such authoritative revolutionaries as Lenin and Trotsky, Serrati's political defeat was inevitable.

The fight against him was to go on for several years, during which he was bitterly and personally attacked by all the Bolshevik leaders. Serrati proved his courage and foresight in a letter he wrote to Lenin at this time:

Your Party has six times as many members now as before the Revolution, but notwithstanding the strict discipline and frequent purges, it has not gained much so far as quality is concerned. Your ranks have been joined by all the slavish elements who always serve the powerful. These elements constitute a blind and cruel bureaucracy which is creating new privileges in Soviet Russia.

Those elements which became revolutionary on the day after the Revolution have made of the proletarian Revolution which cost the masses so much suffering, a source of enjoyment and domination. They are making a goal of that Terror which to you was only a means.

The fate of this man, loved and honoured as few Socialist leaders have been outside their own countries, foreshadowed the fate of Leon Trotsky—a very different type of leader—in a later period. Already in 1920 the Bolsheviks had undermined Serrati's popularity as well as the unity of his party. Here is one of the abject manœuvres they were to use against him a year later:

During the war, we had been surrounded by spies and *agents provocateurs*. One of these who pretended to be a pacifist and sympathizer was introduced to Serrati by an *Avanti* correspondent in Vienna, who wrote that this man, having an opportunity to travel, could serve as a link between the Vienna correspondent and the *Avanti* headquarters in Milan. Under this pretext the man became a friend and visitor at Serrati's home. Knowing that Serrati needed some furniture which he could not afford to buy immediately, this agent had offered to lend him the necessary sum. After a time, Serrati's suspicions had become aroused. He immediately went to the Party Central Committee in Rome, told them the story, borrowed the same sum of money, and placed it with a public notary. Just before coming to Russia, he had published a notice in his paper, stating where this agent could get the money.

When Serrati was leaving Moscow, after the Second Congress, he had mentioned this incident as one of the reasons why he wished to return to Italy immediately. He wanted to be back in Milan to expose the whole affair. Both Bukharin and Zinoviev laughed at his concern.

"Is it worth while even to speak of such trifles? Such things happen to every revolutionary—we have all been denounced as German agents. Who would dare to question your integrity?"

[276]

On the day before the inauguration of the Third Comintern Congress in 1921, about a year after this conversation, the Russian News Agency in Rome spread throughout the world the news that the Italian leader, Serrati, had accepted money from a police agent. Up to this time no Italian paper, even Mussolini's *Popolo d'Italia*, had ever dared to question Serrati's honesty. But after this story had been launched by the Russian agency, all the Italian dailies published it as a "news release." It was then reprinted in all the Russian newspapers, under sensational headlines, as a dispatch *originating in Rome*.

This was the year in which Marcel Cachin, the agent of French nationalism, the violent antagonist of Zimmerwald, and the wooer of the Russian masses for Allied imperialism, was elevated to membership in the Comintern.

To those of us who had left the Second International and created the Zimmerwald movement, who had made the support of the World War a line of demarcation between ourselves and the Right, these two events constituted an irreparable blow. By 1921 I had renounced all relations with the Comintern, and when I was told that at the Third Congress my service as a translator would be indispensable, I refused to participate. To prove that it was not illness which prevented my taking part, I attended some of the sessions. To Lenin, whom I met in the courtyard of the Kremlin and who seemed surprised to see me, I remarked that I was not there to participate but to emphasize my boycott of the affair.

When I read the article about Serrati in the Russian papers, I felt that something more terrible than anything that had gone before now divided me from the Bolsheviks. I had the feeling that they were capable of anything. The recent Moscow "trials" and purges, the executions of dissident revolutionaries by the Communists in Spain, are part of a chain in which the persecution of Serrati constituted the first link.

When Serrati returned to Italy after the Second Congress, his report was approved by a large majority of the Party members, and immediately Bolshevik agents were sent to Italy to fight Serrati, to split the Party, and to organize from its more docile section an official Communist Party. For a whole year this struggle between Zinoviev and Serrati went on.

In 1921, when the split in the Party took place, only about a third of the membership joined the new Communist organization. But this split did not put an end to Moscow's intrigues within the Italian Socialist ranks. New subdivisions, new splits, had to be provoked. In spite of the fact that the Party majority, led by Serrati, still insisted that it should try to maintain its affiliation with the Comintern under certain conditions, a more naïve element, fomented and flattered by the insidious strategy of new Bolshevik agents, became worried lest they lose contact with the leaders of the victorious Russian Revolution and grew more inclined to accept any terms upon which this contact might be renewed. These were led to believe that Serrati was the only obstacle to "complete revolutionary unity." In 1924, after three more years of internal struggle, and after the tide of Comintern self-confidence had somewhat subsided, they prevailed upon Serrati to join a delegation that was going to Moscow for more of these interminable consultations.

"He is the only one who can induce the Russians to compromise on their conditions of affiliation," they declared. "He must make this attempt."

Once in Moscow, all the arts and pressures of the Bolshevik machine were mobilized to induce Serrati to accept a compromise, a tentative arrangement. He had no faith in it and he tried to convince the Bolsheviks of the new Fascist reaction which was ripening in Italy. (Up to this time the Party had been able to function, under difficulties, but in 1924 a new period of persecution began which was to end with the final triumph of the Totalitarian State in 1926.) He told them how dangerous were the tactics they were proposing. Finally, under the hammer blows of the Russian leadership, the sense of growing defeat in Italy, his own nervous exhaustion after the years of sterile struggle with Moscow, his power of resistance gave way and he committed what was for him an act of spiritual suicide. He promised the Bolsheviks to advocate the acceptance of their conditions and returned to Italy.

In Italy, he found the Party situation changed. The splitting off of the Italian Communists had so weakened the Socialist Left Wing that it no longer had a decisive majority in the Party. The majority would not agree to the conditions he had accepted; they now defended their autonomy with the same arguments Serrati had used for years. In a final outburst of temperament, of despair and nervous weakness, Serrati announced that he had become a "rank-and-file member" of the Communist Party. On his way to an illegal meeting, he suddenly died.

To those who knew him intimately and who understood the tragedy of his last years there is no doubt that death was welcome to him. He did not wish to survive what he had loved and served so passionately all his life—Italian Socialism. He realized then that the sacrifices the Bolsheviks had imposed upon him had been in vain. Though he was too proud to admit it, the fact that he had been the victim of people who had abused his attachment to his Party, undermined his existence. He had been put into a condition in which all kinds of extortions and "confessions" are possible. His physical death was only a belated echo of his suicide in Moscow—a suicide induced by his devotion to the Revolution.

I have often been asked if Italian Fascism would have triumphed without the splits provoked by the Bolsheviks. I should like to indicate here the difference between the Italian and German "triumphs." In Germany the working-class defeat was due almost wholly to division and demoralization in the years preceding 1932 and the Communist line of "social fascism" which made impossible any kind of united front; for in Germany, the organized workers numbered many millions and their simultaneous mobilization under one slogan could have prevented the triumph of Hitler. In Germany, too, a great many new Communist voters deserted to the Nazi ticket in 1932, because of discouragement and disgust with the divisions within the labour movement and because in the beginning they had been attracted to Communism for much the same reason they were attracted later to Fascism.

In Italy, Fascism as an *idea* never triumphed. There was merely a victory of castor oil, the dagger, the bomb. The workers' faith in Socialism, their hatred of Fascism, remained intact. How I wish that all those who speak and write of Italian Fascism would read the works in which Professor Gaetano Salvemini, by using documents from Fascist sources, in the most rigorously scientific method, illustrates this fact, as well as the tragedy and courage of the Italian people. I can only emphasize that for three and a half years the Italian masses resisted the bloody vandalism of the Fascist bands and preferred to have their institutions destroyed rather than cede them to their oppressors. The German Fascists had no difficulty in occupying thousands of working-class headquarters throughout the country. I would also like to emphasize that while Parliament still existed in Italy, in spite of savage persecution of voters and deputies, the number of votes given to the labour parties never varied. It was probably this fact which finally convinced the Italian Fascists that only physical extermination and the abolition of parliamentarianism would serve their purposes.

The splits within the ranks of the revolutionary parties both facilitated and prepared the way for the victory of the Fascist terror, the annihilation of the workers' institutions, the physical extermination of anti-Fascists. Here, as in Germany, moreover, the Bolsheviks had asked nothing but obedience of their members, and many individuals without moral or intellectual scruples—individuals whom the war had trained in violence— had been attracted to the anti-Socialist Bolshevik groups. As soon as it became dangerous to be "red," these people were as ready to serve a "black" boss as a "red" one. Soon these individuals were among the leaders of the attacks and atrocities perpetrated against Socialists, Anarchists, Republicans—anti-Fascists of any sort.

Perhaps the heaviest responsibility borne by the Comintern for that defeat of the world labour movement, which began with the victory of Italian Fascism, was the general discouragement it brought to the honest rank and file in the years to come. Thousands drifted out of the movement into inactivity, resentful and disillusioned, as thousands more are becoming today as the result of recent events in Russia. They were lost to the working-class cause forever after.

22

A DAY OR TWO AFTER THE CLOSE OF THE SECOND
Congress, John Reed asked me to come and see him.

"I have a little wood," he said, "and do you know what—I still
have some potatoes I brought back from my last trip. I shall bake
them for you."

He looked ill and depressed and it seemed to me that he had
aged ten years in the past few weeks. I understood what a blow
the Congress had been to him.

"And now comes the farce of Baku," he said. "Zinoviev has
ordered me to leave tomorrow. I will not go. I will tell Zinoviev
I can't do it."

Louise was on her way to Russia, but he had no idea of when
she would arrive or how. But I understood that this was not the
reason why he did not want to go to Baku. Baku would be a
repetition, on a smaller scale, of the Moscow Congress, and he
had already made up his mind that he had nothing in common

with the Comintern. Nevertheless, I heard the next day that he had gone. He knew that Zinoviev and Radek would stop at nothing to discredit him, and he would not give them the excuse of attacking him on the basis of indiscipline.

Two days after he had left, Louise arrived. She had had to make her way across Finland, which was then at war with Russia, disguised as a sailor. From Stockholm she had written Jack in care of Zinoviev's office the probable date of her arrival, but he had never received the message. We saw each other nearly every day after she arrived.

I had been determined to leave Russia with the Italian delegation, and as it was impossible to obtain an Italian visa in Moscow, I decided—providing I could get permission to leave—to go to Reval in Esthonia with them, and to try for a visa there.

When I went to see Lenin, I was so agitated, internally, by the importance of my decision to leave the first Workers' Republic and all that this meant in my life, that I was able to raise the question only indirectly, to speak of something which had never been of the slightest interest to me.

"Look here, Vladimir Ilyitch," I said, "now that I have given up all offices and have decided to leave Russia, I haven't a scrap of paper for my identification."

Lenin pretended that he did not notice the seriousness of my decision to leave the country.

"Your identification?" he asked. "But who would not know you? Perhaps some one in the remote Ukraine?"

He was referring to something that had happened a few evenings before, when we were leaving the Kremlin. A Red soldier had let me pass with a nod, but had stopped Lenin and asked, "Your credentials, comrade. I do not know you."

"But," Lenin went on, "if you really wish an identification, I shall give you one with all my heart." The warm tones in which these words were expressed surprised and touched me. He had never spoken so to me before. While he wrote at his desk, I took a newspaper so as not to disturb him. I had expected him to fill out the regular formula, but to my surprise he handed me a sheet of note paper on which he had written in ink:

Comrade Angelica Balabanoff has been for many years a member of the party. She is one of the most prominent militants of the Communist International.

I was so moved by this unexpected statement that Lenin, noting my hesitation, said:

"How difficult it is to satisfy you! We once offered to make you ambassador to Italy and you refused. If we prevented you from leaving Russia, you would be unhappy. Now you are free to go and you still seem unhappy. What do you object to in my note?"

"Object?" I repeated. "Why should I object? Any other Communist would give ten years of his life to have such a certificate from you—but to me ——"

"Well, what can I do to satisfy you, to make you happy?"

"What I would like most you cannot give me, Vladimir Ilyitch —the political and moral possibility of remaining in Russia the rest of my life."

"Then, why don't you?" he asked. "Why must you leave?"

"You know very well, Vladimir Ilyitch. Russia does not seem to need such people as I."

"But we do," he answered. "We have so few."

He made this statement so seriously that whenever I recall it I feel that Lenin was becoming aware of what might happen to the Revolution. I know that he despised some of his collaborators, but he would never show it as long as he needed their services for the movement. For example, in the years preceding the Revolution, Zinoviev was his most intimate associate; but when the moment came when Lenin decided that power must be seized while Zinoviev hesitated and doubted, Lenin disavowed him immediately, declaring that he had always known that Zinoviev was a coward. I know that he despised Radek for his lack of character and inconsistency, but he encouraged those very traits in him when he considered these useful to the achievement of his own ends. Personally, he had not liked Trotsky, because the latter had opposed him for so many years and because of certain traits in his character. But when he realized the services which Trotsky could render the Revolution, he saw in him only the revolutionary and elevated him to the highest office—

[283]

even when by doing so he encouraged the traits of which he disapproved. When I am asked about his attitude towards Stalin at this time, I can only answer that in 1920 no one seemed to have an "attitude" towards Stalin, because in the political life of the movement he was so unimportant. Lenin's concern about Stalin developed later—in the last year of his own life.

At the Esthonian border I found that it was impossible to obtain an Italian visa. (I suspected later that Zinoviev had a hand in this.) Bidding good-bye to my comrades with a heavy heart, I returned to Moscow. On the very day of my arrival— September 20th—I received a message from Lenin saying that he wished to see me, to talk over certain matters he had discussed with the English delegation. Krupskaya was not well and he asked me to come to their apartment in the Kremlin. The Lenins lived in Russia much as they had lived in exile, and as I entered the rather shabby, low-ceilinged apartment which had served as the quarters of a lady-in-waiting before the Revolution, I was amused to think of the stories that appeared in certain foreign papers about Lenin's way of life. I shared their simple meal in the room which was both dining-room and bedroom, and was touched when Krupskaya opened a treasured bottle of preserves in honour of my visit.

There was no hint in Lenin's manner that he was conscious of the many differences which had arisen between me and the Party leaders in the Comintern. He talked about the English delegation, and only as I was leaving did he speak casually of the news which had just arrived from Italy—"the seizure of the factories" and the peasant demonstrations there. Lenin showed no enthusiasm over this news. When he asked me my opinion, I replied:

"If you are asking about these new developments, I know no more than you do—we have read the same dispatches. If, however, you are alluding to conditions in general in Italy, I can only say that I think that in no country in Europe are the masses so prepared for the social revolution and for Socialism as in Italy."

"For social revolution?" he replied in an irritated tone. "Why, don't you know that Italy has no raw material? What about

[284]

bread, what about coal? How long could the workers resist a blockade? No, we don't want a repetition of the Hungarian defeat." He went on to elaborate upon the fatal consequences of a revolution in Italy at that time.

"But neither had we bread when the Revolution began," I objected.

"Italy has neither our geographic advantages nor our material resources. And how can you compare the masses of Western Europe with our people—so patient, so accustomed to privation?"

I am inclined now to believe that Lenin was right about that specific situation, but the conversation has both a psychological and an historical significance. Lenin was actually apprehensive that the sit-down strikes and demonstrations in Italy would precipitate a revolutionary situation. Yet, after the defeat of the Italian workers, the Communist press, in Moscow and throughout the world, proclaimed that only the timidity and betrayal of Serrati and the other Italian Socialists had prevented a successful social revolution. While these events were taking place, Serrati was on his way home from Moscow by way of Finland, Sweden, and Germany. When he reached Italy, the movement had already collapsed. The attitude of some of the other leaders in Italy had been inspired by the same doubts which Lenin had expressed to me.

Later, of course, I was to receive a more authoritative picture of what was happening in Italy, and because the events of 1919 and 1920 have assumed such historic importance in the Italian labour movement, I should like to deal with them here.

The strike of the metal workers in Turin, in September, 1920, is generally alluded to as the first attempt at seizure of the factories. As a matter of fact, the first attempt at expropriation was made in March, 1919, in Dalmine by workers who did not even belong to the Federation of Labour and who, if they had any philosophy at all, were good Catholics and "patriots." They were animated by resentment against the government which had promised to compensate so generously the "defenders of the fatherland" and had then failed to do so. They had no program, no special demands; their movement was a chaotic and impulsive protest, a gesture of impatience and a menace, of course, to the ruling class. The strikers wanted to get, immediately, the fruits of the so-called "revolutionary war." They had no leadership, as neither the trades-unionists, Socialists nor Anarchists took the movement seriously and did not want to be responsible for a turbulent act that was doomed to fail. The one "leader" who did arrive—and incite the workers to violence—was Mussolini. These workers were merely following the tactics he had preached since the end of the war—violent expropriation and the extermination of any individuals who stood in the way. At this time Mussolini was much impressed by the methods of the Bolsheviks in Russia and was urging these same things—in nationalist, rather than Marxist, terms—upon the Italian working class. This was the period in which the newly organized Fascist bands were talking expropriation and uttering direct threats to the "exploiters." (In 1937 the Communist Party, in exile, issued an offer for a united front with the Italian Fascists on "the basis of the 1919 Fascist program.")

Mussolini's record of betrayal, the meagre results of the war which he had hailed as a war of revolutionary liberation, had made him very unpopular. The bourgeoisie no longer needed him. The job he had been paid for was finished. But the general atmosphere was tense and rebellious, the ruling classes were dominated by fear. The example of Russia was inspiring. Following the main current, as always, and offended at rebukes from above, Mussolini tried to approach the labour movement, offering his collaboration to the Socialist unionists. Naturally they refused to have anything to do with him. Nothing was left to him but to fish in troubled waters. There was unrest in Dalmine and it was there that he went. At meetings and in articles he emphasized that this seizure of the factories was the first step on the road towards the social revolution—that the Socialists who had refused his collaboration were betrayers whom the workers must denounce. Down with the capitalists! Hang them to trees—there are enough in Italy.

The occupation of the factories in Turin, which began on September 20, 1920, had quite a different character. These strikes were not inspired by any illusion that private property was to be abolished immediately. They constituted one phase of the economic struggle for concrete social and industrial reforms—reforms which had been granted verbally, but not in practice. They represented a spontaneous act of self-defence on the part of the workers whose conquests were being sabotaged. Only after the movement had spread from one factory to another, and after the entire press had denounced this act of self-defence as an attempt at revolution, did the leaders of the Socialists meet with the leaders of the Federation of Labour in order to discuss whether or not this fight could be extended to all categories of workers and be transformed into a political and revolutionary movement. The vote showed that the majority were hostile to such a program. Among those who advocated the extension of the strikes into a general struggle were reformists, whereas, among those who stood against it were those Socialist elements who were the most ardent followers of Moscow (and who were later to join the Communist Party when it was organized). These details may be of little importance now. I recall them to prove how history has been falsified both by Fascists and by the Bolsheviks. In the post-war period all of Europe was shaken by serious strikes and land seizures. The Italian strikes were merely one aspect—possibly the most dramatic—of this general unrest. The apologists of Mussolini, in the United States and in Europe, have pointed to these demonstrations as proof that Mussolini and his Fascists "saved" Italy from Bolshevism. The Italians themselves know that the strike movement had subsided and that an industrial up-swing was under way long before the March on Rome.

After the Second Congress, and the failure of my attempt to obtain a visa, my own situation in Russia became more and more painful to me. I continued to speak as a general propagandist for the Soviet institutions and I received as many invitations to address factory and public meetings as I was able to accept. But this type of activity alone did not satisfy me. I had either to speak out or seem to be an accomplice, yet there was no way in which I could express my disagreement with dominant policies either through the Soviet papers or in public meetings. The thought that I would become a parasite in a country where work was so necessary tormented me and crushed my health once more.

I was still living at the National, which was called the First Soviet House, where many leading Communists and members of the government lived. The food shortage was acute and dinner usually consisted of soup made from canned fish, a piece of the same fish with a slice of bread. Once a week, extra food would be distributed—sugar, oil or raisins, herring, and sometimes caviar.

In the Kremlin there was a deposit of extra food for those who were ill or too undernourished, and though I was entitled to take my meals there I never did so. When my doctor, who became a devoted friend of mine, tried to convince me that I must ask for some white bread, I thought he must be joking. Some time later, when my condition became so serious that my life was in danger, he prescribed a special diet of Nestlé's food which had been sent in by the Swedish comrades for Russian children.

It was during this period that I received another indication of the effect of Soviet power, prestige, and stage management upon even the most intransigent of revolutionaries.

I have already mentioned the rôle of Clara Zetkin in the German revolutionary movement and as founder and leader of the Marxist movement among women throughout the world. When Clara arrived in Moscow in the fall of 1920, she was ill and hysterical. Instead of being brought to the National, she was taken to another hotel, where there was no one, except a secretary, to look after her. One evening, after he had visited her there and had found her in an extremely overwrought condition, Lenin had come to my room.

"Clara should have a heated room and regular food," he said. "She should be where she can get personal care—not a hospital, of course."

I told Lenin that I thought I could find a proper place for her. When the representatives of the Italian coöperatives established a headquarters in Moscow, I had succeeded in obtaining for them the former Swedish Embassy, and had assisted Rondani, the deputy in charge, in various ways. The use of the house had been granted in my name, to give the group immunity from the Cheka. I knew that there was a vacant bedroom at the house, and that there Clara could have the comfort, warmth, and quiet she needed. I had no difficulty in obtaining permission to use the apartment, and a day or two later I moved into the place with Clara. I slept on a couch in her room.

As her condition improved somewhat, she was called upon to address huge mass meetings. She was still so weak she had sometimes to be carried on and off the platform. Knowing that she was being used for demonstration purposes by Zinoviev, I urged her to refuse these invitations or to cut her speeches to a few words of greeting and solidarity.

But I did not realize how Clara was fascinated by the platform itself and by the applause that greeted her.

"Look at this white-haired veteran of the movement," Zinoviev would say when he introduced her. "She is a living testament to the approval which all great revolutionaries give to the tactics of our great, invincible Party. Long live the glorious Communist Party!"

Then, as soon as Clara would begin to speak, Zinoviev would write in a note to the translator: "Abbreviate; cut her speech. We can't waste so much time on her eloquence."

I soon discovered that Clara really loved the atmosphere with which she was surrounded and that she would speak for the sake of the applause. The Bolsheviks availed themselves of this weakness to the full; they flattered her, invited her for personal audiences, let her think that she was influencing their policies. Instead, they were laughing at her naïveté—especially when she criticized them for the fatal mistakes they had imposed upon the German Communists. Yet, knowing their tactical errors and the fruits of these errors in Germany, Clara could not resist their flattery. After my departure from Russia, when she was surrounded completely by the tools of Zinoviev, she let herself become one of these tools. She emphasized her adherence to the dominant Bolshevik leadership—which meant the leadership of the Russian government—even while she knew that the nonconformist minority in Germany was right.

[289]

This attitude of Clara was one of the bitter personal dis-illusionments of my life. I had been not only her ardent disciple, but also her friend. She had once assured me that after the loss of Rosa Luxemburg, for whom she had had an unlimited devo-tion, she looked upon me as her closest friend. At the time of our last encounter in Russia I realized that I could no longer look to her either as a friend or as a teacher. I had told her of my refusal to collaborate any longer with the Bolsheviks and of my determination to leave Russia as soon as possible. She insisted that I should remain.

"You can be appointed secretary of the International Wom-an's movement, Angelica," she said. "This will leave you in-dependent of the other Comintern institutions. You must re-main, Angelica. You are one of the few honest people left in the movement." There were tears in her eyes as she said this.

I shook my head. "No, I can't do it, even for Clara Zetkin."

This was the second time in my life when I found it neces-sary to resist the appeal of some one for whom I had had the most profound admiration and whose happiness was dear to me. I remembered the experience with Plekhanoff in Geneva at the beginning of the war. When I had met him in Petrograd after the first 1917 Revolution, he would not even greet me. Had I yielded to pressure in either case, my life would be quite dif-ferent from what it is, but I would have missed the greatest sat-isfaction of my life—the knowledge that I have been strong enough to swim against the stream.

One day in October, as I was leaving the Comintern build-ing where I had gone to send a message by courier to Sweden, I ran into Borodine and the English sculptress, Clare Sheridan. Kamenev had brought her from England early in September and I had heard that she was doing the heads of Lenin and the other Bolshevik leaders, some of whom had seemed rather flat-tered by the attention of this glamorous and adventurous cousin of Winston Churchill. Borodine introduced me to her and asked me if I would take her in my car to the guest-house where she was staying, as he himself would be detained. On the way, she talked of her work, her impressions of the various leaders, and the impression which she seemed to have made. I disapproved of the whole idea of thus "immortalizing" the leaders of proletarian revolution and suggested to her that it would be far more fitting to take as her models typical representatives from among the workers and peasants—particularly the workingwomen whose suffering and heroism were expressed so graphically in their faces.

Shortly after this, when I mentioned to Lenin that I had met Clare Sheridan, he shrugged his shoulders and smiled. It was obvious that he, at least, was not seriously impressed.

Towards the end of the month John Reed returned to Moscow and he and Louise came to see me. Both of them looked unhappy and tired, and we made no effort to hide from each other what was in our minds. Jack spoke bitterly of the demagogy and display which had characterized the Baku Congress and the manner in which the native population and the Far Eastern delegates had been treated. A few days later I heard that Jack was ill and had been taken to a hospital. I was told that he had expressed an urgent wish to see me. To my everlasting regret, I postponed my visit, not realizing how ill he was. On the very morning that I was preparing to go to the hospital I received the news of his death.

I did not go to the funeral because I knew that I could not bear to listen to the speeches that would be made over his coffin. Any speech that I might make which did not allude to the tragedy of the last months of his life would be a lie and a profanation. I knew that Louise understood my absence. Poor girl! She had to stand for hours in the rain and snow while interminable speeches were made in Russian, French, German, and English. Even after she had finally fainted from exhaustion and grief, no attempt was made to take her away. The speeches went on over her unconscious body. Clare Sheridan, who was present at the funeral, later remarked at the callous indifference of this performance.

After the funeral, Louise spent much of her time with me while she regained her strength. I was probably the only person with whom she talked freely and bitterly of Jack's experiences in Russia and his disillusion. She was convinced that this disillusion had robbed him of that will to live which might have saved his life.

Early in 1921 diplomatic relations were established between Russia and Norway. The man who was appointed as Russian ambassador, the former mayor of Petrograd, was a friend of mine. Knowing of my desire to leave Russia even though I was still eager to work for the Soviets, he offered me an opportunity to collaborate with him in Norway as a member of the embassy staff. After I had expressed my gratitude, he made the application for my appointment. It was necessary to obtain the authorization of the Russian Central Committee, as the activities of all the Russian Party members were under its jurisdiction.

Soon after the application had been made, I decided to call on Lenin. From his manner I would be able to tell what the decision of the Central Committee would be.

After we had talked of a number of other things, I asked him:

"Do you know, Vladimir Ilyitch, what the Central Committee has decided about my departure?"

"I don't," he replied, "but if you wish I shall tell them to let you know as soon as possible."

From this evasive answer I understood that he was unwilling for me to go. I then emphasized how futile it was for me to stay in Russia. My disapproval of the Party tactics made me useless for any real work. In Norway, where no political activity would be involved, I could be of some use to Russia.

He understood from my remarks that diplomacy was futile.

"Well," he said finally, looking at me with one eye closed, "if you are permitted to leave, will you write a pamphlet against Serrati?"

My whole future depended upon my answer and I tried not to show my emotion.

"You are the one to write that pamphlet, Vladimir Ilyitch," I replied. "Serrati's position is my own." I turned and left the room.

I knew then that I would never be able to leave Russia as a

member of the Embassy staff or in any other official capacity. My health suffered another relapse.

In the months that followed, my thoughts turned towards Sweden and my friends and comrades there. During the summer, Strom came to Moscow for one of those innumerable conferences about the differences that had arisen between the Comintern and the Swedish Left Socialists over the conditions imposed upon the affiliated parties by the second Comintern Congress—differences which finally resulted in the refusal of the Swedish Party to affiliate with the Comintern.

I discussed the matter of getting a Swedish visa with Strom, who was shocked by my situation and the condition of my health. He suggested that Hjalmar Branting, who had become the Social Democratic premier of Sweden, might be willing to grant me a visa providing I could get a doctor's certificate to the effect that the state of my health required that I leave Russia for medical care. I knew that this last would be easy to obtain.

In time, after Strom returned to Stockholm, I received word that Branting had granted the visa. As soon as I could obtain permission from the Central Committee to leave Russia, Strom would come to Moscow to get me.

When weeks had gone by without any answer to my latest application, I decided to go direct to the Central Committee and demand a decision. I found Molotov, who was then secretary of the Party, very much embarrassed by my visit.

"Are you really so ill, Comrade Balabanoff, that you have to leave Russia?" he asked, nervously. "Perhaps you could recover here. We have some of the best doctors and hospitals . . ."

"My health is my private affair," I answered. "The Central Committee knows very well why I wish to leave."

"But what will you do in Sweden?"

"Sweden is only a doorway," I replied. "I want to return to Italy. I have been an active member of the movement for twenty years and I intend to go my own way. I insist upon my right to leave."

"I'm sorry," he said, very humbly, "but we cannot renounce the work of such a prominent Party member . . ."

I interrupted him. "This prominent Party member has been living in Moscow for over four years, but you have never given her any real work. You have treated me like a prima donna. I wanted to work. Now it is too late. I disagree with the Party line and I cannot work under such conditions."

"Look, comrade," he insisted, "you can chose whatever work you wish. The Central Committee could make you Commissar of Propaganda. What an activity!"

"Let's not waste our time," I said, getting up. "I must leave very soon. The Swedish comrades are on their way to get me."

Several days after this conversation I received a sealed envelope on which was written the words: "Quite confidential." Inside was a statement which read:

Comrade Balabanoff is authorized to leave Russia on her own responsibility. She is prohibited to express her opinion, verbally or in writing, on the Italian question.

I doubt if the answer would have come so speedily had not Strom arrived with a few Communist sailors from Sweden.

On the day of my departure I received proof of the fact that, though he had given me up as politically "hopeless," Lenin bore me no personal ill-will. When I returned home after bidding good-bye to some of my comrades, I was told that he had telephoned twice during my absence. I called back his office, but he was not there. When I asked his secretary if she knew why he had called, she replied:

"Oh yes. Comrade Lenin wished to know if he could assist you in any way. He knows that you are not well and he is anxious that you should leave under the best circumstances, that you should have what money you need."

"I have everything I need," I told her. "But please give him my thanks and my greetings."

I left Russia at the very end of 1921, four and a half years after I had returned with such hope and eagerness to participate in the consolidation of the Workers' Revolution.

23

ON THE TRIP FROM MOSCOW TO STOCKHOLM
I had an experience which was to have a profound effect
upon my own inner life in the next few years and which helped
to lift me from the depths of despair in which I had left Russia.

When we left the train to board the boat at Reval, I went into
a drug store to buy something to ward off the seasickness I
anticipated. The girl behind the counter smiled sympathetically.

"I can't give you anything that will be of any use to you,"
she said, "except some advice—that is, to sing. Try to sing on
the boat."

I was much more impressed by her kindness and human approach than I was by her advice, which remained, however, on
the surface of my memory.

I recalled that advice when the boat got under way and a
storm began. Sing? How could I? I had never sung in my life.
Then the meaning of her words dawned upon me. It had some-

[295]

thing to do with the movement of the waves. As the storm grew worse I began to recite to myself poems which I had learnt in my adolescence, especially those dealing with the sea. Then I translated them, in my mind, into different languages. The rhythm in these translations was suggested by the rhythm of the waves.

I was amazed to find that I had survived those terrible hours of storm better than any of the passengers on the boat, including the Swedish sailors.

Months later, while I was still absorbed by my illness and my new surroundings which offered such a contrast to Russia, I received a visit from a member of the Soviet Embassy staff who had long been a personal friend of mine. I spoke to him about a book on Leopardi which I had begun to write and showed him part of the manuscript. On the cover were some strophes I had jotted down.

"Who translated these?" he asked as he read them.

"Translated? What do you mean?"

"Why these verses. This is Lermontoff! A perfect translation of Lermontoff. Who did it?"

I was deeply surprised. Music and poetry had always seemed to me the highest form of human expression, but I had never dreamed of being able to create anything in these fields. My mother and governesses had killed any appreciative gift I might have had for music by their pedagogical, discouraging approach, and I had given up my musical studies during my early years at school. In Italy during the days of my political activity I had always asked my audience to sing after my speeches. These moments when the enthusiasm of the masses found an outlet in revolutionary songs were moments of intense joy to me. But I would stand amidst the crowd without singing, sure that I had no voice, no ear. In Russia, music and song had become a sort of revolutionary rite, almost a religious function. . . .

The encouraging words of my visitor were a revelation to me. I began to write poetry in various languages with the greatest facility. I seemed to be overwhelmed, carried away by a flood of rhythm.

My organism had been so weakened by work and undernourishment that I had felt like an old woman at forty-three. Now a new life began for me. In the pure joy of creation I felt born again. I realized that this new activity was a continuation of my work as a speaker and I understood now what people had meant when they had written of my "art" of speaking. Unconsciously I had expressed in my speeches that same aspiration towards harmony and rhythm which I was now expressing in verse.

As long as I was too ill to work, I dedicated myself entirely to this new form of expression. During these months I was overwhelmed by the kindness of my Swedish friends. Only in Stockholm did I realize what the past four years of overwork and semi-starvation could do to a normally strong and healthy body. Once the doctor asked me what I had lived on in these years to reduce myself to such a state. I was at a loss for a reply. Even after I began to recover, I found it hard to look at food on the table or in the stores without recalling how the children in Russia had crowded about the doors of the bakeries, hoping to get a few crumbs; how a child would sell in the illegal market—that is, in the street—one cube of sugar, not being able to resist the temptation to lick it occasionally with his tongue. From the money he might get for it, he could purchase black bread for his family. Unable to forget these tragic realities, I found it difficult to adjust myself to a normal life.

As I grew stronger I felt the need to return to my work. The agitation among conservatives against my admission to Sweden was still going on. Hjalmar Branting had been bitterly attacked for granting me a visa. (I have mentioned in a previous chapter that the girl who had acted as an agent for the Anti-Bolshevik League in an attempt to assassinate me and other Russians and who had been imprisoned since 1918, was released as a concession to this clamour.) I was still a member of the Communist Party and any political activity whatever in Sweden would be a violation of the understanding on which my visa had been granted.

I decided to leave Stockholm as soon as possible. A visa for Italy was out of the question at this time and I thought of Vienna. Social Democratic strength had increased enormously in Austria and there was a possibility that because of old friendships with some of its leaders a visa could be arranged. Besides, the cost of living was much lower in Vienna and I knew that now I must make my own living in some other way than as a political journalist.

An Italian friend in Trieste wrote to Freidrich Adler, leader of the Austrian Socialists, and asked him to use his influence for my admittance. Undoubtedly the Austrian Foreign Office knew of my break with the Comintern and the visa was obtained without serious difficulty.

For years before the war, gay and beautiful Vienna had charmed visitors from all over the world. The splendour of court life, the feudal relationships between the classes, the graciousness and picturesque quality of life in general, had attracted in particular the rich and frivolous from the more industrialized countries.

After the war, this attraction disappeared. With the monarchy dismembered, the country deprived of its rich resources, industry localized in and around Vienna, the capital became a dying city which only a class dominated by faith in its own future could resuscitate and rebuild. This class was the industrial workers of Vienna, trained in endurance and guided by their Socialist faith.

In the starving capital which war and famine had ruined the Socialist workers were laying the foundation of a new society. Great houses were being built—not for individual aristocrats or capitalists, but for working-men and -women who had never had a decent dwelling-place. Education had become the privilege of all; cleanliness, hygiene, sun, air, physical and mental culture, were being made accessible to the people. A feeling of social equality was stimulated by these beautiful new workers' apartments. Little by little, a new world was being built inside the old. The Socialist movement was acquiring enormous prestige; most of the city's institutions were headed by Socialists; the Party had the largest single representation in Parliament. There was a time when every eighth person in Vienna was a member of the Party, when every sixth person was a member of a trade union.

In Vienna I began a new life. I decided to earn my living as a teacher of languages—an unknown worker among a million other workers. I knew that this would not be easy in a poverty-stricken city and in the uncertain condition of my health, but after I had settled in a cheap boarding-house I began to advertise for pupils. Standing in the crowded street cars or giving lessons at home, stretched out upon a couch because of pain and exhaustion, there were times when I felt too ill to go on. Yet I was happier than I had been at any time during my past three years in Russia.

As a member of the Communist Party and as a "leader" whom they hoped to win back to active participation in their movement, I received invitations to various affairs at the Soviet Embassy. The only one I ever attended was the anniversary celebration of the Revolution. The diplomatic receptions of Soviet embassies seemed to me a proof of the revolutionary decay of Russia itself, the revival of the petit-bourgeois spirit. They were supposed to encourage and facilitate commercial and diplomatic relations, but it seemed to me naïve to suppose that capitalists or governments wishing to reap profit from business with Russia would be influenced by the quantity of caviar and champagne served at these receptions. Even commercially, I believed that the prestige of Russia would be enhanced by some consistency between its slogans and their application.

At this time there were already two kinds of Soviet receptions in Vienna—one for the bourgeoisie and the diplomats, another for the Communists and sympathizers among the workers. The anniversary reception which I attended was of the latter kind. Towards eleven in the evening a delegation of unemployed Viennese workers came to the Embassy with greetings. They were not received. I left the Embassy immediately.

The news of Lenin's death in January, 1924, came as a blow to everyone whose life had been intimately connected with the Russian Revolution and the international labour movement. As soon as I heard of it I rushed over to the Embassy for further details. To my surprise, I was asked by the attaché in charge (the ambassador, Schlichter, had gone to Moscow for the funeral) to make the memorial speeches in Russian and German at a private meeting of people connected with the Embassy on the following day.

"But you know I am a nonconformist," I said. "You may have complications with Moscow."

"Perhaps," he answered, "but I hope you won't refuse. . . ."

It seemed strange and tragic to commemorate Lenin to a small audience—officials, stenographers, Austrian Communists—when those for whom he had worked and fought were outside.

A few months later I had proof that the Bolsheviks still hoped to win me back. I had just returned from some lessons and had stretched out on my couch when the telephone rang. It was Schlichter, the ambassador.

"How do you do, comrade," he said. "We haven't seen you for a long time."

"Yes," I replied, "I live quite far from you and I have not been well."

"I am sure you will feel much better very soon. You will be able to have care in a sanatorium. . . ."

"What do you mean?" I asked, surprised at this sudden concern for me.

"The Executive of the Party has charged me to find how you are getting on and has sent me some money. . . ."

"Money?" I interrupted. "Please send it back immediately."

"But look here, comrade," he insisted. "The Executive is eager to have you return to Moscow. They offer you some interesting activity. . . ."

"What has that to do with money? If I could be useful to the Soviet Republic, I would return. For this purpose I don't need money. When I feel better, I shall come to see you and hear more about this letter."

When I went to the Embassy a few days later, Schlichter said that he had mislaid the letter from Moscow. I was naïve enough to believe him. As the courier was leaving the same day for Russia, he suggested that I write my reply in an adjoining room. When he and his attaché came to get it, they found me in a serious state, lying in an arm-chair. The writing of the letter and all it involved had so shaken my nerves that I had had a new attack of pain.

I had written to the Central Committee, thanking them for the offer of money and refusing it. My condition of return was that my work should have nothing to do with the Communist International. "As I have told you before," I wrote, "you are demoralizing the movement throughout the world. I will not share the responsibility for this crime. On the Italian question my opinion has not changed. But even if I disagreed with my Italian comrades, I would not desert them now. They are being defeated. You are victorious. They are defending Socialism with their lives; you are destroying it."

In about a fortnight the ambassador called me once more. He had received a telegram summoning me to Moscow. Again he pretended that he could not find it.

"I sent it to another office," he said when I arrived at the Embassy. "It contained certain diplomatic orders. But the Central Committee wants you to come to Moscow to account for an article you have published in an Italian paper."

"If this is the purpose," I replied, "I don't intend to go. If the article has been published, they have read it. I have nothing to modify. I wrote what I have thought on the Italian question ever since it arose."

Now I understood the whole strategy. Since I had begun to write for the Italian Socialist papers, they had tried first to induce me to go to a sanatorium, hoping that this would break my contact with the Italians. Failing this, they wanted to get me to Moscow. My health, the work they offered, were only pretexts.

This was my last interview with any official representative of the Bolshevik government. In August I received a couple of telegrams from Russian Communists residing abroad. They wanted me to know that they considered me the most devoted and consistent revolutionary. This made me wonder what had happened. A few days later I saw a copy of *Pravda* which contained a decree expelling me from the Communist Party for my "Menshevik" approach and my collaboration with a "social fascist paper." I had never belonged to any Menshevik organization and the "social fascist paper" was *Avanti,* the headquarters of which had just been attacked and burned for the third time by the Fascist Blackshirts!

The same copy contained an article by a certain Jaroslavsky, who developed into a specialist in denouncing and defaming at the orders of the Central Committee. I was the first of the leading Party members whom he was ordered to denounce. The second was Trotsky; the third, Zinoviev himself!

At that time expulsions from the Party were taken very seriously. My case was the first of an internationally known revolutionist. It was necessary, therefore, to promulgate a decree which made questions and answers superfluous. This decree stated that my membership had been an error, a mistake from the first, and a dishonour to the Party.

When I had arrived in Austria the leading Social Democrats had been very cordial to me. I had made them understand that I would never again join a Social Democratic party. I believed that Social Democracy would never regain its vigour as the world conditions which had made this type of party necessary had disappeared. I had much admiration for the movement in Austria and much sympathy with its leaders, but I did not participate in its activities, except when I spoke occasionally on Fascism or took part in informal discussions.

Mussolini's rise to power and the triumph of the Blackshirts in October, 1922, had been a terrible blow, but in spite of the stories which reached me every day of the atrocities practised against the Italian movement and its leaders, I did not believe that our movement could be crushed. As long as it could function, I knew that it would fight back. When the murder of Matteotti, in 1924, aroused the indignation even of the foreign capitalist press, it still seemed that the workers in the rest of the world must see that this was no isolated phenomenon and that they would come, somehow, to the aid of their Italian comrades. It was at this time that I received the final blow to my faith in Bolshevism. After the murder of Matteotti, Mussolini was practically boycotted by most of the foreign ambassadors in Rome. Yet, a month after this event he was invited to lunch at the Russian Embassy. The newspapers published a photograph of Mussolini and his friends, sitting under a picture of Lenin and the hammer and sickle, in the Soviet Embassy in Rome!

In Vienna, in those years, I had an opportunity to watch the genesis of the Austrian tragedy which came to a head in 1934. As long as the workers and their Socialist leaders had dedicated themselves to the reconstruction of what the war had destroyed, the Austrian ruling classes were comparatively indifferent to their growth in strength. But as soon as they had succeeded in reorganizing the financial situation and had embarked upon a vigorous program of economic and social reforms for which the bourgeoisie had to pay higher taxes, the situation changed immediately. This was the germ of reactionary discontent. Why should they have to pay more for theatre and concert tickets in order that the slums could be replaced by model apartments? Why should the house-owner have to tolerate the competition of municipally-owned, low-priced apartments? And the terrible strikes! As long as the workers had died in the trenches while their wives and children endured starvation without complaint, all was well. But when those who survived the slaughter demanded a more human standard of living, the "rebels" had to be treated as enemies, rather than patriots.

The Austrian Socialists at that time were considered the spiritual leaders of the world Social Democracy. They had in their ranks such outstanding theoreticians as Otto Bauer; administrators like Breitner and Danneberg; pedagogues like Glockel; such incomparable journalists as Austerlitz; militants like Karl Seitz, mayor of Vienna, who for several decades was the most beloved man in the country. The Party had a disciplined rank and file, unmatched by any other political organization in Austria, men and women with an unshakable faith in their cause and in its leaders, from whom they were not divided by any bureaucratic barriers.

And yet these leaders did not know how to use this wonderful instrument of human energy. Though they considered themselves quite different from both the German Social Democrats

[303]

and Communists, their movement was to meet the same fate as that of Germany.

Since the death of Victor Adler, Otto Bauer had been the Party's outstanding leader. With his return to Austria, after his war captivity in Siberia and a short sojourn in post-revolutionary Russia, Bauer became the leading Marxist of the Second International, the authoritative mouthpiece of its Left Wing. His writings were brilliant and persuasive but there seemed to be no link between his masterful application of the dialectic method, his astute analysis of the past and the contemporary events and situations in which he was a leading figure. Though a passionate friend of the workers, he was no leader for an historical period in which strategy is as necessary as scientific interpretation. His ability as a tactician was absorbed by his parliamentary activities—by what the French call "the parliamentary kitchen."

The Austrian workers had come to rely more and more upon the political strength of their Party and less and less upon their own class action. Otto Bauer was both a factor and a victim of this situation. The one thing he wrote which seemed to me inferior to his own capacities was his explanation of the Austrian tragedy after it had taken place. I had expected from him a profound and courageous statement of the errors of his Party from the very rise of the Austrian Fascist movement. Instead of this, he gave an official account of the steps taken by the Socialist representatives to arrive at an agreement with the other parties and with Dollfuss. These were facts which the newspaper related —the result of the situation rather than an analysis. One might have expected from the leader of a defeated movement something which would enlighten those who have to learn from such defeats. Bauer was too much of a diplomat and a Party official to make such a confession. Then, too, all of us taking part in a movement which has so many enemies and obstacles are tied by a strong sentiment of solidarity with our co-workers. The time comes, however, when such sentiment means a lack of solidarity with the working class itself.

On more than one occasion, in private conversation with the

Austrian leaders, I expressed my fear of Fascist developments in Austria.

"Don't worry, comrade," they would say. "With us, Fascism is impossible. Our workers are too class conscious and united. Look what enormous demonstrations we have! Our people would never tolerate a Mussolini—a cheap actor and adventurer. . . ."

"Well," I answered, "your approach to the problem shows how little you know of how Fascism came to power in Italy and what it really represents. Unity is a requisite of the labour movement, but it is not enough. An inactive unity means nothing. It is a kind of barometer. But it cannot replace action."

Because of this confidence in their strength, the Austrian Socialists made the same mistake as the Germans—although, in the end, they were to fight with a courage and heroism that was to electrify the world. But at this time, they were more democratic than socialistic. They thought and acted like democrats, whereas their enemies, encouraged by the example of the Italian Fascists, thought and acted like terrorists. After each Fascist assault, the reaction of the masses was violent and spontaneous. The Socialist press would publish revolutionary articles of protest and denunciation; the trade unions would organize overwhelming demonstrations for the funerals of their martyrs— and nothing more. The movement was the victim of its own success, of its own sense of responsibility. It was responsible for institutions which had been built and won at the cost of so much sacrifice to the working class, and these were the source of so much pride and joy that its leaders would not take a chance on losing what they had gained. These institutions became an obstacle as soon as they were no longer a means, but a goal in themselves.

The result was the first and chief factor of Fascist success—a feeling of impunity. As soon as the rulers got the impression that they could use terroristic methods with impunity, the workers came to the same conclusion. Failure to strike back at the enemy paralyses the forces of those who are attacked. In this case it also gave confidence to the bystander—the lower middle class, the white-collared workers—who is attracted more or less unconsciously by power and violence. What greater power is there than the ability to destroy human life without paying for one's crime?

In the autumn of 1926, a new act of provocation had been committed—the killing of a worker and a child by Austrian Fascists. The *Arbeiterzeitung* had announced on previous occasions that this was the very last time they would tolerate such terrorism. But the Party reacted in the same way—an incendiary article ending with an appeal to the masses for calm and discipline. The Socialist militia sent a large delegation to the funeral; Otto Bauer and Deutsch, the militia leader, were to be the speakers.

"All the phases of this tragedy are so like the Italian one," I said, when we met in the special train that was to take us to the funeral.

"But don't you see how popular our Party is?" Bauer replied, alluding to the greetings of the train employés, the way in which the train was cheered as it passed through the proletarian sections.

"Do you think that in Italy we did not have such demonstrations?" I asked. "But when terror begins to function, many of those who greet us now become passive, indifferent or hostile —not because they are cowards or traitors, but because most people identify power with right."

Several months after this conversation, the Viennese workers, indignant at the mild sentences passed upon the murderers, attempted to burn the tribunal. In the riot that followed, ninety-five of them paid for this attempt with their lives. In the central cemetery in Vienna there is an area occupied exclusively by the victims of this incident—men, women, and children buried together.

This massacre was the beginning of the final stage of defeat. Terroristic acts became more frequent, the labour movement more isolated and intimidated, their enemies more arrogant. The Socialists were still fearful the Italian or Hungarian Fascist armies would march in if they ordered a general strike or insurrection. When everything was lost, when the Fascists were already in power, a general strike was called. The masses did not respond partly because they had become exhausted during this period of weakness and defeat and had lost confidence in their own strength and partly because these orders could no longer reach them.

The militiamen, the men and women who fought to their last drop of blood, knew that their cause was defeated and that they were defending only their ideals. These men and women, so numerous in this small country, saved the honour of Austrian Socialism.

In Red Vienna, gallows were erected for the survivors, including the wounded. The monuments which had symbolized human progress and freedom were removed. The houses built for the workers, as forerunners of a new society, were destroyed or mutilated—at the order of a man who was later to fall a victim to the Nazi bullets of his collaborators.

As in the case of Italy, the survivors of this tragedy are still meeting in secret or in exile, waiting and working for their day to come again.

24

BY 1926, THE TOTALITARIAN RÉGIME WAS COMpletely triumphant in Italy. Every anti-Fascist paper, institution, and party had been suppressed—after they had been bombarded and burned over a period of four years, after their leaders and followers had been beaten, tortured, and killed. Among those who survived—Socialists, Anarchists, Republicans, Liberals—many attempted to leave Italy, both to escape persecution and in order to fight Fascism from a freer country. Among the refugees there were also many people who had never belonged to any organization at all, but whose sense of justice and dignity was so violated by Fascist despotism that they preferred to emigrate. The various radical groups established their headquarters mostly in Paris.

At the same time, a growing number of parties and individuals had realized the incompatibility between revolutionary Socialism and the Communist International. An attempt was made to unite them into a central, international organization.

The originator of this movement was a well-known French Marxist and journalist, Paul Louis. He had been the editor of the Communist daily paper, *Humanité*, but had resigned for the same reasons I had left the Comintern. He had now formed a new party in France with the hope of uniting all reliable Socialist elements and putting an end to the splits in the French labour movement. By gathering all the dissident Marxist groups together, he also hoped to achieve unity on an international basis.

I was elected secretary of this new organization to which French, Italian, German, Rumanian, Norwegian, and Russian Socialist Revolutionary parties adhered. I accepted reluctantly because I did not want to leave Vienna, but realizing what sacrifices these small parties were making to achieve their goal, I felt that I could not refuse. When I came to Paris to an international meeting, the Italian Socialists began to insist that I become the editor of *Avanti*, which was being published in Paris since its suppression in Italy.

The leadership of a party and a paper of *émigrés* without funds or resources of any kind, cut off from their own people, is a complicated and difficult task. The time it requires is so out of proportion to the results achieved. Conflicts and splits among *émigrés* are more violent and frequent than under normal conditions. Yet, how could I refuse? I knew how much the Socialists in Italy, unable to express themselves, would appreciate my acceptance. I decided to move from Vienna, but to return there for a visit every month or two.

By this time a number of the leading Socialists, who since the split in the Italian Party had become Social Democrats, were living in Paris—Turati, Treves, Modigliani—as were famous Republicans and former members of Parliament, including the former premier, Nitti. The thousands of *émigrés*, political refugees and others, were divided into numerous groups and were scattered throughout Paris. Though I maintained friendly relations with all the leading anti-Fascists I was very soon dedicating all my time to the Italian Socialist Party and *Avanti*.

Once more I seemed to live on an Italian "island." Political refugees from Italy—except for the Communists—visited me daily so that I kept in constant touch with the situation in Italy. During those ten years in Paris, between 1926 and 1936, I came to know and to love my Italian comrades as I never had before, to experience the cheerful self-sacrifice of these under-paid workers whose material situation was so precarious and who were yet determined to maintain their paper and return it to their comrades in Italy when their hour of triumph came.

Once a week, the Executive of the Party met in one of the cheaper cafés of Paris. As most of us were unemployed, we had to order our food very carefully—sometimes the choice would be made between dinner and carfare. Yet no one missed these meetings. Once a month, on Sunday afternoon, the general membership would meet in a room of the same restaurant and on these occasions the meetings would become so noisy the owner of the café would come upstairs to find out what was the matter.

During these years in France I met Emma Goldman and Sasha Berkman, when they happened to be in Paris or when a lecture tour took me into the neighbourhood of Nice or Saint-Tropez. They were always busy, always thinking of America and their friends there, and longing for wider activity. After I had come to the United States, the news of Sasha's death reached me in a Chicago hospital. In the letter, which I received from him two days later and which had been written a few days before his death, there was no hint of any intention to commit suicide.

In Paris, Henry Alsberg, whom I had met in Russia with Emma and Sasha, called on me and told me that Louise Bryant had been in a sanatorium but that her health had not improved and that there seemed to be little hope for her. As soon as she returned to Paris she got in touch with me. I scarcely recognized her. She was now separated from her second husband, William Bullitt, and had been ill for more than a year. I would not have believed that any one could change so, not only in appearance, but in her manner of speaking, her voice and tone. Only at intervals when I continued to see her was she the old Louise I had known with Jack. Whenever we met, she spoke of him with deep sadness, of his disappointment in Russia, his illness and death.

"Oh, Angelica," she would say in these moments of lucidity and confidence, "don't leave me, I feel so lonely. Why did I have to lose Jack? Why did we both have to lose our faith?"

Shortly after this I heard of her death.

On the first day of one of my visits to Vienna, where I had gone to deliver a lecture on Fascism, I received an early call from a woman comrade. She handed me a paper and pointed to a dispatch which read:

"Last night, Angelica Balabanoff died in Leningrad."

After this came a long account of my public activities. Later, I discovered the origin of this story. A woman named Balabanoff had died in Leningrad and the news had been telegraphed by a Viennese correspondent in Moscow who thought it was I; the paper had then added the rest of the material from their files.

The Italian Fascist papers spread the news all over the world and many years after, when my name was mentioned, people would ask, "But isn't she dead?"

Looking over the various accounts which reached me, I found that on the whole the press had been fair to me. One of my German colleagues had gone so far as to describe the place where I had been buried—under the Kremlin wall! Being sure there was no one alive to dispute his story, he had also described incidents in my life which had never taken place. He was probably badly in need of funds. An Italian journalist, meeting me on the street a few days later, could not conceal his disappointment.

"Look here," he cried. "I was just going to mail a story about you to a South American paper, describing how you sold your fur coat to help the Italian *émigrés*, including myself. It would have been such a nice story and I needed the money to pay my rent."

Few of the Italian exiles remained in Vienna. They were for the most part manual workers, and as there were so many

Austrian unemployed, they could not hope to find work. But when they arrived, the reception they received from the Austrian Socialists helped to compensate for what they had suffered. A barracks had been taken over by the Socialist mayor and transformed into apartments for the Italians, with a common kitchen. It was when I realized how badly in need of clothing some of them were that I had sold the fur coat I had been given in Russia. This was the episode to which the Italian journalist referred.

Those who believe that the Italian masses entrusted Mussolini with power or assented to the Fascist régime should have been compelled to listen to some of these *émigrés*. There was one man of forty-five who had worked for twenty years in the same factory, who had been elected to the county council, where he worked a revolution in the hygienic conditions of his district. When the Blackshirts attacked and set fire to the People's House, he had fought for its defence until the smoke became so thick he could not see. Then he had jumped from a window and escaped in the darkness.

"But I did not escape alone," he told me. "I took her with me." He placed his hand over his heart, with a triumphant glance, as though he were speaking of a beloved woman. The "her" was the red banner of the People's House. "I ran with her until I found a place where I could hide her. Those brigands will never find her. Only a few comrades know where she is. When we shall be free again, we shall show them how we have protected our banner."

For more than two years this man had been unable to sleep at home, for fear of endangering his family. Each evening the Blackshirts had come to search for him. "For two years," he said, "I lived with my hand on my revolver. I can scarcely straighten my fingers now."

His experience is typical of that of hundreds of thousands and his spirit is a symbol of the fact that the Italian rebels have not been subjugated by defeat.

I was in Vienna when Tagore, the Indian poet and philosopher, was lecturing there, about two years after the assassination of Matteotti. This murder had evoked such a reaction to the Fascist régime that *émigré* opinion was shocked at the announcement that Tagore had been a guest of the Fascist government in Italy. Modigliani, who had participated as an attorney in the "trial" of Matteotti's murderers, was in Vienna at this time and he asked me to accompany him to an appointment with Tagore and to act as his translator.

Tagore was staying at a fashionable hotel, where he was obviously an object of idolatry among the wealthy patrons.

"There is no need to tell me the details of what is going on in Italy," he said. "I have been there and I do not know anything I could say or do about it."

I would have left immediately had not Modigliani begun to speak in Italian. As I started to translate his remarks, Tagore interrupted me.

"Are you the person who gave the interview about Mussolini that was published a few months ago?"

His secretary answered before I could speak. "Yes, this is the lady whose interviews and articles have interested you so much."

The whole atmosphere changed and Tagore became an understanding and even apologetic human being.

"Your interpretation of Mussolini's character," he said, "coincides with the impression he made upon me—a coward and an actor. When I asked the English ambassador if he thought my impression was correct, he said it was not—that Mussolini was a great and courageous man. However, he did not convince me and I was glad to have a confirmation, in your interview, of my own impression. I should like you to tell me more."

"I shall have to begin by saying," I answered, "that the Italian people who have attempted, more than any other people, to apply your own attitude towards war do not deserve that you should accept the hospitality of a man who came to power through violence and assassination."

"Please don't misunderstand me," he interrupted. "When I came to Italy, I knew nothing about the situation nor could I get in touch with reality. You are the second person who has given me any idea of what Fascism is. The first one I met also after I had left Italy. You may be sure that I will make a statement of what I think about the Fascist régime."

The secretary told me that Tagore had numerous clippings on Fascism which he was eager to have translated.

One of the next issues of the Viennese daily *Neue Freie Presse* contained a long article by Tagore dealing with this subject. It ended with the statement: "To be ruled by a tyrant is a great misfortune for any country. But to know that one has worshipped an individual who owes his success only to his negative qualities is a tragedy. . . ." This comment, which I quote only from memory, contains the kernel of the tragedy of Italy. When all the factors which contributed to Mussolini's rise to power are unveiled—which can happen only after his fall—most of those who today pretend that "he must have some good qualities" will declare that they have always known that he was an impostor and an adventurer.

Their recognition of this fact may come too late. They themselves may be the victims of some similar demagogue in their own countries whose rise they have encouraged through similar tolerance and by ignorance of the conditions which make for Fascism. Hitlerism in Germany and Austria, undeclared wars in Abyssinia, China and Spain would not be possible were it not for the complicity of public opinion in the social and economic conditions from which war and Fascism arise.

After reading this chronicle of my collaboration with the international labour movement in its periods of victory and defeat, the reader is entitled to ask where I stand now. At sixty I am drawing conclusions from those experiences. My belief in the necessity for the social changes advocated by that movement and for the realization of its ideals has never been more complete than it is now when victory seems so remote. I am more than ever persuaded that a militant international labour movement must be the instrument of those changes. The experience of over forty years has only intensified my Socialist convictions, and if I had my life to live over again, I would dedicate it to the same objective. This does not mean that I do not recognize my own mistakes or those of the groups in which I have worked.

The social and physical defeats administered by Fascism to the working class and to humanity in general can be overcome and compensated for if the spirit of that movement is not killed. The news I receive from underground sources in all the Fascist countries confirms my conviction that it cannot be killed, though the price paid for its conservation has been so high. I know that the Italian masses are not Fascist in spirit; that the German masses are not anti-Semitic or jingoist. The reports of journalists or of casual visitors to those countries whose people have been terrorized into silence and deprived of any means of expressing their true feelings do not impress me. Fascist Italy has been described by some of these people as an orderly Paradise—no strikes, no disorder, no irregularity in train service; its leader the object of unanimous adoration. These who would have laughed at Mussolini, his appearance and gesticulations, in his "soap-box" days, are carried away by his eloquence when his performances are given from the balcony of a palace. Auto-suggestion induces such people to believe that this eloquence has also carried away the Italian masses.

So far as personal ability is concerned, Mussolini is an average, self-made semi-intellectual, a type of which there are so many varieties in Italy. The verbal violence of his Romagnolo inheritance and his capacity for vulgar bluffing have been enormously exaggerated by his inherent exhibitionism. Absence of scruples has enabled him to assume contradictory attitudes and slogans, and the impunity which the servility of public opinion grants a successful bluffer has made it possible for him to pose as a genius. If the economic situation in Italy were to collapse beneath him, those who flatter him today would see in him a comic and ambitious adventurer, tortured by an inferiority complex. Unlike Hitler, Mussolini is aware that his methods will never be able to achieve the aim at which he aspires. He knows enough of economic forces to know that he can never completely suffocate the labour movement or prevent the development, eventually, of Socialist collectivism. He still

[315]

hates the ruling classes, the monarchy and the Church, quite as much as in the days when he was fighting them openly; and he knows that they mistrust him. But they have been his accomplices in his march to power. After having been their tool, he has become their master.

The foreign visitor knows nothing of this, nor of the discontent behind the scenes, the attempts at strikes or demonstrations which are quickly suppressed and then arise again without the slightest allusion to them in the press. These are the sparks of light which visitors do not see and of which even many Italians know nothing.

Shortly before I left Paris for the United States, I wrote, in a letter to Leon Blum, then editor of *Populaire*, the French Socialist daily, that Mussolini would never hesitate to break any treaty or alliance he might make as master of Italy—just as he had betrayed his Party in 1914.

In contemporary Spain, Fascist assault, aided by outside mercenaries, assumed from the beginning such an obviously reactionary and military character that the Spanish masses as well as large sections of the middle class were galvanized into action against it. Here, too, the workers had been better prepared psychologically to defend themselves by the experiences of their Italian and German comrades and by the mistakes of the Social Democratic and Communist leadership in Germany.

In spite of the economic backwardness of the country, the Spanish labour movement was the most militant in Europe—completely permeated by a revolutionary Socialist and Anarcho-Syndicalist tradition. More than other European workers, perhaps, they were convinced that they had "nothing to lose but their chains." Their desperate and heroic struggle against the combined forces of Spanish, Italian, and German Fascism, the almost incredible endurance they have displayed, as well as the support and sympathy which their struggles have received from revolutionaries and liberals in other countries, are a light which helps to illumine the whole world in the dark years through which we are living. So, too, is the less conspicuous and less dramatic struggle carried on by the victims of Fascist suppression in Italy, Germany, and Austria.

[316]

I have said that the spirit of international Socialism cannot be killed. There is, however, a possible exception to that generalization, an exception which the events in Russia bring to mind. *That spirit might be killed by those who have been its prophets and who seem to have personified it.* The situation which has matured in Russia in the past few years has threatened it as Fascism has been unable to do. The germs of this situation induced me to leave Russia less than five years after I had returned there in 1917 and to sever all relationship with its leaders. At that time other revolutionists were denying or ignoring their existence, or believed that they could exterminate them. Many of these, like Trotsky, or like others who were unable to leave Russia, have become the victims of methods which they tolerated for too long. Today that system of repression has reached outside of Russia to Spain and, through the mechanism of aid to the Spanish workers in their military struggle, threatens the unity and the very life of the Spanish labour movement—after it has already destroyed some of its bravest leaders.

Soviet Russia! How the significance of those words has changed in the past twenty years! At the time of the October Revolution only a few of the liberals and intellectuals supported it. In Russia, the struggles implied in a social revolution in a backward country frightened them. Outside of Russia, tales of starvation, cruelty, terror, loss of individual liberty—tales both true and false—did not make a seductive picture.

But later, with the growing inequality between the manual workers and the intellectuals, with the new privileges which accrued to those belonging or attached to the bureaucracy, the liberals became reassured. And when the Russian government became more concerned with liberal than with working-class opinion and when the adaptation to the capitalist world had penetrated its organs and agencies at home and abroad, the intellectuals and liberals accepted Russia, began to extol its institutions and to feel at home there. Everything was praised without discrimination. Their articles and books, many of them less than mediocre, put them in a privileged position—a world of their own—so that in Russia they could not see what was

[317]

going on above or below. In Europe and the United States, they automatically achieved a large audience and a status which was all the more attractive because it provided an illusion of "daring" and moral courage. This was particularly true after the economic catastrophes in the western countries had deprived the intellectuals of that "security" which they had more or less taken for granted.

The savage ruthlessness of Nazi anti-Semitism, which made social and economic pariahs of so many of the German intellectuals and their liberal followers, was even more effective in augmenting Russian influence. To many of these the military might of Russia and of what they thought of as "international Communism" seemed the only force capable of resisting their persecutors and they were either blind or indifferent to other considerations—the persecutions of political dissidents and other groups in Russia. Their books could be neither published nor sold at home, but abroad they were paid well and flattered for writing books in behalf of Stalinist Russia and its leaders. What did it matter that Russians of their own sort—intellectuals and political dissidents—were imprisoned, exiled, executed, or left without work to starve in this new Holy Land? Or that 160,000,000 human beings were subject to the political whims of an individual? Nor did it matter, of course, that this situation was completely incompatible with the spirit in which the first Workers' Republic was created. Their enthusiasm is probably the greatest insult which genuine revolutionaries, in Russia and throughout the world, have had to bear in the past few years.

I believe that large sections of the Russian masses feel and know this and that while they cherish the basic program of the Soviet régime, they resent more and more—though they are unable to express the fact—the corruption of the spirit and purpose of their Revolution. Otherwise the elaborate system of repression, the enormous expansion of the OGPU, the trials and executions of the past few years, would have been unnecessary. Not even a small percentage of the older generations in Russia believe in the accusations against Trotsky and the other builders of the Revolution. *But they must behave as though they believe.* But, the reader may ask, do not the "confessions" of some of these men prove that they were guilty? To one who has known these men—and the Russian system—they prove nothing of the sort.

It is this that kills the spirit of the labour movement—not only in Russia, but throughout the world: that an Idea which has inspired whole generations to matchless heroism and enthusiasm has become identified with the methods of a régime based upon corruption, extortion and betrayal; and last, but not least, that the sycophants and assassins of this régime have infected the world labour movement. In this, Bolshevism identifies itself more and more with the methods of Fascism.

I am among the few people who have not been surprised at the various abrupt changes in the tactics of the Communist International. I knew that its tactics were always imposed, rather than accepted, and as they never corresponded to conviction, there has been no need of any psychological adaptation. These changes have been the result of bargains, or the failure of bargains, between Stalin and the military and diplomatic authorities of other countries.

If a new world war—which can no more make the world safe for democracy than did the last—does not plunge us into a new nightmare within the next few years, I believe that the international labour movement can be built again, and that in this movement and its courage and solidarity lies the only hope for humanity. Such a movement will have learnt from its past defeats at the hands of Fascism and from the mistakes and the betrayals of the Russian experiment. A new world war, with the inevitable rise of totalitarianism of various sorts within the democratic countries, can very well kill the possibility of such international action for decades to come.

I am proud to have lived and worked with the artisans of a new social order. Many of them are now dead or defeated—in exile or in their own countries. But a new generation will take their place—to build more wisely and more successfully on the foundations we have laid.

ANGELICA BALABANOFF

January 1938

[319]

INDEX

Philips, Dr. Marian, 131
Picard, Edmond, 14
Pirro Incident, 233-35
Platten, Fritz, 136, 145, 214, 215
Plenkhanoff, George, 18-20, 24, 66-67, 69-70, 73, 75, 120-21, 226, 290
Politiken, 174
Popolo d'Italia, 126, 127, 128, 277
Pravda, 301

Quelch, Harry, 82

Racovsky, Christian, 180, 211, 212, 216, 218, 224, 226-28, 230, 236
Radek, Karl, 143, 163, 167, 169, 171, 172, 174, 177, 210, 243, 246-48, 257, 275, 282, 283
Reclus, Elie, 14
Reclus, Elisée, 13-14, 18
Red Trade Union Congress, 223, 266, 276
Red Week, 1914, 111-12
Reed, John, v, 177-79, 243-46, 253-54, 272, 274, 275, 281-82, 291-92, 311
Reinstein, Boris, 214
Resto del Carlino, 124, 127
Rolland-Holst, Henriette, 85
Rühle, Otto, 139
Russell, Bertrand, 258
Russian Purges, 318
Russian Revolution, 1905, 53
Russian Revolution, 1917, March, 142-144; November, 170-74; 151-53, 160, 161, 165, 167, 317
Russian Social Democratic Party, Fifth Congress, 47, 70-75; 19, 67

Sadoul, Jacques, 213, 224
Salvemini, Gaetano, 280
Sarfatti, Cesare and Margherita, 55-56
Saumoneau, Louise, 131
Schlichter, 299-301
Second International, Executive Committee, 1-4, 19-20, 114-18; Stuttgart Congress, 79-86; 79, 87, 113-18, 132, 134, 209, 226, 227, 304
Seitz, Karl, 303
Serrati, Giacinto Menotti, 43, 127, 128, 129, 221, 240, 261, 262-67, 268-73, 275-77, 278-79, 285, 292

Shaw, Tom, 246, 258
Sheridan, Clare, 290, 291
Singer, Paul, 71, 84
Snowden, Mrs. Philip, 258-59
Socialist Propaganda League, 166
Spanish Fascism, 316
Spiridonova, Maria, 53-54
Stalin, Joseph, 185-86, 221, 284, 319
Stockholm Conference, 1917, 153-55, 163-64
Stocklitsky, 272
Strom, Fred, 162, 293, 294
Su, Compagne, 35-38
Sudecum Episode, 121-22
Swedish Socialist Party, 161-63, 272, 275, 293

Tagore, R., 312-14
Ten Days that Shook the World, 177-78
Terror, Red, 179-80, 183-86, 187, 225, 228
Terror, White, 184-85, 225, 228
Third International, Bolsheviks advocate, 132, 136, 154-55; Executive, 222-24, 236, 241-42, 245, 263, 267; First Congress, 209-12, 213-14, 219-22; methods, 268-72, 273-77, 301, 319; Second Congress, 263, 267, 268-69, 272-76; Third Congress, 277; 162, 176-77
Tillett, Ben, 258
Treves, Claudio, 29, 64, 99, 100, 121, 275, 309
Trotsky, Leon, Character, 249, 251; 69, 70, 73, 155-57, 161, 203, 209, 216-18, 222, 226-27, 237-38, 243, 245, 247, 267, 276, 283, 302, 317, 318
Tseretelli, Iraki, 73, 147
Turati, Filippo, 29, 62-64, 101, 211, 275, 309
Turner, Ben, 240, 258

Ukrainian Civil War, 225, 228, 230-35
Université Nouvelle, 11-14, 20
University of Sapienza, 24-25

Vandervelde, Emile, 14-16, 18, 81, 134, 154
Vladeck, B. Charney, 74

[323]